Pelican Books
Pelican Geography and Environmental Studies
Editor: Peter Hall

Urban and Regional Planning

Peter Hall was educated at the University of
Cambridge, and has taught at Birbeck College and the
London School of Economics. He is now Chairman
of the School of Planning Studies and Professor of
Geography at the University of Reading. He has
published a number of books including *The World
Cities* (1966); *Theory and Practice of Regional
Planning* (1970) and *The Containment of Urban
England* (1973).

Urban and Regional Planning

Peter Hall

Penguin Books

Penguin Books Ltd, Harmondsworth,
Middlesex, England
Penguin Books Australia Ltd, Ringwood,
Victoria, Australia
Penguin Books Canada Ltd,
41 Steelcase Road West, Markham, Ontario, Canada
Penguin Books (N.Z.) Ltd,
182–190 Wairau Road, Auckland 10, New Zealand

Published in Pelican Books 1974

Copyright © Peter Hall, 1974

Filmset in Photon Times
Richard Clay (The Chaucer Press) Ltd, Bungay, Suffolk
and printed in Great Britain by
Fletcher & Son Ltd, Norwich

To Magda

Contents

Acknowledgements   xi
List of Illustrations   xiii
List of Tables   xvii
Preface   1

1. *Planning, Planners and Plans*   3

    The Application to Urban and Regional Planning
    'Planning' as an Activity
    Objectives in Planning – Simple and Complex
    Structure of This Book
    Further Reading

2. *The Origins: Urban Growth from 1800 to 1940*   19

    Planning before the Industrial Revolution
    The Impact of Industrialism
    The Phenomenon of Urban Spread
    The Reaction against Sprawl
    Further Reading

3. *The Seers: Pioneer Thinkers in Urban Planning,
    from 1880 to 1945*   42

    The Anglo-American Tradition
    The European Tradition
    A Verdict on the Seers
    Further Reading

4. *The Regional Economic Problem and the Barlow Report,
    from 1930 to 1940*   81

    The Nature of the Regional Economic Problem
    The Barlow Commission and its Report, 1937–40
    Further Reading

5. *The Creation of the Postwar Planning Machine, from 1940 to 1952*   99

   The Foundation Reports
   The Legislation
   A Tentative Verdict
   Further Reading

6. *National/Regional Planning from 1945 to 1972*   125

   The Pattern of Regional Change, 1945–70
   Policy Changes, 1960–72
   A Verdict on Regional Economic Policies, 1960–72
   Further Reading

7. *Planning for Cities and City Regions from 1945 to 1972*   155

   The Reality of Change in Postwar Britain
   Planning in the 1950s: Cities versus Counties
   The Major Regional Studies of the 1960s
   The New Regional Structure and Local Government Reform, 1965–72
   City Region Planning and Local Government, 1965–72
   The Changing Content of Planning
   Further Reading

8. *Planning in Western Europe since 1945*   200

   French Postwar Planning
   The German Experience
   Regional Development in Italy
   Scandinavian City Region Planning
   The Netherlands: Randstad and Regional Development
   The European Experience: Some Conclusions
   Further Reading

9. *Planning in the United States since 1945*   244

   Economic Development Problems
   Machinery for Economic Development
   Metropolitan Growth and Change
   Planning Powers and Planning Policies
   Some Conclusions
   Further Reading

10. *The Planning Process*   269

Planning as a Continuous Process
Goals, Objectives and Targets
Forecasting, Modelling and Plan Design
Plan Design and Plan Evaluation
Implementing the Plan
Further Reading

Index   295

Acknowledgements

My thanks go to the following for the use of illustrations as listed:

Aerofilms, 4, 6, 8, 13, 23, 24, 26, 27, 37, 41, 43, 55; Artemis Verlag, 22; British Steel Corporation, 35; Cadbury Brothers Ltd, 9c; California Division of Highways, 76; Cumbernauld Development Corporation, 38; Faber & Faber Ltd, 10, 11; Ford Motor Company, 36; French Embassy, 60; Greater London Council, 44; Her Majesty's Stationery Office, 28; Leonard Hill Books, 7; KLM Aerocarto n.v., 69; City Engineer and Surveyor's Department, Manchester, 14; New American Library, 19; Regional Plan Association, 72, 73, 74; Stevenage Development Corporation, 29, 30; Swedish Embassy, 67.

List of Illustrations

1. British Isles: Population distribution: (a) 1801; (b) 1851
2. Deaths from cholera in the Soho district of London, 1854
3. Early 'industrial dwellings', London
4. Aerial photograph of Preston in the 1930s
5. The growth of London, 1800–1960
6. Edgware, North West London: (a) 1926; (b) 1948
7. A house-agent's advertisement of the early 1930s
8. The Great West Road, London, in 1951
9. (a) New Lanark (Robert Owen, c. 1800–1810); (b) Saltaire (Titus Salt, 1853–63); (c) Bournville (George Cadbury, 1879–95); (d) Port Sunlight (William Lever, 1888)
10. Ebenezer Howard's Three Magnets
11. Ebenezer Howard's Social City
12. Plan of Letchworth Garden City, 1903
13. Letchworth from the air
14. (a) and (b) Barry Parker's parkway principle; (c) Its expression at Wythenshawe, 1930
15. The 'neighbourhood unit' principle
16. Two views of Radburn, New Jersey, USA
17. Sir Alker Tripp's precinct diagram
18. Abercrombie's Bloomsbury Precinct
19. Broadacre City
20. The Linear City, 1882
21. The Radiant City (La Ville radieuse)
22. La Ville radieuse, as from the air
23. Aerial photograph of Roehampton
24. Slough
25. Relative growth of population in Great Britain: (a) 1861–91; (b) 1921–39
26. Jarrow in the 1930s
27. The Team Valley Trading Estate
28. The Abercrombie Plan for Greater London, 1944

29. The master plan for Stevenage
30. Stevenage town centre
31. The London Green Belt, 1944–64
32. The structural effect on regional employment change, 1959–67
33. Regional unemployment differentials, 1961–8
34. (a) Median net annual incomes (before tax) in the United Kingdom, 1969–70; (b) Areas where the percentage of net incomes (before tax) of less than £900 per annum is greater than the national average,1970–71
35. Aerial view of Port Talbot steel mill, Glamorgan, South Wales
36. Ford factory, Halewood, Merseyside
37. Reconstruction in central Glasgow
38. Cumbernauld new town, Dunbartonshire, Scotland
39. (a–d) The pattern of regional development in Britain, 1945–72
40. (a) Birth rates in England and Wales, 1871–2004; (b) Population growth in Great Britain, 1871–2004
41. Suburban development at Heswall, Cheshire
42. Major restraints to development in Great Britain
43. A view of the London Green Belt at Cockfosters, North London
44. Reconstruction in London's East End
45. Population growth in the London region, 1951–61 and 1961–71
46. New towns in Britain, 1946–70
47. Plans for expansion in the South East, 1964–70: (a) The *South East Study*, 1964; (b) The *Strategy for the South East*, 1967; (c) The *Strategic Plan for the South East*, 1970
48. Population growth in Great Britain, 1961–71
49. The South Hampshire Plan, 1972
50. Local government reform proposals, 1969 and 1972: (a) The English Royal Commission, 1969; (b) The Local Government Act, 1972; (c) The Scottish Royal Commission (Wheatley), 1969
51. Car ownership in Great Britain and the USA, 1900–2010
52. The transportation planning structure
53. Alternative levels of urban redevelopment in part of London's West End, from the Buchanan Report: (a) Maximal; (b) Minimal
54. Country parks: (a) Wirral Way Country Park, Cheshire; (b) A picnic place on Wirral Way; (c) Location of country parks in England and Wales, 1972
55. Elvaston Castle, Derbyshire
56. The European Economic Community in maps: (a) Density of population mid-1960s; (b) Population change, 1958–68; (c) Gross

Regional Product *per capita*, 1971; (d) Development programmes and problem areas
57. The administrative structure of French regional planning
58. French planning regions and the *métropoles d'équilibre*
59. The Paris regional plan of 1965
60. Reconstruction of La Défense, Paris
61. Development areas in the German Federal Republic
62. The development plan for the Ruhr
63. The Mezzogiorno
64. Plans for Copenhagen: The 1948 Finger Plan, and the 1960 Plan 'B'
65. Plans for Stockholm: 1952 and 1966
66. Stockholm: schematic diagram of a suburban group
67. Aerial view of Farsta, Sweden
68. Map of Randstad Holland
69. View of Randstad Holland near Rotterdam
70. The principle of 'concentrated deconcentration', from the *Second Report on Physical Planning in the Netherlands*
71. Area development programmes in the USA
72. Levittown-Fairless Hills, New Jersey, USA
73. Milford Center, Milford, Connecticut, USA
74. A ghetto area
75. The Atlantic Urban Region: (a) Population densities, *c.* 1960; (b) Potential development by the year 2000
76. Freeway interchange in Los Angeles
77. Three concepts of the planning process: (a) Brian McLoughlin; (b) George Chadwick; (c) Alan Wilson
78. The Garin–Lowry model structure
79. The plan implementation process, according to Brian McLoughlin

List of Tables

1. Insured workers, 1923 and 1937
2. Industrial building completions and employment changes, 1956–60 and 1966–70
3. Total employment changes by industrial orders: Great Britain, 1953–9, 1959–63, 1963–5
4. Regional relatives for unemployment, activity rates and incomes, 1961–6
5. Migration, gross and net, 1965–6

Preface

It is important to stress what this book is and what it is not. It is not a textbook of planning; there are excellent examples of those now available, including especially J. B. McLoughlin's *Urban and Regional Planning: A Systems Approach* and G. Chadwick's *A Systems View of Planning*, as well as the bulkier and wider-ranging text by F. Stuart Chapin, *Urban Land Use Planning*. Rather, it is an introduction to planning, written both for the beginning student and for the general reader. I hope that it will be found useful by students of applied geography and of town and country planning; by university and college students concerned to fit modern planning into its historical context; and by a wider audience which may want to know how planning has evolved.

Two points must be made about the treatment. First, it is deliberately historical; it traces the evolution of urban and regional problems, and of planning philosophies, techniques and legislation, from the Industrial Revolution to the present day. Secondly, it is necessarily written from a British standpoint for a British readership (though hopefully Commonwealth readers will find it relevant). Throughout most of the book the exclusive emphasis is on the British experience, though the survey of early planning thought in Chapter 2 is international, and Chapters 8 and 9 deliberately range out to compare the experience of other advanced industrial countries. Even in those chapters the comparison deliberately excludes the developing world; doubtless, another useful book is to be written there, but there is no space in this book to do the subject justice.

The book is a by-product of nearly ten years of lectures on introductory applied geography, first at the London School of Economics, then at the University of Reading. I am grateful to successive waves of students who endured these courses and who unfailingly, by their reactions, indicated the places where material was boring or unintelligible. More particularly, I am indebted to two academic colleagues and friends: to Brian McLoughlin for his characteristically generous and thoughtful comments on a first draft; and to Marion Clawson for bringing his immense experience to bear on the

1

account in Chapter 9. I must add the usual disclaimer: that for errors and omissions, the author is solely responsible.

To two devoted helpers – my secretary, Monika Wheeler, who typed the manuscript meticulously despite unnaturally heavy departmental burdens, and my cartographer, Kathleen King – I offer my best thanks. Lastly, I dedicate this book to my wife Magda for her imperturbable patience in the face of gross provocation. I hope that she will find the result some small recompense for many delayed dinners and obsessed weekends.

1. Planning, Planners and Plans

Planning, the subject matter of this book, is an extremely ambiguous and difficult word to define. Planners of all kinds think that they know what it means; it refers to the work they do. The difficulty is that they do all sorts of different things, and so they mean different things by the word; planning seems to be all things to all men. We need to start by defining what exactly we are discussing.

The reference in the dictionary gives one clue to the confusion. Whether you go to the *Oxford English Dictionary* or the American *Webster*, there you find that the noun 'plan' and the verb 'to plan' have several distinct meanings. In particular, the noun can either mean 'a physical representation of something' – as for instance a drawing or a map; or it can mean 'a method for doing something'; or 'an orderly arrangement of parts of an objective'. The first meaning, in particular, is quite different from the others: when we talk about a street 'plan' of London or New York, we mean something quite different from when we talk about our 'plan' to visit London or New York next year. But there is one definition that combines the others and blurs the distinction, as when we talk about a 'plan' for a new building. This is simultaneously a physical design of that building as it is intended to be, and a guide to realizing our intention to build it. And it is here that the real ambiguity arises.

The verb 'to plan', and the nouns 'planning' and 'planner' that are derived from it, have in fact only the second, general group of meanings: they do not refer to the art of drawing up a physical plan or design on paper. They can mean either 'to arrange the parts of', or 'to realize the achievement of', or, more vaguely, 'to intend'. The most common meaning of 'planning' involves both the first two of these elements: planning is concerned with deliberately achieving some objective, and it proceeds by assembling actions into some orderly sequence. One dictionary definition, in fact, refers to what planning does; the other, to how planning does it.

The trouble arises because, although people realize that planning has this more general meaning, they tend to remember the idea of the plan as a physical representation or design. Thus they imagine that planning must include the preparation of such a design. Now it is true that many types of planning might require a physical design, or might benefit from having one: planning often is used in the production of physical objects, such as cars or aeroplanes or buildings or whole towns, and in these cases a blueprint of the desired product will certainly be needed. But many other types of planning, though they will almost certainly require the production of many symbols on pieces of paper, in the form of words or diagrams, may never involve the production of a single exact physical representation of the entity which is being produced.

For instance, the word 'planning' is today applied to many different human activities – in fact, virtually all human activities. One almost certainly needs a plan to make war; diplomats make contingency plans to keep the peace. We talk about educational planning: that does not mean that every detail of every class has to be planned by some bureaucracy (as happens, by repute, in France), but merely that advance planning is necessary if students are to find classrooms and libraries and teachers when they arrive at a certain age and seek a certain sort of education. We talk about planning the economy to minimize the swings of boom and slump, and reduce the misery of unemployment; we hear about a housing plan and a social-services plan. Industry now plans on a colossal scale: the production of a new model of a car, or a typewriter, has to be worked out many years in advance of its appearance in the shops. And all this is true, whatever the nature of the economic system. Whether labelled free enterprise or social democratic or East European socialist or Maoist, no society on earth today provides goods and services for its people, or schools and colleges for its children, without planning. One might regret it and wish for a simpler age when perhaps things happened without forethought; if that age ever existed, it has gone for ever.

The reason is the fact of life everybody knows: that modern society is immeasurably more complex, technically and socially, than previous societies. Centuries ago, when education involved the simple repetition of a few well-understood rules which were taught to all, and when books were non-existent, the setting up of a school did not involve much elaborate plant or the training of specialized teachers. The stages of production were simpler; wood was cut in the forest, men wrought it locally into tools, the tools were used by their neighbours, all without much forethought. But today, without elaborate planning, the whole complex fabric of our material civilization would begin to crack up: supplies of foodstuffs would disappear, essential water and power supplies would fail, epidemics would rapidly break out. We see these things happening all too readily, after natural or human disasters like earthquakes or wars or major strikes of railwaymen or power workers. Though some of us may decide to opt out of technological civilization for a few years or for good, the prospect does not seem likely to appeal to the great mass of mankind even in the affluent world. Those in the less affluent world are in much less doubt that they want the security and dignity that planning can bring.

The point is that the sorts of planning which we have been discussing in these last two paragraphs either may not require physical plans at all, in the sense of scale blueprints of physical objects, or may require them only occasionally or incidentally. It is more likely to consist, for the most part, of written statements accompanied by tables of figures, or mathematical formulae, or diagrams, or all these things. The emphasis throughout is on tracing an orderly sequence of events which will achieve a predetermined goal.

Consider educational planning as an example. The goal has first to be fixed. It may be given externally, as a situation which has to be met: to provide education which will meet the expected demands ten years hence. Or there may be a more positive, active goal: to double the numbers of scientists graduating from the universities, for instance. Whatever the aim, the first step will be a careful projection which leads from the present to the future target date, year by year. It will show the number of students in schools and colleges and the courses that will be needed to meet whatever objective is stated. From this, the implications will be traced in terms of buildings, teachers and materials. There may need to be a crash school-building programme using quickly assembled prefabricated components; a new or a supplementary teacher-training programme, or an attempt to win back married women into teaching; a new series of textbooks or experiments in closed-circuit TV, all of which in turn will take time to set in motion and produce results. At critical points in the process, alternatives will be faced. Would it be more economical, or more effective, to increase teacher supply or concentrate on a greater supply of teaching material through the TV system? Could better use be made of existing buildings by better overall coordination, rather than by putting up new buildings? Ways will need to be found of evaluating these choices. Then, throughout the lifetime of the programme, ways will need to be found of monitoring progress very closely to take account of unexpected failures or divergences from the plan or changes in the situation. In the whole of this complex sequence the only scale models may be the designs of the new schools or of the TV system and a few other details – a small part of the whole, and one which comes at a late stage in the process, when the broad outlines of the programme are determined.

To summarize, then: planning as a general activity is the making of an orderly sequence of action that will lead to the achievement of a stated goal or goals. Its main techniques will be written statements, supplemented as appropriate by statistical projections, mathematical representations, quantified evaluations and diagrams illustrating relationships between different parts of the plan. It may, but need not necessarily, include exact physical blueprints of objects.

The Application to Urban and Regional Planning

The difficulty now comes when we try to apply this description to the particular sort of planning that is the subject matter of this book: urban and regional planning (or, as it is often still called, town and country planning). In many advanced industrial countries, such as Britain, the United States, Germany or Japan, the phrase 'urban planning' or 'town planning' is strictly a tautology: since a great majority of the population are classed in the statistics as urban and live in places defined as urban, 'town planning' seems simply to mean any sort of planning whatsoever. In fact, as is well known, 'urban' planning conventionally means something more limited and precise: it refers to planning with a spatial, or geographical, component, in which the general objective is to provide for a spatial structure of activities (or of land uses) which in some way is better than the pattern existing without planning. Such planning is also known as 'physical' planning; 'spatial' planning is perhaps a more neutral and more precise term.

If such planning centrally has a spatial component, then clearly it only makes sense if it culminates in a spatial representation. Whether this is a very precise and detailed map, or the most general diagram, it is to some degree a 'plan' in the first, more precise meaning of the term. In other words, it seems that urban planning (or regional planning) is a special case of general planning, which does include the plan-making, or representational, component.

Broadly, in practice this does prove to be the case. It is simply impossible to think of this type of planning without some spatial representation – without a map, in other words. And whatever the precise organizational sequence of such planning, in practice it does tend to proceed from very general (and rather diagrammatic) maps to very precise ones, or blueprints. For the final output of such a process is the act of physical development (or, in some cases, the decision not to develop, but to leave the land as it is). And physical development, in the form of buildings, will require an exact design.

A great deal of discussion and controversy in recent years tends to have obscured this fact. In most countries spatial or urban planning as practised for many years – both before the Second World War and after it – was very minute and detailed: the output tended to consist of very precise large-scale maps showing the exact disposition of all land uses and activities and proposed developments. After 1960 such detailed plans were much attacked: planning, it was argued, needed to concentrate much more on the broad principles rather than on details; it should stress the process, or time sequence, by which the goal was to be reached, rather than present the desired end-state in detail; it should start from a highly generalized and diagrammatic picture of the spatial distributions at any point of time, only filling in the details as they needed to be filled in, bit by bit. This, as we shall see later, is the essential difference in Britain between the system of local town and country planning introduced by the historic Town and Country Planning Act of 1947, and the system which is replacing it under the Town and Country Planning Act of 1968.

The central point, though, is that this type of planning is still essentially spatial – whatever the scale and whatever the sequence. It is concerned with the spatial impact of many different kinds of problem, and with the spatial coordination of many different policies. Economic planners, for instance, are concerned with the broad progress of the economy, usually at national and sometimes at international level: they look at the evolving structure of the economy, in terms of industries and occupations, at the combination of the factors of production which brings forth the flow of goods and services, at the income thus generated and its reconversion into factors of production, and at problems of exchange. The regional economic planner will look at the same things, but always from the point of view of their particular *spatial* impact: he is considering the effect of the variable, geographical space and distance on these phenomena. Similarly social planners will be concerned with the needs of the individual and the group; they will be concerned with the changing social structure of the population, with occupational mobility and its effect on life styles and housing patterns, with household and family structure in relation to factors like age and occupation and educational background, with household income and its variation, with social and psychological factors which lead to individual or family breakdown. The social planner in the urban planning office shares the same interests and concerns, but he sees them always with the spatial component: he is concerned, for instance, with the effect of occupational mobility on the inner city – as against the new suburb – on changing household structure as it affects the housing market near the centre of the city, on household income in relation to items like travel cost for the low-income family whose available employment may be migrating to the suburbs.

The relationship between urban and regional planning and the various other types of specialized planning, in these examples, is

8

interestingly like the relationship of geography, as an academic subject, to other related social sciences. For geography also has a number of different faces, each of which stresses the spatial relationships in one of these related sciences: economic geography analyses the effect of geographic space and distance on the mechanisms of production, consumption and exchange; social geography similarly examines the spatial impact upon patterns of social relationship; political geography looks at the effect of location upon political actions. One can argue from this that spatial planning, or urban and regional planning, is essentially human geography in these various aspects, harnessed or applied to the positive task of action to achieve a specific objective.

Many teachers in planning schools would hotly deny this. They would argue that planning, as they teach it, necessarily includes many aspects which are not commonly taught in geography curricula – even those that stress the applications of the subject. The law relating to the land is one of these; civil engineering is another; civic design is another. This is true, though many would argue – both inside the planning schools, and out – that not all these elements are necessary to the planning curriculum. What does seem true is that the central body of social sciences which relate to geography, and whose spatial aspects are taught as parts of human geography – economics, sociology, politics and psychology – does form the core of the subject matter of urban and regional planning. By 'subject matter' I mean that which is actually planned. It is, however, arguable that there is another important element in planning education, not covered in this body of social science: that is the study of the *method of planning* itself, the way men assume control over physical and human matter and process it to serve their defined ends. According to this distinction 'planning method' would be what is common to the education of all kinds of planners – whether educational, industrial, military or any other; geography and its related social sciences would constitute the peculiar subject matter of that particular division of planning called urban and regional.

Urban and Regional Planning

'Planning' as an Activity

What then would this core of planning education — the study of 'planning method' — comprise? This is a basic question, which ought to have been the subject of intense debate in schools of planning. But curiously, for a long time it was avoided — the reason being, apparently, that planning education was seen as education in making physical plans, not education in planning method. The first people to raise the question seriously were not teachers of physical planning, but teachers of industrial or corporate planning, in the American business schools. There, up to about 1945, education in management was usually based on a rather narrow spectrum of skills in applied engineering and accounting; the aim was to obtain maximum efficiency in plant operation, both in an engineering sense and in an accounting sense, and little attention was given to the problems of decision-taking in complex situations. But, partly as the result of the work of such fundamental thinkers as Chester Barnard, Peter Drucker and Herbert Simon, management education was transformed. First, it developed into a science of decision-making, which borrowed freely from concepts in philosophy and politics, but which in effect consisted of a new branch of academic study; and secondly, it harnessed the thinking of a number of social sciences, such as economics, sociology and psychology. It was this new tradition in corporate planning which began, after about 1960, to affect the direction and content of education for physical planning.

By this time, however, management education had further evolved. With the development of computerization in management and planning of all kinds there was increasing interest in the development of sophisticated control systems which would automatically control machinery. Such systems, of course, were only a development of earlier experiments in automation, which can be dated right back to the origins of the Industrial Revolution; but progress in this field took a big leap forward with the rapid development of more complex computers during the 1950s. Yet even before this, a remarkable original thinker, Norbert Wiener of Harvard, had anticipated the development, and much more. In a book published in 1950, *The*

Human Use of Human Beings, he had suggested that automation would liberate the human race from the necessity to do mundane tasks. But further, he proposed that the study of automatic control systems was only part of a much larger science of cybernetics,* which he defined in the title of a book published in 1948 as the science of 'Control and Communication in the Animal and the Machine'. According to Wiener, animals and especially human beings have long possessed extremely complex communication and control mechanisms – the sort of thing the computer was then replicating. Human societies, Wiener suggested, could be regarded as another manifestation of this need for communication and control.

Thus a new science was born. Rapidly developing in the late 1950s and 1960s, it had a profound influence on research and education in management, and particularly in planning. For if human arrangements could be regarded as complex interrelating systems, they could be paralleled by similar systems of control in the computer, which could then be used to monitor developments and apply appropriate adjustments.

The best analogy here is manned space flight. In an expedition to the moon most of the adjustments to the spacecraft are made not by the astronauts but by an extraordinarily complex computer-control system on earth at Houston, Texas. This system does not consciously 'see' the spacecraft in order to pilot it: it receives information from it electronically, and responds by feeding this information to models, or artificial simulations, of the course of the spacecraft in relation to the movement of the earth and the moon; it then processes this information, calculates the correct controls to be applied and automatically applies them. Similarly, it is argued, the development of cities and regions could be controlled by a computer which received information about the course of development in a particular area, related this to the objectives which had been laid down by the planners for the development during the next few years and thus produced an appropriate series of adjustments to put the city or the region 'on course' again.

In practice this insight has been very useful for the way we think

* The word is derived from an ancient Greek word, meaning 'helmsman' or 'steersman'.

about physical or spatial planning. As we shall see in later chapters of this book, it has profoundly affected the way planners think about their job and the way they produce plans. In essence it has led to a swing away from the old idea of planning as production of blueprints for the future desired state of the area, and towards the new idea of planning as a continuous series of controls over the development of the area, aided by devices which seek to model or simulate the process of development so that this control can be applied. This in turn has led to a complete change in the sequence of the planner's work.

Formerly, at any time from about 1920 until about 1960, the classic sequence taught to all planning students was *survey–analysis–plan*. (It had first been worked out, and taught, by a remarkable British pioneer in planning, Patrick Geddes; his work is discussed in more detail in Chapter 3.) The terms were self-explanatory. First the planner made a survey, in which he collected all the relevant information about the development of his city or region. Then he analysed these data, seeking to project them as far as possible into the future to discover how the area was changing and developing. And thirdly, he planned: that is, he made a plan which took into account the facts and interpretations revealed in his survey and analysis, and which sought to harness and control the trends according to principles of sound planning. After a few years – the British Planning Act of 1947 laid down that the period should be every five years – the process should be repeated: the survey should be carried out again to check for new facts and developments, the analysis should be re-worked to see how far the projections needed modifying, and the plan should be updated accordingly.

The new planning sequence, which is rapidly replacing this older one as orthodoxy, reflects the new emphases in cybernated planning. It is more difficult to represent in words because it is a continuous cycle; more commonly, it is represented as a flow diagram. But, to break into the flow for purposes of exposition, it can be said to start with the formulation of goals and objectives for the development of the area concerned. (These should be continuously refined and re-defined during the cycles of the planning process.) Against this background the planner develops an information system which is continuously updated as the region develops and changes. It will be used to produce various alternative projections, or simulations, of the state of the region at various future dates, assuming the application of various policies. (The aim is always to make this process as flexible and as varied as possible, so that it is possible to look at all sorts of ways of allowing the region to grow and change.) Then the alternatives are compared or evaluated against yardsticks derived from the goals and objectives, to produce a recommended system of policy controls which in turn will be modified as the objectives are re-examined and as the information system produces evidence of new developments. Though it is difficult to put the new sequence into a string of words like the older one, it might be succinctly described as *goals—continuous information—projection and simulation of alternative futures—evaluation—choice—continuous monitoring*. Something like this sequence, with some differences in words and in ordering, can be found in several important and well-known accounts of the planning process written in the 1960s and early 1970s.

Objectives in Planning – Simple and Complex

In practice, as has been said above, this is a great improvement. It means that the whole planning process is more clearly articulated, more logical and more explicit. It is obviously better that planners should start with a fairly exhaustive discussion about what they are seeking to achieve and that they should go on having this discussion during the whole planning process. It is better, too, that different alternatives for the future should be developed, so that they can be openly discussed and evaluated. And the emphasis on specific evaluation, using certain fixed criteria, is an advance. Planning is now much more flexible, working with much greater information. And it is more rational – at least potentially so.

Nevertheless, the new system creates many new problems and pitfalls of its own. The development of computerization does not make planning easier, in the sense that it somehow becomes more automatic. There may be many automatic aids to smooth out tedious processes, such as detailed calculations; but they do not diminish the area of human responsibility – the responsibility to take decisions. And the basic difficulty is that it is more difficult, and finally just less feasible, to apply cybernation to spatial planning problems than it is to apply it to the job of getting men on the moon.

At first sight this may seem absurd: nothing could be more awe-inspiring than space travel. But this is to mix up levels of difficulty. Moon travel presents many technical problems, but there are two features that make it basically simple. First, the objective is clearly understood: there is one aim only, to get men on the moon. Secondly, the processes involved are nearly all physical: they are subject to laws of physics, which are much better understood, and which appear to be more regular in their application, than laws of human behaviour. (There are human beings involved, of course, but in practice they are reduced to little more than biological units for most of the voyage.) The sort of planning which we are discussing here is, conversely, more complex. First, the basic objective is not well understood; there are clearly more than one, and perhaps dozens (economic growth, fair distribution of income, social cohesion and stability, reduction of psychological stress, a beautiful environment – the list seems endless). Secondly, most of the processes which need controlling are human processes, which are less well understood and work with much less certainty than laws in the physical sciences. Anyone who has studied any of the social sciences such as economics, sociology, psychology or human geography is familiar with this fact. Just as in these sciences we have to work with laws of statistical tendency rather than with laws which are constantly reliable in producing experimental results, so it will be in much of spatial or physical planning.

One point made in the last paragraph is relevant for our understanding of the particular nature of spatial planning. Earlier, we said that its method was shared with other sorts of planning activity; its subject matter was distinctively spatial, so that at some time, in some sense, it would produce spatial representations of how activities should be ordered on the ground. We now see that spatial planning, as we are using the term in this book – urban and regional planning, as it is conventionally termed – has another essential feature: it is *multi-dimensional* and *multi-objective* planning. It is necessary to

14

specify these two linked attributes, because there are many types of planning which are 'spatial' in the sense that they are concerned with spatial arrangements on the earth's surface, but have only a single dimension and a single objective. When a sanitary engineer considers a sewer plan, his work certainly has a spatial component, but it is neither multi-dimensional nor multi-objective. (Or, to be more precise, even if the engineer thinks he has more than one objective, these are all engineering objectives within the same basic dimension.) This engineer, or his colleagues the highway engineer or telephone engineer, are doubtless all working with plans which are spatial representations of their territory. But none of them will be trying (for instance) to balance the advantages of preserving a long-established inner city society against the advantages of building better housing on an estate some distance away, or the problem of reconciling higher car ownership with the preservation of public transport for those who have no access to cars, or the merits of segregating factory zones versus the merit of having local factories nearer to people's homes – all these, and many more, being considered as part of the same planning process, and having finally each to be considered *vis-à-vis* all the others. This is the essence of the job of the urban and regional planner; this is why, compared with most other sorts of job regarded as planning, it is so difficult.

It is clear by now that it is difficult in two ways. First of all, the amount of necessary information and specialized expertise is so much greater than in most other planning activities: it covers almost the whole of human experience. The ideal urban and regional planner would have to be a good economist, sociologist, geographer and social psychologist in his own right, as well as having several other necessary physical-scientific skills, such as a good understanding of civil engineering and of cybernetics. To judge the quality of the information he was receiving, he would need to be a sophisticated (and even slightly cynical) statistician. And he would need to be a highly competent systems analyst in order to develop the relationships with the computer control system with which he related. All of which, of course, constitutes an impossible specification – and a daunting task for the educationist.

But secondly, and even more problematically, there is the need to frame and then weigh up different objectives. Consider a very typical (and very topical) type of planning controversy, repeated almost daily: the line of a new urban motorway. Some critics say that it would be quite unnecessary if public transport were adequate: some that the line should be shifted. The fact is that car ownership is rising, and this seems outside the planner's control; it is set for him by the political or social framework within which he acts. The projections (which may not be entirely reliable) suggest that the traffic will overwhelm the present road network, giving an environment to many thousands of people which, by current standards, is judged intolerable. The quality of public transport is declining, but the available evidence shows that better quality would not have much result in tempting people back from their cars and reducing the case for the motorway. One possible line for the motorway goes through a slum district due for early demolition and re-building; some sociologists say that the community should be re-housed *in situ*, others argue that many of the people would lead happier lives in a new town. Another line goes through open space which contains playing fields as well as the nesting grounds of several species of birds; local sports clubs and nature conservationists are united in opposing this line. The costs to the public purse are known in the two cases, but the benefits are dependent on the valuation of travel time for the likely motorway users, on which two groups of economists are hotly disputing. And the costs, or disbenefits, for different groups of the public affected by the building of the motorway are almost incalculable. There are many varying interests and many special academic skills, some of the practitioners of which cannot agree among themselves; the only person who seems competent to take any decision at all is someone whose training and thinking are supposed to encompass them all. This, of course, is the general urban and regional planner.

This is not the point at which to discuss the resolution of the problem just mentioned; in fact, there simply is *no* clear resolution, and the most the planner can do is to try to reach a decision within a clear and explicit framework – which, hopefully, the new style of planning helps him to do.

The example has been given simply to illustrate the unique quality, and the unique difficulty, of the sort of planning that is the subject matter of this book. To sum up: urban and regional planning is *spatial* or *physical*: it uses the general methods of planning to produce a physical design. Because of the increasing influence of these general methods, it is oriented towards *process* rather than towards the production of one-shot (or end-state) plans. Its subject matter is really that part of geography which is concerned with urban and regional systems; but the planning method itself is a type of management for very complex systems. And, further, it is necessarily multi-dimensional and multi-objective in its scope; this is what distinguishes it from the work of many other professionals whose work can fairly be described as planning with a spatial component.

Structure of This Book

The remainder of this book falls into five parts. Chapters 2 and 3 outline the early history of urban development in Britain, with special references to the changes brought about by the Industrial Revolution, and the contributions of notable early thinkers and writers on urban planning during the period 1880–1945. Chapters 4 and 5 take the British story through the 1930s and 1940s, describing the new challenge of regional imbalance which appeared in the Great Depression of 1929–32, and the subsequent creation of the postwar planning machine, following publication of the Barlow Report of 1940. Chapters 6 and 7 analyse the postwar history, and attempt to pass judgement on the performance of the planning system, first at broad regional level in respect of economic planning, then at the scale of the town and the city region in respect of urban planning. Chapters 8 and 9 attempt a comparative look at planning experience in other developed industrial countries, Chapter 8 for Western Europe and Chapter 9 for the United States. Lastly, Chapter 10 provides an outline of the sequence of urban and regional plan making, with an introduction to some of the more important techniques involved at various stages of this process; it is deliberately written to provide a bridge to the more advanced textbooks of planning, which deal with these processes in more detail. But this book, as I have stressed in the Preface, must end there; it does not try to compete with those textbooks, but to provide the necessary historical framework of introduction to them.

Further Reading

Peter Hall, *The Theory and Practice of Regional Planning* (Pemberton, 1970). Chapters 1 and 2 contain an extended treatment of some of the problems of definition discussed here.

2. The Origins: Urban Growth from 1800 to 1940

Modern urban and regional planning has arisen in response to specific social and economic problems, which in turn were triggered off by the Industrial Revolution at the end of the eighteenth century. It is important to notice that these problems did not all come at once, in the same form; they changed in character, and in their relative importance, so that the questions uppermost in the minds of city-dwellers in the 1930s were by no means the same as those experienced by their great-grandfathers in the 1840s. As problems were identified, solutions were proposed for them; but because of the inertia of men's minds, and still more the inertia of social and political processes, these solutions – especially the more radical ones – might not be put into action until decades afterwards, when the problem itself had changed in character and perhaps also in importance. That is a most important common theme which runs through this and the next two chapters.

Planning before the Industrial Revolution

There were important cities before the Industrial Revolution: Ancient Rome had an estimated population of 800,000–1,200,000 in the third century A.D.; Elizabethan London numbered about 225,000 people. Correspondingly, these cities had problems of economic and social organization: Rome had to be supplied with water brought over considerable distances by aqueduct (the word itself is Roman in origin), and the city developed immense problems of traffic congestion – which, unfortunately, have been inherited by the modern city two thousand years later. London by the fourteenth century had to draw on coalfields by the River Tyne, 270 miles away, for fuel, and on distant countries for more specialized provisions, such as dyestuffs or spices; by the seventeenth century it, too, was drawing water from 35 miles away by aqueduct. (The New River, which still runs through North London, is part of it.) These problems in turn brought forth a host of regulations for the better ordering of the city, sometimes dealing with strangely modern problems: Rome banned chariots at night to deal with the first recorded case of urban noise pollution; in London in the fourteenth century a man was hanged for burning 'sea coal' – a somewhat draconian penalty for medieval air pollution.

Furthermore, many cities both in the ancient and the medieval world were planned, at least in the sense that their existence and their location were laid down consciously by some ruler or some group of merchants; and among this group, a large proportion even had formal ground plans with a strong element of geometric regularity. In Britain the group of medieval planned towns is larger than many people think: a small town like Baldock, on the Great North Road (A1) before it was by-passed, was actually a creation of the Knights Templar, and the name itself is a corruption of Baghdad; Winchelsea on the Sussex coast, and small towns in North Wales like Flint, Conway and Caernarvon, were all fortified towns created by Edward I in the late thirteenth century, and were deliberately modelled on the Bastide towns established by the French kings as part of their conquest of Provence a few years earlier.

The greatest flowering of formal town planning before the Industrial Revolution, though, came in what is known in continental Europe as the Baroque Era: the seventeenth and eighteenth centuries. There, it produced such masterpieces of large-scale architectural design as the reconstruction of Rome during the late sixteenth and early seventeenth centuries; or the great compositions of the Tuileries gardens and the Champs-Élysées, in Paris; or the palace of Versailles and its bordering planned town; or the completely planned town of Karlsruhe, in Germany; or the seventeenth-century quarters of Nancy, in the province of Lorraine in eastern France; as well as many other smaller, but fine, examples. These were nearly all expressions of absolute regal or papal power, and some commentators have claimed to see in them the expression of a new style of warfare;

instead of the medieval walled town, cities must now be planned along broad formal avenues where mobile armies could deploy themselves. Britain, after Cromwellian times, had no such absolute monarchy; here the aristocracy and the new merchant class dominated the growth of cities, and determined their form. The result was a different but equally distinctive form of town planning: the development of formal residential quarters consisting of dignified houses built in terraces, or rows, generally on a strongly geometrical street plan which was modified by charming squares with gardens. The original development of many of the quarters of London's West End, now sadly decimated by later reconstruction – areas like St James's, Mayfair, Marylebone and Bloomsbury – still provides the best examples in Britain of this type of planning attached to an existing major city; Edinburgh's New Town, facing the medieval city across the deep cut now occupied by the railway, is another. But perhaps the best example of eighteenth-century British town planning is the development of Bath, up to then a small medieval town, as the result of a new enthusiasm for spa cures among the aristocracy at that time.

All these examples, and many other imitations, have great interest for the student of architecture or the origins of planning. And similarly, the creation of the rural landscape of Europe – a process which involved much more conscious planning than most people, looking at the result casually, would imagine – is important for the planner, understanding how previous generations adjusted to the opportunities and the limitations the region presented. But the subject deserves much fuller treatment than it can receive here; and it is excellently written up in another book in this series, *The Making of the English Landscape* by W. G. Hoskins. Our main concern now is a subject that has little relation with the past: the unprecedented impact of modern industrialism on urban development and upon consequent urban planning problems.

The Impact of Industrialism

Oddly, at first the Industrial Revolution had no striking effect on urban growth. The earliest of the new inventions in textiles or in iron-making, developed in England between 1700 and 1780, seemed rather to be dispersing industry out of the towns and into the open countryside. By the end of this period – and even later still, into the early nineteenth century – typical industrial landscapes, such as the cotton-making areas of south Lancashire or south Derbyshire, the woollen areas of the Colne and Calder Valleys in the West Riding of Yorkshire, or the iron-making and working areas of Coalbrookdale (Shropshire) or the Black Country, essentially consisted of a straggle of small industrial hamlets across an area fundamentally still rural. In some industries this tradition survived even longer: D. H. Lawrence's early novels describe it in the Nottinghamshire coalfield as late as 1900.

But it was coal that changed the situation. As soon as it became a principal raw material of industry – replacing water power in textiles after 1780, for instance – it tended to concentrate industry where supplies could be made available: on the coalfields themselves, and then adjacent to bulk transport. Britain, because it industrialized earlier than any other country, experienced special constraints on its industrial location pattern: the early machinery consumed great quantities of coal because it was inefficient, and the coal was very expensive to transport because there were no railways, only canals. After about 1830 (the first steam-driven railway, the Stockton and Darlington, came in 1825) both these conditions changed, and industry was freer to locate. But by then its pattern was fixed.

This fact alone created a new phenomenon: the new industrial town, developed almost from nothing – or perhaps from a small and obscure village origin – within a few years, on the coalfields of Lancashire and Yorkshire and Durham and Staffordshire. Simultaneously some towns – those which were neither port towns nor on coalfields – stagnated industrially. But many older-established medieval towns – because they were near enough to coalfields, or because they were on navigable water, or because they became railway junctions soon after the railways arrived – were also able to become major centres of the new factory industry: Leicester, Nottingham and Bristol are good examples. Port towns, indeed, were just as important as pure industrial towns in the whole process of industrialization, because they effected the critical exchange of raw materials and finished products on which the whole system depended: thus cities like Liverpool, Hull, Glasgow and, above all, London were among the fastest-growing places from 1780 onwards.

Some of the resulting growth patterns are extraordinary – even by the standards of the twentieth century, which has become used to mushrooming growth in the cities of the developing world. The most spectacular cases were, of course, some of the new industrial towns which developed almost from nothing. Rochdale in Lancashire, for instance, numbered about 15,000 in 1801, 44,000 in 1851 and 83,000 in 1901; West Hartlepool in County Durham grew from 4,000 in 1851 to 63,000 by 1901. But though their percentage rate of growth was necessarily more modest, many bigger and older-established centres managed to maintain an amazing rate of growth throughout most of the century. London doubled from approximately 1 million to about 2 million between 1801 and 1851; doubled again to 4 million by 1881; and then added another $2\frac{1}{2}$ million to reach $6\frac{1}{2}$ million in 1911.

The parallel with the cities of the developing world is, in several ways, only too exact. The people who flooded into the burgeoning nineteenth-century industrial and port cities of Britain were overwhelmingly coming from the countryside. They tended to be drawn from the poorer section of the rural population – those who had least to lose and most to gain by coming to the city. Many of them had found it increasingly difficult to get work after the enclosure movement which, approved and planned by Parliament, transformed so much of midland and southern England during the eighteenth century. Some of them – like the Irish who flooded into Liverpool and Manchester and Glasgow after the failure of the potato harvest in 1845–6 – were truly destitute. They had little or no knowledge of the technical skills needed by the new industry, or of the social and technical necessities of urban life. And though the industry of the towns provided economic opportunities in plenty for an unskilled labour force, the social arrangements in the towns were quite incapable of meeting their needs for shelter, for elementary public services like water and waste disposal, or for health treatment.

This last point is critical: these towns had only the most elementary

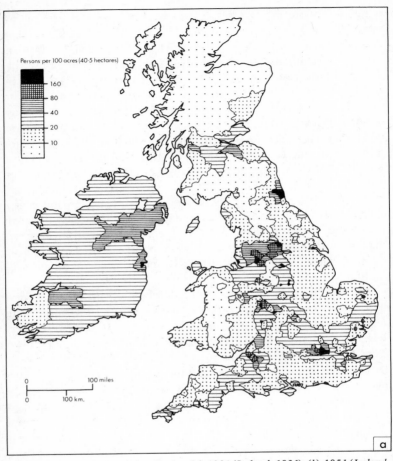

1. *British Isles: Population distribution: (a) 1801 (Ireland, 1821); (b) 1851 (Ireland, 1841). In the first half of the nineteenth century, population concentrated in the towns – especially on the newly developed coalfields of the north. Here, towns grew without plan or control.*

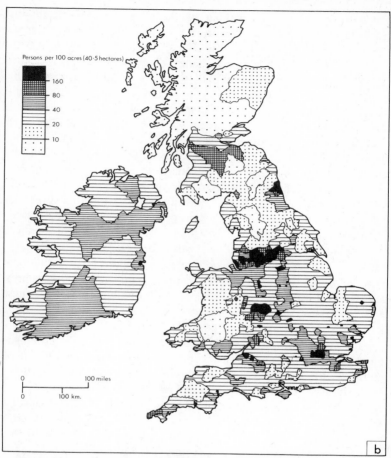

Persons per 100 acres (40·5 hectares)

160
80
40
20
10

100 miles

100 km.

b

arrangements, or none, for providing water, or clearing refuse or sewage, or for treating mass epidemics. Many of the towns, having sprung up so rapidly from villages, had virtually no arrangements at all. Even in the larger towns they had been very elementary; and they tended to be quite overwhelmed by the influx. In a stagnant or slowly growing city, or in a relatively small town, the consequences might not have been so dire: wells might not have become polluted so easily by sewage; new dwellings could be constructed quite easily outside the existing town limits without overcrowding. But in the rapidly growing towns these solutions were not open. Because there was no system of public transport to speak of, the new population like the old must be within walking distance of work in the factories or warehouses. Within the limits thus set, population densities actually tended to rise during the first half of the nineteenth century; the census records for London or Manchester show this quite clearly. The results could have been predicted. Limited water supplies were increasingly contaminated by sewage; there were quite inadequate arrangements for disposal of waste, and filthy matter of all kinds remained close to dense concentrations of people; water supplies were lacking or fitful, and personal hygiene was very poor; over-crowding grew steadily worse, both in the form of more dwellings per acre and more people per room; cellar dwellings became all too common in some cities, such as Manchester or Liverpool; medical treatment, and above all public health controls, were almost completely lacking. And, to make things worse, the greater mobility induced by trade meant that epidemics could move more rapidly across the world than ever before. This, plus polluted water supplies, was the basic cause of the terrible cholera epidemics that swept Britain in 1832, 1848 and 1866.

The results for public health became clear only after the establishment of an efficient government organization for charting the state of public health: the General Register Office, set up in 1837. William Farr, the first Registrar General and one of the founding fathers of the modern science of statistics, showed as early as 1841 that the expectation of life at birth – 41 years in England and Wales overall and 45 in salubrious Surrey – was only 26 years in Liverpool: two years later in Manchester, it was only 24. Much of this difference arose because of the shockingly high infant-mortality rates in the northern industrial towns: 259 out of every 1,000 children born died within the first year of life in Liverpool in 1840–41, and for the early 1870s the average was still 219. (The corresponding figure for Liverpool in 1970 was 21; an eloquent testimony to the improved quality of life.)

It was a situation which society could not tolerate for long. Even in the most cynical view, the more privileged members of society –

the industrialists and merchants − were likely to suffer from it: less so than their workers, to be sure, but still the statistics showed that the risk was considerable. Yet the struggle for reform was a difficult one; it had to surmount at least three major hurdles. The first was the will to act; and this took some time to spread to a large section of the controlling interests who dominated Parliament and the local authorities. Until 1832, it must be remembered, Parliament was totally

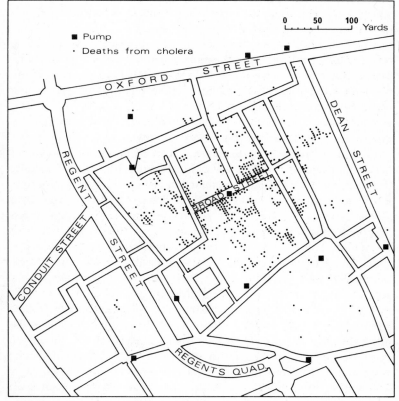

2. *Deaths from cholera in the Soho district of London, September 1854. Dr John Snow's celebrated map, which established the connection between the cholera outbreak and a single polluted water pump in Broad Street. This emphasized the importance of supplying pure water to the inhabitants of the growing cities of Britain.*

unrepresentative of the experience and the views of those in the new industrial towns. The second was knowledge of how to act; and on many critical questions, such as the germ-borne causation of disease and its treatment, and above all the origin of cholera, medical experts were sadly ignorant until after the turn of the century. (Cholera was first identified as a water-borne disease in 1854 by a London doctor, John Snow, in an early piece of spatial analysis; he proved that the outbreaks in a slum district of London were systematically associated with the water supply from a single pump. But it was not until some time after this that the mechanism was understood.) The third need was for effective administrative machinery, including finance, for instituting the necessary controls and providing public services; and this, in an era of rampant *laissez-faire*, was in many ways the hardest of all, involving as it did the upsetting of existing and ineffectual local governments.

The position here was confused. An Act of 1835, the Municipal Corporations Act, had reformed borough government; but usually it did not make the boroughs exclusively responsible for public services or sanitary controls, and in any case, many towns had new building beyond their boundaries. Two major Blue Books, or official reports – the Select Committee on the Health of Towns (1840) and the Royal Commission on the State of Large Towns (1844–5) – recommended that there should be a single public health authority in each local area to regulate drainage, paving, cleansing and water supply; they also called for powers to govern the standards of construction of new buildings. From the mid-century a series of Acts – the Public Health Act of 1848, which set up a Central Board of Health and allowed it to establish Local Boards of Health, the Nuisance Removal Acts from 1855 and the Sanitary Act of 1866 – aided the control of the more obvious sanitary problems. And, from the 1860s, there was increasing interest in the control of building standards. The Torrens Acts from 1868 onwards allowed local authorities to compel owners of insanitary dwellings to demolish or repair them at their own expense; the Cross Acts, from 1875 onwards, allowed local authorities themselves to prepare improvement schemes for slum areas. The last of these Acts – the Public Health Act of 1875 – produced a long-overdue fundamental reform of local government in England and

3. *Early 'industrial dwellings' in Bethnal Green, London. From the mid-nineteenth century onwards, these were a reaction by private philanthropic landlords to the slum problem of the Victorian city. They offered superior working-class accommodation and yet gave a return on capital. Now, a century or more later, many are in turn condemned as slums.*

Wales, outside the boroughs: the country was divided into urban and rural sanitary districts, which would be supervised by a central government department already set up in 1871, the Local Government Board. The word 'sanitary' in their title amply indicates the original scope of these authorities; but soon they were incorporated in a comprehensive local government reform. Three Acts – the Municipal Corporations Act of 1882 and the Local Government Acts of 1888 and 1894 – gave new local government structures to the boroughs, the counties (plus new county boroughs or large towns) and county districts. This system survived almost unchanged until the major reform of English local government, carried through by the Act of 1972.

These local authorities, but above all the boroughs, increasingly began to adopt model by-laws for the construction of new housing from the 1870s onwards. By-law housing, as it came to be known, can readily be recognized in any large British city. It tends to occur in a wide ring around the slums of the earlier period (1830–70), most of which were swept away in the great assault on the slums between 1955 and 1970. Drably functional, it consists of uniform terraces or rows of two-storey housing in the local building material (brick in most parts of the country, stone on the upland borders in Lancashire and the West Riding). The streets have a uniform minimum width to guarantee a modicum of air and light; each house has a separate external lavatory with access to a back alley, which runs parallel to the street. (This was necessary for the emptying of earth closets; for even in the 1870s it was impossible to provide for water-borne clearance of waste from many of these houses. It was also thought desirable for clearance of solid refuse.) Usually, unless reconstructed in the twentieth century, these houses have neither inside lavatory nor inside bath – indeed, they have no fixed bath at all. They represent a major problem in British housing policy for the 1970s and 1980s; but since they were built according to some minimal standards, some at least of them are capable of being upgraded to reasonable modern standards without the need for total demolition.

Commonly, even with the more generous standards of street width which were required, by-law housing was built at net densities of about 50 houses to the acre. (The term 'net density', often used in this book, means density of housing or people on the actual housing area, including local streets; it does not include associated open space, public buildings, or industry.) Given the large families of 3 or 4 children then prevailing, this could mean densities of 250 people to the acre or more. In London, densities of over 400 to the acre persisted in places as late as the Second World War.

The Phenomenon of Urban Spread

But by and large the period after 1870 marks a significant change in the development of British cities – and, as far as can be seen from international studies by the economist Colin Clark, in other countries' cities too. In fact, the trend is quite marked for London after the 1861 census. Up to that time, as we noted earlier, densities were actually rising within a radius of about 3 miles from the centre of

British cities – the radius within which people could walk to their work within about an hour, there being no effective public or private transport of any kind for most of the population. If we look at a town like Preston (Illustration 4), which had changed little in the 100 years or so between the time when most of the buildings were erected and the time of the photograph (taken about 1935), we should realize that most of the people living in these gardenless houses, without public parks, nevertheless could walk to open fields within about twenty minutes. (This was true in 1935 as in 1835.) And since the cotton mills – the chief and almost the sole source of work for many

4. Aerial photograph of Preston in the 1930s. This demonstrates the high density and closely built-up nature of the early industrial town. Though open space is lacking, the town is small and open countryside is not far away (though not visible here); and, with factories scattered among houses, the journey to work is short.

– were scattered fairly evenly across the town, journeys to work on foot were quite extraordinarily short: an average mill hand could walk to and from work four times a day, coming home for a midday meal, in rather less time than the average modern commuter spends on his outward morning journey. Even the biggest European city, London, grew relatively little in area as it doubled in population from 1 to 2 million people between 1801 and 1851.

But then, between about 1870 and 1914, virtually all British cities rapidly acquired a cheap and efficient public-transport system, first in the form of horse trams and buses, then, about the turn of the century, electric trams, and lastly in the form of motor buses, just before the outbreak of the First World War in 1914. In very large cities like London there were also commuter trains. The early railways had neglected the possibilities of suburban traffic, even in London, but most of them awoke to the possibilities after 1860; and one, the Great Eastern serving north-east London, was compelled by Parliament to run cheap trains for workmen, allowing them to live in suburbs as distant as Edmonton and Leytonstone. London even had a steam-operated underground railway, the world's first, by 1863; its first electric tube railway opened in 1890 and its first electrified suburban lines in 1905–9.

The impact on urban growth was profound, as can clearly be seen in the series of maps for London at different dates (Illustration 5). London in 1801, with 1 million people, was still a remarkably compact city, mainly contained within a radius about 2 miles from the centre; and by 1851, with double the number, the radius had not increased to much more than 3 miles, with higher densities in the inner areas. Then the city began to spread in all directions, but particularly to the south and north-east – as seen in the map for 1880 and, even more clearly, for 1914. This last represents the apogee of what can fairly be called the early public-transport city – just as the London of 1850 represented the pre-public-transport city. The steam trains gave fairly easy and rapid access to middle-class commuters (and, in east London, the working class too) at distances up to 15 miles from the centre. But they accelerated and decelerated poorly; stops tended to be widely spaced; and feeder services, in the form of horse buses or trams, were poorly developed, or slow. The

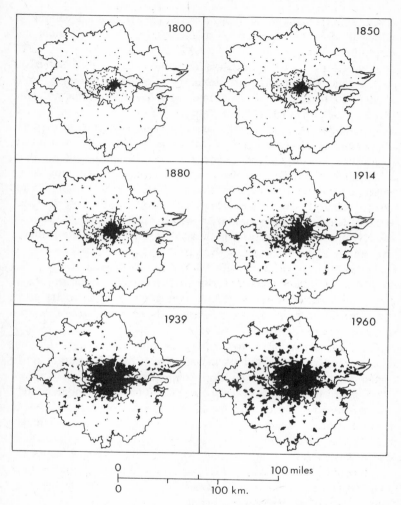

1800	1850
1880	1914
1939	1960

0   100 miles
0   100 km.

5. *The growth of London, 1800–1960. Until the development of the suburban railways (from 1860) London remained physically small; densities actually increased near the centre as population doubled between 1800 and 1850. Then the city spread – particularly between 1914 and 1939 under the influence of electric trains and motor buses. After 1939, the green belt limited London's growth.*

result is a typically tentacular form of growth, with development taking the form of blobs (or beads on a string, to change the metaphor) around each station.

Between the two world wars the whole process of suburban growth and decentralization began to speed up; in doing so it changed its form. The forces behind the suburban movement during those years were partly economic, partly social, partly technological. Economic forces in the world outside – world depression between 1929 and about 1934, a general depression in the prices of primary products – meant that both labour for construction and building materials were cheap. Social changes, too, were produced by economic development: more and more workers were becoming white-collar employees in offices or shops or other non-factory occupations, enjoying regular salaries which allowed them to borrow money on credit, and regarding themselves as members of an enlarging middle class. In large numbers, these people began to aspire to buy a house of their own with the aid of a mortgage. Lastly, and perhaps most fundamentally, further developments in transport technology extended the effective commuting range: electric trains in London, motor buses elsewhere, allowed the effective area of the city to extend up to four or five times the previous limits.

This was particularly well marked in London. In 1914 London had a population of about $6\frac{1}{2}$ million; by 1939, $8\frac{1}{2}$ million. Yet in that period, the capital's built-up area extended about three times. The underground railways before 1914 had barely extended beyond the existing developed area; but after 1918 they began to colonize new territory, extending quickly above ground on to previously undeveloped areas. The result was as predicted: a vast flood of speculative building, cheaply built for sale. Illustration 6 shows the result around just one station: Edgware in Middlesex, some 12 miles from central London, in 1926 – two years after the line was opened – and 1948 – a quarter of a century later.

The precise impact of this sort of development upon the urban structure can be well seen by comparing the maps of London, in 1914 and 1939, respectively, in Illustration 5. London in 1914, as we already noted, had the characteristically tentacular shape associated with the early public-transport city – the city of the steam

6. Edgware, north-west London: (a) 1926; (b) 1948. The impact of the extension of the underground railway (station in centre of pictures) on suburban development. Typical are the uniform rows of semi-detached housing, built at about 12 dwellings to the acre, with generous gardens. Better transportation allowed the city to spread.

train and the horse bus. By 1939 London had assumed a completely different shape: growth was much more even in any direction, producing a roughly circular city with a radius about 12 to 15 miles from the centre. The basic reason for this was a change in the technology of transportation. First, electric trains were more efficient carriers than the steam trains had been: accelerating and decelerating rapidly, they could serve more frequently spaced stations. Secondly, and even more importantly, the motor bus allowed a fairly rapid urban-transport service to penetrate in any direction from these stations, along existing roads, without the need for elaborate capital investment on the part of the operator; it therefore served as a highly efficient feeder service. These changes altered the pattern of accessibility within the urban area. The isochrones (lines of equal accessibility to the centre, in terms of time) were in 1914 very irregular; they fingered out a long way along the rail lines. By 1939 they had become more even and circular (or concentric) in form; and the development of the urban area followed accordingly. This form we can call typical of the later public-transport city; it was not at all a creation of the private car, since in London by 1939 only about one family in ten owned one.

The same process was repeated around the provincial cities too; it was merely on a smaller scale, and dependent on the tram or bus rather than the train. In some of the bigger cities – Manchester, Liverpool and Leeds – the local authorities themselves contributed to the process. They re-housed many thousands of slum dwellers and other people in need of public housing by developing new estates of single-family homes – generally at distances from 4 to 7 miles from the city centre, in the case of the biggest cities, and connected to it by rapid, frequent and cheap public transport. Like the private housing, this was cheaply built (and, unlike most of the private housing, it was aided by central-government subsidy as the result of a 1919 Housing Act). It was also of a standard never before reached in public housing: equipped with basic facilities like bathrooms, and with generous private garden space around. These authorities built fairly faithfully according to the recommendations of an influential official report, the Tudor Walters report, which had been published at the end of the First World War in 1918; it had recommended develop-

7. *A house-agent's advertisement of the early 1930s. At this time house prices, aided by cheap labour and materials, were probably cheaper in relation to white-collar salaries than ever before or since. Commuting on the new electric lines round London was easy. There was a striking contrast with the poverty in the depressed industrial areas of the north.*

ment of single-family homes at about 12 per net residential acre, or about one quarter the density of the old by-law housing.

This also was the density of much of the private housing developed around London and other big cities; many private estates were built at even lower densities: 10 or 8 or even 6 houses to the acre. For the general feeling was that more spacious housing standards were a healthy reaction to the cramped terraces of the nineteenth-century industrial town; the bus and the electric train had liberated the manual worker in his rented council house and the white-collar worker in his mortgaged semi-detached house alike. And because the improved transportation made so much land potentially developable, the price of land was low. Indeed, it is clear from later research that land prices and the house prices which are always so closely related reached a low point in relation to income in the 1930s that has never been equalled before or since. It was actually easier for the average clerical or skilled manual worker to buy a house in the 1930s than it is in the more affluent Britain of 40 years later.

The Reaction against Sprawl

A minority of thinking people, however, were alarmed at the result. They included both town planners, who by then existed as a

8. *The Great West Road, London, in 1951. Ribbon development of the 1920s and 1930s alongside an interwar arterial road. This consumed some of the best agricultural land in southern England, and aided the movement in the 1930s for more effective controls on urban growth. It also compromised the original purpose of the road as a through route, so that by the mid 1960s a replacement motorway was needed.*

profession – the Town Planning Institute had been incorporated in 1914 – and rural conservationists. They were concerned at the fact that the development was uncontrolled by any sort of effective planning. Though Acts of Parliament had provided for local authorities to make town-planning schemes for their areas – in 1909, in 1925 and then, most decisively, in 1932 – basically these Acts gave them no power to stop development altogether where such development was not in the public interest; the developer could build almost wherever he liked, provided he followed the general lines of the local town-planning scheme. And this, the planners and conservationists argued, had two bad effects.

First, it was using up rural land – the great majority of it agricultural land – at an unprecedented rate. By the mid 1930s, as subsequent research showed, some 60,000 acres each year (out of 37 million acres in all) were being taken from agriculture in England and Wales for all forms of urban development. Because the development was completely uncontrolled, it was no respecter of the quality of agricultural land: the suburban spread of London, for instance, took much of the finest market gardening land in all England, on the gravel terrace lands west of the capital (and ironically, later on, Heathrow Airport took much of the rest). The result, critics argued, was a major loss in home food production – a loss Britain could ill afford in times of war. And in the late 1930s, with war threatening, this seemed an important argument.

Secondly, the critics argued that the effect on the townsman was equally bad. Homes were being decentralized at greater and greater distances from the city centre, but jobs were not being decentralized nearly as rapidly. In London and in some of the bigger provincial cities, between the two world wars, some factory industry was moving outwards to the suburbs in search of space: new factory estates were developed like Park Royal and the Lea Valley in London, Slough just outside it, Witton Park in Birmingham, or Trafford Park in Manchester. But much industry remained in inner urban locations, and the growing volume of so-called tertiary industry – service occupations like work in offices and shops – seemed to be firmly locked in city centres. As a result, traffic congestion in the cities appeared to be growing; and journeys to work, it was assumed, must be becoming longer all the time. As cities grew larger and larger, as their suburbs sprawled further and further, it was argued that they imposed an increasingly insufferable burden on their inhabitants. And as new arterial roads were built to relieve traffic congestion on the old radial arteries out of the city, so these in turn were lined by ribbon development of new housing, compromising their function and reducing their efficiency. Ribbon development was partially controlled by an Act of 1935, but the real answer to the problem — motorways for through traffic, with limited access, already being opened in Italy and Germany — were not introduced to Britain until the Special Roads Act of 1949.

Thus a small, but powerful and vocal, movement, built up to limit urban growth through positive planning. Essentially, it represented a working coalition between people interested in town planning — some, but not all of them professional planners — and rural preservationists, who had been instrumental in organizing the Council for the Preservation of Rural England in 1925. One strong figure spanned both camps and united them: Patrick Abercrombie, Professor of Planning in the University of London and founder of the CPRE. Though they were persuasive, they might not have been so effective if they had not been joined by a third group: the representatives of the depressed industrial areas of northern England, south Wales and central Scotland. We shall see in Chapter 4 how this happened. But meanwhile, we need to retrace our steps in time, to look at some of the most important ideas circulating among urban planners, and others interested in the subject, at this time.

Further Reading

A standard textbook of modern economic and social history will provide indispensable background. Good examples include: E. J. Hobsbawm, *The Pelican Economic History of Britain, Vol. 3: Industry and Empire* (Penguin, 1968); P. Mathias, *The First Industrial Nation: An Economic History of Britain 1700–1914* (Methuen, 1969; paperback edition available); G. P. Jones and A. G. Pool, *A Hundred Years of Economic Development in Great Britain, 1840–1940* (Duckworth, paperback reprint, 1966). These texts should be supplemented by W. Smith, *A Historical*

Introduction to the Economic Geography of Great Britain (Bell, 1968), which emphasizes the geographical impact of economic change, and then by W. G. Hoskins, *The Making of the English Landscape* (Penguin, 1970), which discusses the impact on the landscape.

On the early history of town planning, see W. Ashworth, *The Genesis of Modern British Town Planning* (Routledge, 1954), and Leonardo Benevolo, *The Origins of Modern Town Planning* (Routledge, 1967). These should be supplemented by Colin and Rose Bell, *City Fathers* (Penguin, 1972), which gives an indispensable picture of early town planning experiments; and by Gordon Cherry, *Urban Change and Planning* (Foulis, 1972).

3. The Seers: Pioneer Thinkers in Urban Planning, from 1880 to 1945

During the whole of Chapter 2 we have concentrated on the evolution of what can be called, broadly, the urban problem in Britain from the Industrial Revolution of the late eighteenth century to the outbreak of the Second World War. We have looked at the facts of urban development and at the attempts – often faltering and not very effective ones – on the part of central and local administration to deal with some of the resulting problems. This was the world of practical men grappling with practical matters. But no less important, during this time, were the writings and the influence of thinkers about the urban problem. Often their writings and their lectures reached only a tiny minority of sympathetic people. To practical men of the time, much of what they asserted would seem utopian, even cranky. Yet in sum, and in retrospect, the influence of all of them has been literally incalculable; furthermore, it still continues.

This delay in the recognition and acceptance of their ideas is very important. Some of these ideas were more or less fully developed by the end of the nineteenth century, and a large part were known to the interested public by the end of the First World War. Yet with the exception of some small-scale experiments up to 1939, nearly all the influence on practical policy and design has come since 1945. One obvious peril in this is that no matter how topical and how appropriate these thinkers were in analysing the problems of their own age, their remedies might be at least partially outdated by the time they came to be taken seriously. We shall need to judge for ourselves how serious this has been.

It is useful to divide the thinkers into two groups: the *Anglo-American group* and the *Continental European group*. The basis of the distinction here is more than one of convenience. Basically the background of the two groups of thinkers has been quite different. We already saw in Chapter 2 that in England and Wales (Scotland in this respect has been rather more like the European Continent) cities began to spread out after about 1860: first the middle class and then (especially with the growth of public housing after the First World War) the working class began to move out of the congested inner rings of cities into single-family homes with individual gardens, built at densities of 10 or 12 houses to the acre. Exactly the same process occurred, from about the same time, in most American cities, though in some cases the process was delayed by the great wave of arrivals of national groups (such as Italians, Greeks, Russians, Poles and Jews from these last two countries) between 1880 and 1910; they crowded together in ethnic ghettos in the inner areas of cities like New York, Boston or Chicago, and took some time to join the general outward movement. Nevertheless, by the 1920s and 1930s there was a rapid growth of single-family housing around all American cities, served by public transport and then, increasingly, by the private car. This was a tradition which, by and large, writers and thinkers in both Britain and the United States accepted as the starting point.

On the Continent of Europe it was quite otherwise. As cities grew rapidly under the impact of industrialization and movement from the countryside, generally several decades later than the equivalent process in Britain (i.e. from about 1840 to 1900), they failed to spread out to anything like the same extent. As public-transport services developed, generally in the form of horse- and then electric-tram systems, some of the middle class took up villa life in new suburbs; but most of the middle class, and virtually all the working class, continued to live at extraordinarily high densities virtually within walking distance of their work. The typical Continental city consisted then, and still consists today, of high apartment blocks – four, five or six storeys high – built continuously along the streets, and thus enclosing a big internal space within the street block. In middle-class areas this might be a pleasant communal green space; in other areas it was invariably built over in the desperate attempt to crowd as many people as possible in. The result by 1900 was the creation of large slum areas in most big

European cities, but of a form quite different from the English slums. In England, even poor people lived in small – generally two-storey – houses of their own, either rented or bought. In Europe they lived in small apartments, and the densities – both in terms of persons per room, and dwellings or persons per net residential acre – were much higher than in typical English slum areas. (Scotland, curiously, developed in the European way: Glasgow, for instance, is a city of tenements, not houses, and standards of crowding have always been much worse there than in big English cities.) Naturally, when Continental Europeans began to think about urban planning, they tended to accept as a starting point this apparent preference for high-density apartment-living within the city.

The Anglo-American Tradition

(i) HOWARD

The first, and without doubt the most influential, of all the thinkers in the Anglo-American group is Ebenezer Howard (1850–1928). His book *Garden Cities of Tomorrow* (first published in 1898 under the title *Tomorrow*, and republished under its better-known title in 1902) is one of the most important books in the history of urban planning. Reprinted several times and still readily available as a paperback, it remains astonishingly topical and relevant to many modern urban problems. From it stems the whole of the so-called garden-city (or in modern parlance, new-town) movement which has been so influential in British urban-planning theory and practice.

To understand its significance it is necessary to look at its historical background. Howard was not a professional planner – his career, if he can be said to have one, was as a shorthand writer in the law courts – but a private individual who liked to speculate, write and organize. As a young man he travelled, spending a number of years in the United States during its period of rapid urban growth before returning to England to write his book. At that time several pioneer industrialists with philanthropic leanings had already started new communities in association with large new factories which they had built in open countryside. (Their motives, perhaps, were not entirely philanthropic: they built their factories cheaply on rural land; it was necessary to house the labour force outside the city in consequence, and they got a modest return in rents for their investment.) The earliest of these experiments, Robert Owen's celebrated experimental settlement at New Lanark in Scotland (*c.* 1800–1810) and Titus Salt's town built round his textile mill at Saltaire near Bradford (1853–63), actually date from the early years of the Industrial Revolution. But the best known and the most important date from the late nineteenth century, when the growing scale of industry was tending to throw up a few very powerful industrialists who saw the advantages of decentralizing their plants far from the existing urban congestion. Bournville outside Birmingham (1879–95), built by the chocolate manufacturer George Cadbury, and Port Sunlight on the Mersey near Birkenhead (1888), built by the chemical magnate William Hesketh Lever, are the best-known examples in Britain. In Germany the engineering and armaments firm of Krupp built a number of such settlements outside their works at Essen in the Ruhr district, of which the best preserved, Margaretenhöhe (1906), closely resembles Bournville and Port Sunlight. Similarly, in the United States, the railroad engineer George Mortimer Pullman (who invented Pullman cars) built a model town named after himself, outside Chicago, from 1880 onwards.

These towns all contain the germ of the idea which Howard was to propagate: in all of them industry was decentralized deliberately from the city, or at least from its inner sections, and a new town was built around the decentralized plant, thus combining working and living in a healthy environment. They are, in a sense, the first garden cities, and many of them are still functional and highly pleasant towns today. But Howard generalized the idea from a simple company town, the work of one industrialist, into a general planned movement of people and industry away from the crowded nineteenth-century city. Here he drew on previous writings: on Edward Gibbon Wakefield, who had advocated the planned movement of population even before 1850, and James Silk Buckingham, who had developed the idea of a model city. But perhaps the strongest intellectual influence on Howard's thinking was that of the great Victorian economist Alfred Marshall; he, if anyone, invented the idea of the

9. (a) New Lanark (Robert Owen, c. 1800–1810); (b) Saltaire (Titus Salt, 1853–63); (c) Bournville (George Cadbury, 1879–95); (d) Port Sunlight (William Lever, 1888). Four pioneer new towns, established by philanthropic industrialists around their works in open countryside.

new town as an answer to the problems of the city, and he gave it an economic justification which only later came to be fully understood. Marshall argued, as early as 1884, that much industry was even then footloose, and would locate anywhere if labour was available; he also recognized that the community would eventually have to pay the social costs of poor health and poor housing, and that these were higher in large cities (as they then existed) than they would be in new model communities.

Howard, however, developed the idea, generalized it and above all turned it into an eminently practical call for action. And of all visionary writers on planning, Howard is the least utopian, in the sense of impractical; his book is packed with detail, especially financial detail, of how the new garden cities were to be built. But first of all Howard had to provide a justification of the case for new towns (or garden cities) that could be readily understood by practical men without much knowledge of economics. He did so in the famous diagram of the Three Magnets (Illustration 10), which in fact is an extremely compressed and brilliant statement of planning objectives. (It is an interesting exercise to try to write out the diagram in suitably jargon-ridden, abstract modern language as a statement of objectives; to say the same thing less clearly takes many pages, whereas Howard got it all in one simple diagram.) Basically Howard was saying here that both existing cities and the existing countryside had an indissoluble mixture of advantages and disadvantages. The advantages of the city were the *opportunities* it offered in the form of accessibility to jobs and to urban services of all kinds; the disadvantages could all be summed up in the poor resulting natural *environment*. Conversely, the countryside offered an excellent environment but virtually no opportunities of any sort.

It is important here to remember the date of Howard's book. In the 1890s material conditions in British cities were better than they had been in the 1840s. Average incomes for many workers were significantly higher; medical standards had improved; and the new housing by-laws were beginning to have effect. Nevertheless, by modern standards they were still appalling. The 1891 census showed that at least 11 per cent of the population, over 3 million people, were living at densities of over 2 persons per room; and this

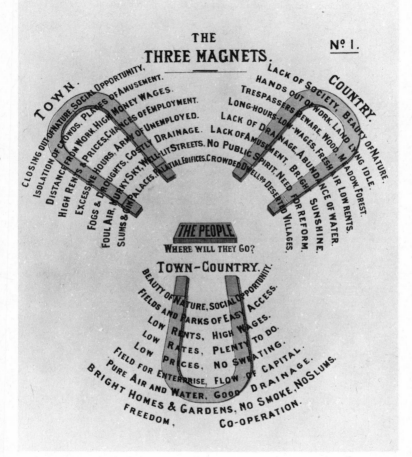

10. Ebenezer Howard's Three Magnets. The celebrated diagram from Garden Cities of Tomorrow *(first published in 1898) setting out the advantages and disadvantages of town and country life. A hybrid form for the future, the planned Town-Country or Garden City, combined the advantages of both with none of the disadvantages – so Howard argued.*

11. Ebenezer Howard's Social City. The lost diagram from the first edition of Howard's book, demonstrating his full conception of garden cities (or new towns) grouped in planned urban agglomerations of a quarter million people or more.

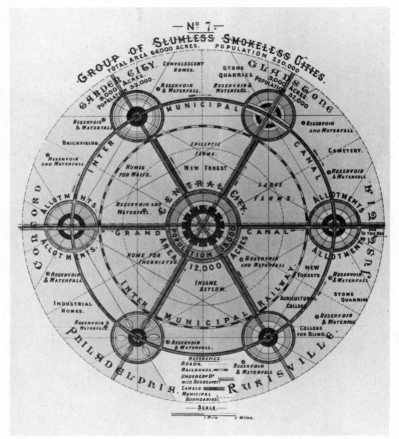

was certainly an underestimate. Even in the 1880s the Registrar General's records showed that the expectation of life in a city like Manchester was only 29 years at birth on average – only 5 years more than 40 years previously. In the late 1880s and early 1890s the shipowner Charles Booth conducted the first modern social investigation, based on strict statistical recording. Aided by the young

Beatrice Webb, he produced a study which is still a classic: it showed that on a strict and minimal standard no less than one quarter of the population of inner East London was living below the poverty line. But on the other hand there was equal distress in the countryside: these were the years of deep agrarian depression, brought about by the mass importation of cheap foreign meat and wheat against which the British farmer was given no protection. The population map of Britain in the 1890s shows losses almost everywhere except for the limited areas of the cities and the industrial districts. Though the towns were beginning to spawn suburbs, there was virtually none of the twentieth-century phenomenon whereby urban workers could afford to live in the countryside; that had to wait for the motorcar. And when Howard's book was published, it was precisely two years since Parliament had removed the requirement that a car must be preceded along the highway by a man with a red flag. He could, perhaps, hardly be expected to foresee the consequences of liberating the car.

Against this background Howard argued that a new type of settlement − Town-Country, or Garden City − could uniquely combine all the advantages of the town by way of accessibility, and all the advantages of the country by way of environment, without any of the disadvantages of either. This could be achieved by planned decentralization of workers and their places of employment, thus transferring the advantages of urban agglomeration *en bloc* to the new settlement. (In modern economic jargon, this would be called 'internalizing the externalities'.) The new town so created would be deliberately outside normal commuter range of the old city. It would be fairly small − Howard suggested 30,000 people − and it would be surrounded by a large green belt, easily accessible to everyone. Howard advised that when the town was established 6,000 acres should be purchased: of this no less than 5,000 acres would be left as green belt, the town itself occupying the remainder.

Two important points about Howard's idea especially need stressing, because they have been so widely misunderstood. The first is that contrary to the usual impression Howard was advocating quite a high residential density for his new towns: about 15 houses per acre, which in terms of prevailing family size at the time meant about 80–90 people per acre. (Today it would mean 40–50.) The second is that he did not advocate small, isolated new towns. His notion was that when any town reached a certain size, it should stop growing and the excess should be accommodated in another town close by. Thus the settlement would grow by cellular addition into a complex multi-centred agglomeration of towns, set against a green background of open country. (And even this was to be fairly densely populated by space-consuming urban activities like public institutions: Howard allowed for one person to every four acres there.) Howard called this polycentric settlement the 'Social City'. The diagram in the first edition of his book showed it as having a population of 250,000 – the target population of the modern 'giant' new town of Milton Keynes in England – but Howard himself stressed that Social City could grow without limit. This point has never been well understood, because the second edition of Howard's book, and all subsequent editions, have omitted the diagram; it is reproduced here in Illustration 11.

Howard, as we have noticed, was very specific about how his new communities could be built. Private enterprise could do it, he stressed, if money could be borrowed for the purpose: land could be bought cheaply in the open countryside for the project, and the subsequent increase in land values would allow the new town company to repay the money in time and even make a profit to be ploughed back into further improvement, or into the creation of further units of the Social City. In fact, Howard was actually instrumental in getting two garden cities started – Letchworth in northern Hertfordshire (1903) and Welwyn Garden City a few miles to the south (1920). Both were built very much on the lines he advocated, with wide green belts around. But both suffered financial troubles, and the vision of private-enterprise new towns on a large scale was never realized. Furthermore, despite insistent and effective propaganda from the Town and Country Planning Association which he founded, governments after the First World War failed to respond to the call for public new towns.

(ii) UNWIN AND PARKER

Between 1900 and 1940 many of Howard's ideas were developed by his faithful followers. Among the most prolific and brilliant of the

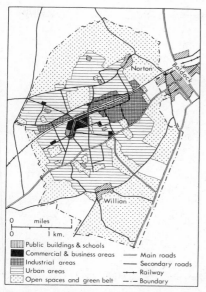

12. Plan of Letchworth Garden City, 1903. This was the first garden city, built in northern Hertfordshire with private capital under Howard's general direction. The architects were Raymond Unwin and Barry Parker.

writers was Sir Frederic Osborn, who lived to see over a score of new towns built in England after the Second World War. In terms of physical realization the opportunities were clearly more limited. The two architects who designed the first garden city, Letchworth, Raymond Unwin (1863–1940) and his young assistant Barry Parker (1867–1947), later went on to build Hampstead Garden Suburb at Golders Green in north-west London (1905–9). As its name indicates, this was not a garden city but a dormitory suburb owing its existence to the new underground line opened in the year 1907; and it was condemned by many garden-city supporters on that ground. But it was an interesting experiment in the creation of a socially mixed community, with every type of house from the big mansion to the small cottage; and in its creation of a range of houses which are all skilfully designed, all varied yet all quietly compatible, it is one of the triumphs of twentieth-century British design.

13. *Letchworth from the air, showing the general physiognomy of the town today. The large open green space in the centre of the town faithfully followed the original schematic plan in Howard's book. Industry is aligned along the railway, which existed before work on the town was started.*

Later, Parker went on to a more ambitious enterprise: the design of a new community for 100,000 people to be built by the City of Manchester at Wythenshawe, south of the city (1930). Wythenshawe in fact deserves to be called the third garden city (or new town) actually started in Britain before the Second World War. It has all the essential features of the design of Letchworth or Welwyn: the surrounding green belt, the mixture of industrial and residential areas, and the emphasis on single-family housing of good design. (The family resemblance between Hampstead Garden Suburb and Wythenshawe is more than coincidental.) It did, however, compromise on the principle of self-containment: because most of its inhabitants came from the city where they held jobs, subsidized public transport was provided for them to commute back. But the intention – never completely realized in practice – was to provide a wide range of jobs in the community itself.

Together, Unwin and Parker developed some important modifications of the original Ebenezer Howard idea. In a very influential pamphlet published in 1912, *Nothing Gained by Overcrowding!*, Unwin argued that housing should be developed at lower densities than were then common. The need for public open space, he pointed out, was related to the numbers of people, so that the saving in land from higher urban densities was largely illusory. He recommended a net density in new residential areas of about 12 houses to the acre – or, in terms of the average family size of the time, about 50–60 people to the acre. This standard was accepted in the important official Tudor Walters report of 1918, as we saw, and became usual in most public housing schemes of the 1920s and 1930s: Wythenshawe, like many other major schemes by city housing departments, was built at about this density.

Both Unwin and Parker consistently argued for the Howard principle of generous green belts around the new communities. In Unwin's graphic term, used in the regional plan he produced for the London area in the late 1920s, they would be cities against a background of open space – not cities surrounded by green belts, in the conventional use of the term. But Parker developed the idea still further. Visiting the United States in the 1920s, he was impressed by the early experiments in building parkways, i.e. scenic roads running through landscaped open country. Parker argued that the 'background of open space' between cities should be occupied by these parkways, giving easy interconnection between them; this in fact was an adaptation to the motor age of Howard's original idea (shown in Illustration 11) of an inter-urban railway. Parker's conception of the parkway is shown in Illustration 14; he actually managed to half-build one in the middle of Wythenshawe, and it was later completed as the M56 North Cheshire motorway, though not as he would have intended it.

Lastly, at Wythenshawe, Parker employed yet another notion he had picked up in the United States, which was in fact a logical development of Howard's own ideas: the idea of dividing the town into clearly articulated neighbourhood units. The ground plan of Wythenshawe as actually completed shows the influence of this idea. To see its origins, we now need to follow across the Atlantic the Anglo-American tradition of thought.

(iii) PERRY, STEIN AND TRIPP

In Howard's original theoretical diagram of his Garden City, published in 1898, he divided the town up into 'wards' of about 5,000 people, each of which would contain local shops, schools and other services. This, in embryo, is the origin of the neighbourhood-unit idea, which in essence is merely pragmatic: certain services, which are provided every day for groups of the population who cannot or do not wish to travel very far (housewives and young children) should be provided at an accessible central place for a fairly small local community, within walking distance of all the homes in that community. Depending on the residential density, the idea of convenient walking distance will dictate a limit of a few thousand people for each of these units. It makes psychological sense to give such a unit a clear identity for the people who live in it, by arranging the houses

---

14. (a) and (b) Barry Parker's parkway principle; (c) Its expression at Wythenshawe, 1930. Parker, Unwin's assistant for Letchworth Garden City, later developed the idea of the parkway – a landscaped road running through wedges of green space between strips of urban development. He tried to apply the idea in the centre of his satellite town of Wythenshawe for the city of Manchester, but it was not completed according to his original conception.

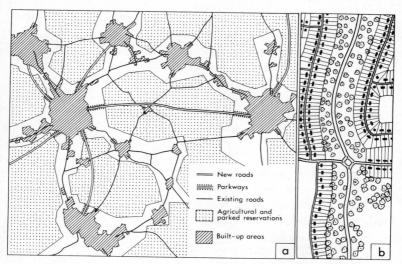

New roads
Parkways
Existing roads
Agricultural and parked reservations
Built-up areas

a

b

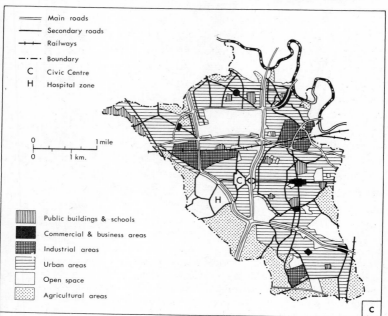

Main roads
Secondary roads
Railways
Boundary
C   Civic Centre
H   Hospital zone

0   1 mile
0   1 km.

Public buildings & schools
Commercial & business areas
Industrial areas
Urban areas
Open space
Agricultural areas

c

and streets so that they focus on the central services and providing some obvious boundary to the outside.

In the United States, however, the idea was taken much further during the preparation of the New York regional plan in the 1920s. (This great multi-volume plan, prepared wholly by a voluntary organization, is one of the milestones of twentieth-century planning; it reflects the influence of the thinker Patrick Geddes, whom we shall discuss shortly.) One contributor to this plan, Clarence Perry (1872–1944), there developed the idea of the neighbourhood unit, not merely as a pragmatic device, but as a deliberate piece of social engineering which would help people achieve a sense of identity with the community and with the place. For this there was no empirical justification, and not much has emerged since; though some important work done for the Royal Commission on Local Government

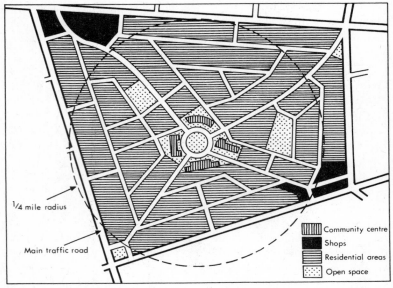

15. The 'neighbourhood unit' principle. First developed by the American architect–planner Clarence Perry in the celebrated New York Regional Plan of the 1920s, this principle was based on the natural catchment area of community facilities such as primary schools and local shops. It was copied by Parker at Wythenshawe and then widely in British plans after the Second World War.

in England, and published in 1967, did suggest that most people's primary sense of identification was to a very small local area. But just in terms of physical planning Perry's work did give firmness to the neighbourhood idea. He suggested that it should consist of the catchment area of a primary school, extending about half or three quarters of a mile in any direction, and containing about 1,000 families – or about 5,000 people, in terms of average family size then. It would be bounded by main traffic roads, which children should not be expected to cross.

The essential idea of the neighbourhood unit, as developed by Perry – though not some of his details, such as putting shops at the corners of the units at the junctions of traffic roads – was enthusiastically taken up by British planners in new towns and in some cities after the Second World War; its influence is everywhere to be seen. Since the early 1960s, however, it has come in for increasing criticism. An influential paper published in 1963 by Christopher Alexander, a young English émigré to the United States, called *A City is Not a Tree*, suggested that sociologically the whole idea was false: different people had varied needs for local services, and the principle of choice was paramount. In his view cities that had grown naturally demonstrated a more complex settlement structure, with overlapping fields for shops and schools; planners should aim to reproduce this variety and freedom of choice. The master plan for the new town of Milton Keynes, published in 1969, is one of the first to reflect these ideas.

Meanwhile a close associate of Perry – Clarence Stein (1882–), an architect–planner working in the New York region – had taken the neighbourhood concept further. Stein was one of the first physical planners, apart from Parker in England and Le Corbusier in France, to face fully the implications of the age of mass ownership of the private car. He grasped the principle that in local residential areas the need above all was to segregate the pedestrian routes used for local journeys – especially by housewives and children – from the routes used by car traffic. In a new-town development at Radburn, northern New Jersey (1933), which was started but never completed, he applied these ideas by developing a separate system of pedestrian ways, reached from the back doors of the houses, which pass through

16. *Two views of Radburn, New Jersey, USA, a town designed in the early 1930s by the American architect Clarence Stein. This was the first recorded case of planned segregation of pedestrians from vehicle traffic, and gave its name to the Radburn Layout, widely used in British plans from the late 1950s onwards.*

communal open space areas between the houses, and thence cross under the vehicle streets. The vehicle streets, in turn, are designed according to a hierarchical principle, with main primary routes giving access to local distributors and then in turn to local access roads designed on the cul-de-sac (dead-end) principle, serving small groups of houses. The Radburn Layout, as it came to be known, was applied by Stein in one or two other developments in the United States in the 1930s, but was adopted in Britain only after the Second World War; in fact, most of the examples date from the late 1950s or later. Few of them have the charm and ease of the design in the surviving section of Radburn itself.

The transfer of Stein's ideas back across the Atlantic to Britain, there to be combined with Perry's neighbourhood idea, came via a curious route. In 1942 an imaginative Assistant Commissioner of Police (Traffic) at London's Scotland Yard, called H. Alker Tripp (1883–1954), published a slim book called *Town Planning and Traffic*. Though there is no direct evidence that Tripp knew of Perry's or Stein's work, it seems possible that he had read of it. The most novel suggestion in the book was the idea that after the war British cities should be reconstructed on the basis of *precincts*. Instead of main city streets which served mixed functions and which had many points of access to local streets, thus giving rise to congestion and accidents, Tripp argued for a hierarchy of roads in which main arterial or sub-arterial roads were sharply segregated from the local streets, with only occasional access, and also were free of direct frontage development. These high-capacity, free-flow highways would define large blocks of the city, each of which would have its own shops and local services. Tripp illustrated the idea graphically in his book by applying it to an outworn (and heavily bombed) section of London's East End.

Tripp's book came at an opportune time. For at that point Patrick Abercrombie – the most notable professional planner in Britain of that age – was working with the chief architect of the London County Council, J. H. Forshaw, and his brilliant assistant Wesley Dougill, on a postwar reconstruction plan for London. In an important section of the plan (which was published in 1943) Abercrombie and Forshaw called for the widespread application of the precinctual

17. *Sir Alker Tripp's precinct diagram. Tripp, a senior traffic policeman at Scotland Yard, applied his ideas to a part of London's East End. Main roads would be largely sealed off from local side access, to give better traffic flow and safety; residential areas would be protected from heavy traffic.*

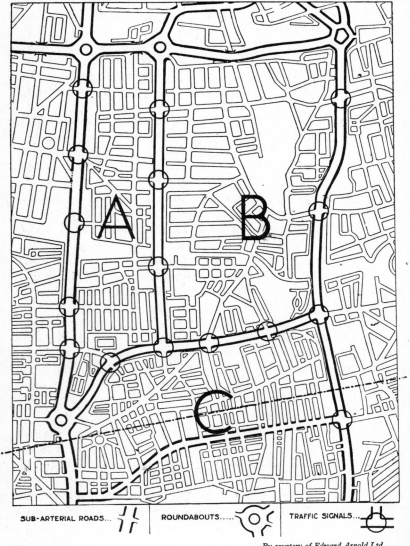

SUB-ARTERIAL ROADS... | ROUNDABOUTS..... | TRAFFIC SIGNALS...

By courtesy of Edward Arnold Ltd.

18. *Abercrombie's Bloomsbury Precinct, from the County of London Plan, 1943. Patrick Abercrombie and J. H. Forshaw applied Tripp's principles to the area around the British Museum and the University of London. Some of the necessary works were completed, but the idea is still not fully realized thirty years later – traffic is actually channelled through the precinct in a one-way system.*

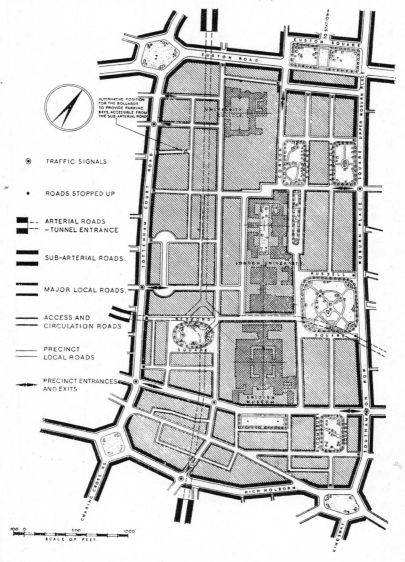

principle to London, and illustrated its application to two critical areas where traffic threatened the urban life and fabric: the zone around Westminster Abbey, and the university quarter of western Bloomsbury. Ironically, in neither area were the ideas ever applied; indeed, at the end of the 1950s a new one-way traffic scheme actually routed through-traffic through the heart of Abercrombie's Bloomsbury precinct. But elsewhere – most notably, in the postwar reconstruction of the centre of Coventry, one of Britain's most heavily bombed cities – the idea was employed to good effect.

(iv) GEDDES AND ABERCROMBIE

Abercrombie's most notable contributions to Anglo-American planning theory and practice, however, were made in extending city planning to a wider scale: the scale which embraced the city and the whole region around it in a single planning exercise. To understand this tradition and the way Abercrombie fits into it, it is necessary to go back some way, and consider how the Ebenezer Howard tradition developed in another, slightly different direction.

From 1883 to 1919 a visionary Scots biologist, Patrick Geddes (1854–1932) taught at the University of Dundee, but did much of his most important work at his famous outlook tower in Edinburgh. Geddes's extraordinary mind soon took him away from conventional biology, into the area we should now recognize as human ecology: the relationship between man and his environment. In turn he was led to a systematic study of the forces that were shaping growth and change in modern cities, which culminated in his masterpiece *Cities in Evolution* (published in 1915, but mostly written about 1910). To understand the nature of Geddes's achievement, as with Howard's, it is necessary to place the book in the context of its time. Human geography, which had developed so finely in France during the first decade of the twentieth century in the hands of such practitioners as Vidal de la Blache and Albert Demangeon, was an almost unknown study in Britain; only one man, H. J. Mackinder, kept the subject alive, at the University of Oxford. But Geddes was fully acquainted with this tradition of study, and with the associated work of the French sociologist P. G. F. le Play. Both stressed the intimate and subtle relationships which existed between human settlement and the land, through the nature of the local economy; in le Play's famous triad, the relationship Place–Work–Folk was the fundamental study of men living in and on their land.

Geddes's contribution to planning was to base it firmly on the study of reality: the close analysis of settlement patterns and local economic systems in relation to the potentialities and the limitations of the local environment. This led him to go right outside the conventional limits of the town, and to stress the natural region – a favourite unit of analysis of the French geographers – as the basic framework for planning. Today, when so many students are trained in the basic principles of human geography at school, all this seems very obvious and familiar. But, published at a time when planning for most practitioners was the study of civic design at a quite local level – a sort of applied architecture – it was quite revolutionary. Howard had already anticipated the change of scale: his analysis of the problem, and its solution, was a regional one. Geddes's contribution was to put the flesh of reality on the bare bones of the regional idea: at last, human geography was to provide the basis of planning. From this came Geddes's working method, which became part of the standard sequence of planning: *survey* of the region, its characteristics and trends, followed by *analysis* of the survey, followed only then by the actual *plan*. Geddes, more than anyone, gave planning a logical structure.

But his contribution did not end there. His analysis of cities in evolution led him to what was then a novel conclusion. Suburban decentralization, we saw in Chapter 2, was already by then causing cities to spread more widely. But in addition certain basic locational factors – the pull of coalfields in the early nineteenth century, the natural nodality conferred on certain regions by the way railways, roads and canals followed natural routes, the economies of scale and agglomeration in industry – had already caused a marked concentration of urban development in certain regions, such as the West Midlands, Lancashire, Central Scotland in Britain, or the Ruhr Coalfield in Germany. Geddes demonstrated that in these regions suburban growth was causing a tendency for the towns to coalesce into giant urban agglomerations or *conurbations* – the first time this word was used in the English language.

The conclusion Geddes drew was a logical one: if this was happening and would continue to happen, under the pressure of economic and social forces, town planning must be subsumed under town and country planning, or planning of whole urban regions encompassing a number of towns and their surrounding spheres of influence. Howard and his supporters had already drawn the same conclusion; and between the two world wars, aided powerfully by the persuasive writing of Geddes's American follower Lewis Mumford – whose 1938 text *The Culture of Cities* became almost the Bible of the regional planning movement – the idea gained a great deal of credence among thinking planners and administrators. Unwin himself was commissioned to prepare an advisory plan for London, though funds ran out in the depression of 1931–3, before it could properly be completed. Already, here, Unwin was applying the ideas of Howard to a planned scheme for large-scale decentralization of people and jobs from London to satellite towns in the surrounding Home Counties.

In this plan can be seen the germ of the Greater London Plan of 1944, which Patrick Abercrombie (1879–1957) prepared at the direct request of the British government. (It is significant that in this case, as elsewhere, extraordinary arrangements had to be made to prepare even an advisory plan for a whole urban region; the existing machinery of local government was quite inadequate in scale for the purpose.) But Abercrombie's great achievement was to weld this complex of ideas, from Howard through Geddes to Unwin, and turn them into a graphic blueprint for the future development of a great region – a region centred on the metropolis but extending for 30 miles around it in every direction, and encompassing over 10 million people. The broad aim of the plan was essentially Howard's: it was the planned decentralization of hundreds of thousands of people from an overcrowded giant city and their re-establishment in a great series of new planned communities, which from the beginning would be self-contained towns for living and working. The method was essentially Geddes's: survey of the area as it was, including the historical trends which could be observed, followed by systematic analysis of the problem, followed by production of the plan. But the great sweep of the study, its characteristic assurance, and its quality of almost cartoon-like clarity, were essentially Abercrombie's own. However, the Greater London Plan essentially belongs to the story of the development of British planning at the time of the Second World War, which we treat in Chapter 4. We shall save a full discussion of it until then.

(v) WRIGHT

For the last important figure in the Anglo-American tradition we have to return across the Atlantic. Frank Lloyd Wright (1869–1959) does not fit readily into the line of development outlined in the previous pages, or into any line at all. It is fitting to put him last in this series, because his ideas about urban planning are so fundamentally at variance with those of the Continental school. Above all, they stand at the opposite extreme from those of Le Corbusier – the only other master of modern architecture whose ideas on planning are significant.

As with Corbusier, Wright's best-known monuments are his individual buildings, several of which are milestones of the modern movement; his ideas for planning on a wider scale never got further than paper. But unlike Corbusier, Wright's ideas were never taken up enthusiastically by a large following, either in Europe or in his native United States. They have, however, continued to exercise an important hold on a few influential thinkers in American planning practice during the 1950s and 1960s, especially in California. This is just, because in the same way that Corbusier's ideas are quintessentially European, so Wright's are typically American.

Wright based his thinking on a social premise: that it was desirable to preserve the sort of independent rural life of the homesteaders he knew in Wisconsin around the 1890s. To this he added the realization, based on the early spread of the motor car among the farmers of North America, that mass car use would allow cities to spread widely into the countryside. With the car and with cheap electric current everywhere, Wright argued, the old need for activities to concentrate in cities had ended: dispersion, not only of homes but also of jobs, would be the future rule. He proposed to accept this and to encourage it by developing a completely dispersed – though planned – low-density urban spread, which he called

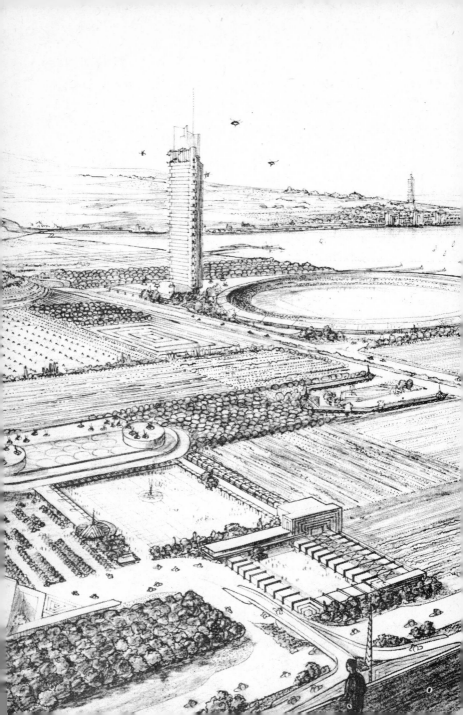

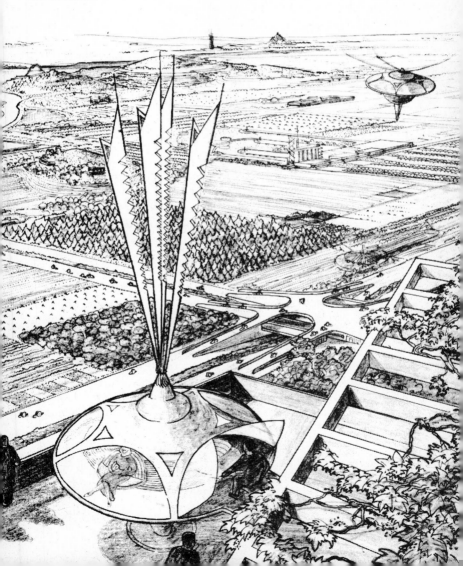

19. Broadacre City – the planning concept of the celebrated American architect and planner, Frank Lloyd Wright, in the 1930s. Single-family homes, each surrounded by an acre of land, allow each family to grow food for its own consumption. Transportation is by car, and the petrol ('gas') station becomes the focus of shopping and services. This concept is in sharp contrast to the ideas of a European planner like Corbusier.

'Broadacre City'. Here, each home would be surrounded by an acre of land, enough to grow crops on; the homes would be connected by super-highways, giving easy and fast travel by car in any direction. Along these highways he proposed a planned roadside civilization, in which the petrol ('gas') station would grow naturally into the emporium for a whole area; thus he anticipated the out-of-town shopping centre some twenty years before it actually arrived in North America. In fact, Wright's description of Broadacre City proved to be an uncannily accurate picture of the typical settlement form of North America after the Second World War – except that today the big half-acre or one-acre lots grow very little food to support their families. The form developed without the underlying social basis that Wright so devoutly hoped for.

The European Tradition

(i) SORIA Y MATA

Like many other thinkers considered here, the first representative of the opposing European tradition, the Spanish engineer Arturo Soria y Mata (1844–1920), owes his place in history to the importance of one basic idea. In 1882 he proposed to develop a linear city (El Ciudad lineal), to be developed along an axis of high-speed, high-intensity transportation from an existing city. His argument was that under the influence of new forms of mass transportation, cities were tending to assume such a linear form as they grew – an argument which, as we already saw in Chapter 2, had some justification at that time. Soria y Mata's ideas were ambitious if nothing else: he proposed that his linear city might run across Europe from Cadiz in Spain to St Petersburg (now Leningrad) in Russia, a total distance of 1,800 miles. In fact, he succeeded only in building a few kilometres just outside Madrid; these still survive, though they are difficult to pick out on the map or on the ground, because they have been swallowed up in the amorphous growth of the modern city. In some ways the form seems archaic today: a main road runs straight through the linear centre of the city, carrying a tramway (since scrapped), with rather geometrical housing blocks on either side.

And there seems no doubt from experience that such a form is difficult and costly to build; furthermore, even though commuter journeys may be fast, they are certainly likely to be long.

Nevertheless, the idea has always enjoyed some popularity among planners on the grounds that it has some good qualities. It does correspond to the need to exploit costly investments in new lines of rapid communication, whether these are nineteenth-century railways or twentieth-century motorways. (In both these cases, though, the settlement form that is most likely to arise is not linear, but rather a series of blobs round the stations or interchanges on the high-speed route.) And it does give easy access to near-by open countryside. Furthermore, it can respond automatically to the need for further growth, by simple addition at the far end; it does not need to operate through restrictive green belts, as Ebenezer Howard's finite garden

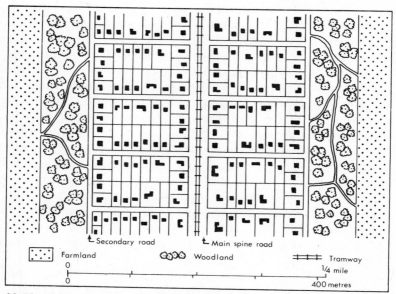

20. *The Linear City, 1882. This concept of the Spanish architect Arturo Soria y Mata, based on a central rapid transit system, was actually begun outside Madrid but has now been swallowed up in the general development of the city. It has been influential in many twentieth-century urban plans.*

city has to. So it is not surprising that the form has often appeared in regional plans as the most obvious alternative to the Howard–Abercrombie tradition. The well-known MARS plan for London (1943), produced by a group of architects, used it; variants of it, in the postwar period, have appeared in plans for Copenhagen (1948), Washington (1961), Paris (1965) and Stockholm (1966). Some of these plans are discussed in more detail in Chapter 8. But one point can be made here: both in Washington and in Paris it proved extremely difficult to preserve the plan in the face of private attempts to build in the spaces left between the fingers or axes of urban growth. The claim that the linear city is a natural form, therefore, does not seem justified.

(ii) LE CORBUSIER

The Swiss-born architect Charles Edouard Jeanneret, who early in his professional career adopted the pseudonym Le Corbusier (1887–1965), stands with Frank Lloyd Wright, Walter Gropius and Mies van der Rohe as one of the creators of the modern movement in architecture; and among the general public his fame is probably greater than any of the others. Yet, though his best-known achievements consist of an astonishing range of individual buildings all stamped indelibly with his personality, from the Villa Savoye at Passy (1929–30) to the chapel of Notre Dame en Haut at Ronchamp near Belfort (1950–53), his most outstanding contribution as a thinker and writer was as an urban planner on the grand scale. Of the scores of designs which Corbusier produced for city reconstructions, or for new settlements – both in France, where he worked all his professional life, and widely across the world – few materialized. The most notable are his Unité d'Habitation (1946–52) at Marseilles in France, and his grand project for the capital city of the Punjab at Chandigarh (1950–57), which will be finished only long after his death.

His central ideas on planning are contained in two important books, *The City of Tomorrow* (1922) and *The Radiant City* (*La Ville radieuse*, 1933), which is now available in English translation. Unfortunately Corbusier does not translate or summarize easily. The words pour out in no particular logical order, accompanied by diagrams which often contain the real sense of what is being said; the books seem to consist of collections of papers put together on no consistent principle; the style is highly rhetorical, and often even declamatory. But in so far as it is possible to make a very summary digest, his ideas seem to reduce themselves into a small number of propositions.

The first was that the traditional city had become functionally obsolete, due to increasing size and increasing congestion at the centre. As the urban mass grew through concentric additions, more and more strain was placed on the communications of the innermost areas, above all the central business district, which had the greatest accessibility and where all businesses wanted to be. Corbusier's classic instance, often quoted, was Manhattan Island with its sky-scrapers and its congestion.

The second was the paradox that the congestion could be cured by increasing the density. There was a key to this, of course: the density was to be increased at one scale of analysis, but decreased at another. Locally, there would be very high densities in the form of massive, tall structures; but around each of these a very high proportion of the available ground space – Corbusier advocated 95 per cent – could and should be left open. The landscape he advocated, which can be seen in countless of his writings from his Paris plan of 1922 onwards, consists, therefore, of skyscrapers separated by very large areas of intervening open space. Thus Corbusier is able to achieve the feat of very high overall densities – with up to 1,000 people to the net residential acre and more – while leaving the bulk of the ground unbuilt on.

The third proposition concerned the distribution of densities within the city. Traditionally, as we noted in Chapter 2, densities of residential population are higher in the centre of the city than at the edge. Since the development of mass urban transportation from the 1860s onwards, this 'density gradient' has flattened somewhat, with lower densities at the centre and rather higher densities farther out than the rural densities which used to obtain; but it is quite noticeable nevertheless, and in Continental European cities (as well as some American cities, such as New York) it is much more pronounced than in Britain. Furthermore, there is an even more pronounced

LA VILLE RADIEUSE

(ZONING)

gradient of employment density, with big surviving concentrations near the centre. Corbusier proposed to do away with all this by substituting virtually equal densities all over the city. This would reduce the pressure on the central business districts, which would in effect disappear. Flows of people would become much more even across the whole city, instead of the strong radial flows into and out of the centre which characterize cities today.

Fourthly and lastly, Corbusier argued that this new urban form could accommodate a new and highly efficient urban transportation system, incorporating both rail lines and completely segregated elevated motorways, running above the ground level, though, of course, below the levels at which most people lived. Corbusier even claimed to have invented, in the early 1920s, the multi-level free-flow highway interchange, long before such structures were built in Los Angeles or elsewhere.

To yield the full promised results, and thus to be open to testing in practice, Corbusier's plans would need to have been applied on a very wide scale. His own diagrams show large areas of Paris, including historic quarters, razed to accommodate the new forms. This is one good reason why it proved so difficult to execute any of his ideas – especially in interwar France, where the pace of physical construction was extremely sluggish. And his notions about density have seldom been applied anywhere in the extreme form he suggested. Nevertheless, in planning cities after the Second World War, Corbusier's general influence has been incalculable. A whole generation of architects and planners, trained in the 1930s and then from 1945 onwards, came to revere the writings of 'Corbu'; and in practice afterwards, they tried to apply his ideas to local conditions. In England, for instance, his influence was particularly strong in the famous London County Council Architect's Department during the 1950s, at a time when it produced much of its best work: the celebrated Alton West estate at Roehampton in south-west London

---

21. The Radiant City (La Ville radieuse). Le Corbusier, the Swiss-French architect and planner, developed during the 1920s and 1930s the idea of a city with very high local concentrations of population in tall buildings, which would allow most of the ground space to be left open. His ideas proved very influential for a whole generation of planners after the Second World War.

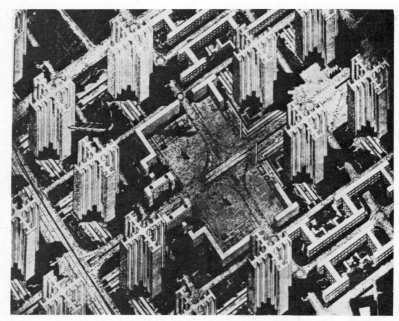

22. La Ville radieuse, as from the air. This is Corbusier's own imaginitive conception of his radiant city. The cruciform tower blocks are designed to admit maximum light to the apartments. Dense flows of traffic on the motorway-style roads are handled by complex interchanges.

(1959), with multi-storey blocks set among acres of finely landscaped parkland, is completely Corbusian in concept (see Illustrations 22 and 23). All over Britain the remarkable change in the urban landscape during the late 1950s and the 1960s – as slum clearance and urban renewal produced a sudden unprecedented crop of skyscrapers – is a mute tribute to Corbusier's influence. Whether it was for good or ill, later generations will have to decide. Certainly, by the end of the 1960s, there was an increasing volume of protest at the inhumanity of the new high blocks; and it seemed doubtful whether many more would be built. Many critics were going further, and questioning the whole philosophy of massive urban renewal which was essential to the realization of Corbusier's ideas.

23. *Aerial photograph of Roehampton – the practical application of Corbusier's ideas after the Second World War, by the architects of the old London County Council in their celebrated Alton West estate in south-west London (late 1950s).*

Corbusier has however had another, more subtle, influence. Though many of his ideas were intuitive rather than scientifically exact, he did teach planners in general the importance of scale in analysis. The notion that densities could be varied locally, to produce very different results while maintaining the overall density unaltered, was a very simple yet at the same time elusive one, which few grasped fully before he demonstrated it. Equally important was his insistence on the elementary truth that dense local concentrations of people helped support a viable, frequent mass-transportation system. This realization, for instance, has been extremely important in the much-admired Stockholm suburbs built in the post-1950 period, where densities are systematically higher around the new underground railway stations than they are farther away.

But in general the basic difference between Anglo-American and Continental European traditions has persisted. The two lines have intermingled more in the post-1945 period than ever before, it is true: in many urban renewal areas of British cities it would really be difficult at first glance to tell whether one was in Birmingham (or Newcastle), Amsterdam, Milan or Warsaw. For many bourgeois home buyers and even some planners on the Continent there has been enthusiasm for the English idea of single-family home living and the creation of new communities in the countryside. Nevertheless, the majority of British people still appear to prefer a single-family home with garden if given the choice, while many people in Continental countries are quite firmly wedded to the advantages of inner-city apartment living.

A Verdict on the Seers

It may seem difficult, on first impression, to pass a general verdict on a group of planners as varied as those considered in this chapter. But in the light of the distinctions made in Chapter 1 of this book, it is possible to draw some conclusions that apply to almost all of them.

The first point is that most of these planners were concerned with the production of blueprints, or statements of the future end-state of the city (or the region) as they desired to see it: in most cases they were far less concerned with planning as a continuous process which had to accommodate subtle and changing forces in the outside world. Their vision seems to have been that of the planner as omniscient ruler, who would create new settlement forms, and perhaps also destroy the old, without interference or question. The complexities of planning in a mixed economy where private interests will initiate much of the development that actually occurs, or in a participatory democracy where individuals and groups have their own, often contradictory, notions of what should happen – all these are absent from the writings of most of these pioneers.

Howard and Geddes are, perhaps, honourable exceptions to most of this criticism. Howard's idea may have seemed utopian, but he never avoided the practical details of how to bring it about. Geddes, even more, was explicitly concerned that planning should start with the world as it is, and that it should try to work with trends in the economy and society, rather than impose its own arbitrary vision of the world. It is perhaps significant that his intellectual background was different from many of the others. An architect, by definition, starts thinking in terms of the structures he would like to build; a biologist turned geographer–sociologist starts by thinking about the nature of the society and the land he is planning for.

This leads us to a second point about most of the pioneers. Their blueprints seldom admitted of alternatives. There was one true vision of the future world as it ought to be, and each of them saw himself as its prophet. This is understandable, because these men were visionaries trying to be heard in a sceptical and sometimes hostile world. But if the idea is too persuasive, there is an evident risk of a stifling orthodoxy.

One last point will be very evident. These pioneers were very much physical planners. They saw the problems of society and of the economy in physical terms, with a physical or spatial solution in terms of a particular arrangement of bricks and mortar, steel and concrete on the ground. This again is understandable; they were trained to think in this way, and their concerns were with physical development. Nevertheless, this attitude carries with it a real peril: that such planners, and those they teach and influence, will come to see all problems of cities and regions as capable of solution in these

79

terms and only these terms. According to this view, problems of social malaise in the city will be met by building a new environment to replace the old – whereupon poor health, inadequate education, badly balanced diets, marital discord and juvenile delinquency will all go away. Similarly, problems of circulation and traffic congestion in the city will be dealt with by designing a radical new system as part of a new urban form – whereupon, of course, the problems will disappear. The notion that not all problems are capable of simple solution in these physical terms – or the still more disturbing notion that there might be cheaper or better solutions to the problems, of a non-physical character – is not often found in the writings of the pioneers of planning thought we have been discussing. Nor, it should be noted, is it often found in the plans of many of those countless planners these men have influenced and inspired. The seers have made their mark as much by their limitations as by their positive qualities – striking though these latter may have been.

Further Reading

Important background will be found in the works of Ashworth, Benevolo, and Bell, already quoted in the reading to Chapter 2.

The best general treatment of several of the writers and thinkers discussed here is in John Tetlow and Anthony Goss, *Homes, Towns and Traffic* (Faber, second edition, 1968), especially Chapter 2. Also useful is Thomas A. Reiner, *The Place of the Ideal Community in Urban Planning* (Philadelphia: University of Pennsylvania Press, 1963).

On (or by) particular writers, the following are important: Ebenezer Howard, *Garden Cities of Tomorrow* (with preface by Frederic J. Osborn and introduction by Lewis Mumford. Faber, 1946; paperback edition, 1965); Walter Creese, *The Search for Environment: The Garden City Before and After* (New Haven and London: Yale University Press, 1966) on Howard, Unwin and Parker; Patrick Geddes, *Cities in Evolution* (Benn, 1968); Marshall Stalley, *Patrick Geddes: Spokesman for Man and the Environment* (New Brunswick, N.J.: Rutgers University Press, 1972; with a reprint of most of *Cities in Evolution*); Le Corbusier, *The Radiant City* (Faber, 1967; English translation of *La Ville radieuse*).

4. The Regional Economic Problem and the Barlow Report, from 1930 to 1940

In Chapters 2 and 3 we have concentrated throughout on planning on the urban scale. But in looking at the writings of Howard, Geddes and Abercrombie we saw that, increasingly from 1900 to 1940, the more perceptive thinkers came to recognize that effective urban planning necessitated planning on a larger than urban scale – the scale of the city and its surrounding rural hinterland, or even several cities forming a conurbation and their common overlapping hinterlands. Here, the development of the idea of regional planning in one commonly used sense of the word begins.

The difficulty – it is elementary but quite serious – is that there is another common meaning to the term 'regional planning' in modern usage. This other meaning only assumed prominence during the 1930s, as the result of the great economic depression which so seriously affected virtually all nations of the western (non-communist) world. It refers specifically to economic planning with a view to the development of regions which, for one reason or another, are suffering serious economic problems, as demonstrated by indices such as high unemployment or low incomes in relation to the rest of the nation. Though it has some clear interrelationships with the other meaning of 'regional planning', it really represents a different kind of problem, demanding a different expertise. And commonly, the 'region' referred to in this other sort of planning is quite differently designed, and is of a different size, from the 'region' of the city-region planners.

This distinction will be discussed in more detail in a later chapter, but one simple illustration can be given here. Within Britain the northernmost part of England – including the Northumberland and Durham coalfields, and the Tyne and Tees estuaries, as well as the northern Pennine uplands and the isolated industrial area of West

Cumberland — has presented economic problems ever since the interwar period. The former basic industries of coalmining, shipbuilding and heavy engineering have declined; heavy unemployment and low incomes were the result in the 1930s, and during the postwar period large parts of the area, or the whole of it, have been designated a Development Area or Development District. The unit appropriate to analysing these problems, and to providing solutions, is a fairly large one; minimally, most people would agree that the Northumberland–Durham industrial area would require treating as a single unit, and many would accept that the smaller populations in the Pennines and West Cumberland should be included for the sake of convenience, as is in fact now done in the Northern Region Planning Council and Board. But such a unit contains quite a number of separate city regions, or cities and conurbations with their surrounding hinterlands: Tyneside, Sunderland, Durham City, Darlington, Teesside and Carlisle, to name a few. The unit appropriate for planning of one sort may not be at all appropriate for regional planning of the other sort. And, of course, the responsibilities of the two sorts of organization will be quite different.

It is, therefore, merely confusing to give them the same name. Elsewhere, I have proposed two terms which resolve the ambiguity. The larger-scale, economic-development type of planning can best be called *national/regional planning* because essentially it relates the development of each region to the progress of the national economy. And the smaller-scale, physical type of planning can conveniently be called *regional/local planning* because it attempts to relate the whole of an urban region to developments within each local part of it.

The need for regional/local planning, as we have seen, was already coming to be recognized when Geddes wrote in 1915. But the need for national/regional planning only became fully evident in the aftermath of the Great Depression of 1929–32.

The Nature of the Regional Economic Problem

In 1914, just before the outbreak of the First World War, Britain was still self-evidently a prosperous industrial giant. It had been overtaken in recent years by Germany and the United States in total industrial production, but it was still unquestionably one of the three industrial great powers of the world. During the nineteenth century, Britain had achieved its position by taking to heart the principle of the division of labour, as enunciated by Adam Smith in his *Wealth of Nations* (1776). For the principle applied to nations as well as individuals: each nation should produce those goods and services in which it had the greatest comparative advantage. Britain in fact had put its eggs not in one basket, but in a limited number of big baskets, representing the staple export industries. Furthermore, the principle of specialization applied not merely *externally,* to Britain's role as 'Workshop of the World', but also *internally*, where several of the major industrial regions had based their prosperity on a very limited economic base.

Britain had taken this principle of specialization further than most nations. Wedded to the principle of free trade, it had allowed its agriculture to decline, and to readapt drastically, in the face of competition from recently settled areas such as western North America, Argentina, Australia and New Zealand; we already saw how Ebenezer Howard's writings were influenced by the great agricultural depression of the late nineteenth century. Some rural countries, by the outbreak of the First World War, had been losing population continuously since the mid-nineteenth century. Even by 1901 Britain was fully urbanized, with 80 per cent of the people living in towns – a higher proportion than any other nation at that time. The population had increasingly concentrated into a few major industrial areas, where – as Geddes noted in 1915 – towns were already merging into conurbations.

Moreover, the industrial base of these workers was very narrow. Just after the First World War the 1921 census revealed that more than half the total employment in the country was in mining and manufacturing. And of these workers, totalling 9 million, no less than 1.5 million were in mining and quarrying; 2.6 million in metal manufacturing and engineering; and 1.3 million in textiles. These three great industrial groups were the staples of the Industrial Revolution, on which Britain's nineteenth-century industrial prosperity had been based. Their importance in the national economy had actually increased since 1851, with especially big increases in coal and heavy engineering in the years just before 1914.

All these staple groups were tied – sometimes for historical rather than for contemporary technical reasons – to coalfield locations. In 1921 two thirds of the total employment in the three staple groups was in northern England (that is, north of the river Trent) and Scotland; the rest mainly in the Midlands and South Wales. Apart from the Midlands, all the major staple industrial areas were either on the coast or near to it, on navigable water: the Clyde Valley, North-East England, Lancashire, the West Riding and South Wales. This, in most cases, reflected the reliance on exporting coal or heavy manufactured goods by water. But there was also a strong tendency for each major area to specialize in a small group of related industries. Thus Clydeside meant ships and heavy engineering; the North East meant export coal, iron and steel, ships and heavy engineering; Lancashire meant cotton and some engineering; the West Riding meant coal and woollens; South Wales meant export coal and iron and steel.

The problem was that virtually all this basic export industry was extremely vulnerable to changes in the world economy, which manifested themselves very rapidly after the First World War. First, there was a complex chain reaction in the critically important relationships between the advanced industrial countries and the less developed primary producers, which had been the central feature of the nineteenth-century world economy: the slowing in the rate of population growth in the advanced countries from about 1870 onwards caused a slackening in the rate of growth in demand for primary products; consequently the primary producer countries suffered an economic crisis; in turn their demand for industrial goods grew slowly, if at all. Secondly, a series of technological changes brought about a weakening of the demand for several of Britain's export staples: oil replaced coal as a fuel; less coal was needed for smelting iron; artificial fabrics began to replace cottons and woollens. Thirdly, other countries began to follow Britain through the stages of industrialization, developing first the industries that were simpler technologically: textiles were the most obviously suitable for early development, so that Japan and the Indian sub-continent were both expanding their cotton industries during the 1920s and 1930s. But fourthly and most critically of all, these changes would not have mattered so much if the British economy had been capable of reasonably rapid adaptation to the new circumstances. What happened, in the interwar period, was that Britain as a whole failed to develop new industries fast enough to compensate for the loss of the old.

Furthermore, in so far as the new industries did develop, they did so in quite different locations from those of the old. The so-called 'new industries', representing twentieth-century rather than nineteenth-century technology (or, as Geddes had put it in 1915, 'neotechnic' as opposed to 'palaeotechnic' industry) — electrical engineering, motor vehicles, aircraft, precision engineering, pharmaceuticals, processed foodstuffs, rubber, cement and a host of others — grew rapidly in and around London, in towns like Slough, and in the West Midlands (Birmingham and the associated conurbation) and East Midlands (Leicester, Nottingham, Derby and the area around). They hardly implanted themselves at all in the areas farther north, where the staple industries were dying. The reasons for this were complex; they were fully analysed in the important Barlow Commission report of 1940, which we shall discuss below. Most of all, they reflected changes in marketing: the home market was more important for these industries than it had been for the older staples, and even exporting tended to be associated with new marketing agencies which were concentrated in London. In addition, it just so happened that the historical roots of many of these industries were put down where they later grew: light engineering and car manufacture developed out of a long tradition of metal working in the Birmingham and Coventry areas; in London, motor manufacture developed out of an older carriage-making trade for an aristocratic and wealthy market; precision and scientific engineering had traditionally been concentrated in London.

All this was not very surprising. In fact, what was perhaps odd in British economic history was the rapid nineteenth-century concentration of the staples on the northern coalfields. This, we already saw in Chapter 2, was due to the accident that Britain industrialized so early, when coal was expensive and very difficult to move far from

24. *Slough. An unplanned 'new town' of the 1920s and 1930s, Slough developed almost as an accident around an industrial trading estate, itself a converted wartime supply base. New industries, such as electrical goods and motor engineering, helped secure its prosperity and continued growth through the depression of the early 1930s.*

where it was mined. Other European countries, industrializing later, found that the new industry developed naturally in the older trading towns, to which coal and then electricity could be moved. In the twentieth century, in effect, the distribution of population in Britain has been steadily moving back to what it was at the start of the Industrial Revolution, as Illustration 25 shows. The movements, in either direction, have not been spectacular when viewed in this way. Nor is Britain a big country – the distressed industrial areas were never more than about 400 miles, and often much less, from the more prosperous ones. Nevertheless, perhaps because of the long social traditions and the relative immobility of the people in the older areas, the resulting strains have been enormous.

These long-term structural shifts in the economy, and their geographical manifestations, were not fully evident to contemporaries in the 1920s and early 1930s. At that time the shorter-term cyclical fluctuations in the national and world economy – above all, the Great Depression of 1929–32, following the Wall Street crash – dominated everyone's consciousness. It was only as the country began to emerge from the depths of the trough, during 1932, 1933 and 1934, that observers began fully to notice the discrepancy between the more prosperous South and Midlands, and the depression in the North, Wales and Scotland. Unemployment, 16.8 per cent in Great Britain among insured persons in 1934, was 53.5 per cent in Bishop Auckland and over 60 per cent in parts of Glamorgan; in London it was only 9.6 per cent. Despite large-scale migration from the depressed areas – 160,000 left South Wales and 130,000 left the North East during the years 1931–9 – unemployment rates remained stubbornly high in those areas right through to the outbreak of war.

---

25. Relative growth of population in Great Britain: (a) 1861–91; (b) 1921–39. The interwar period saw a fundamental reversal of the nineteenth-century pattern of population growth. Population now moved away from the coalfields and towards London and the Home Counties. The imbalance in job opportunities, which brought this about, caused increasing concern in the 1930s and led to the establishment of the Barlow Commission in 1937.

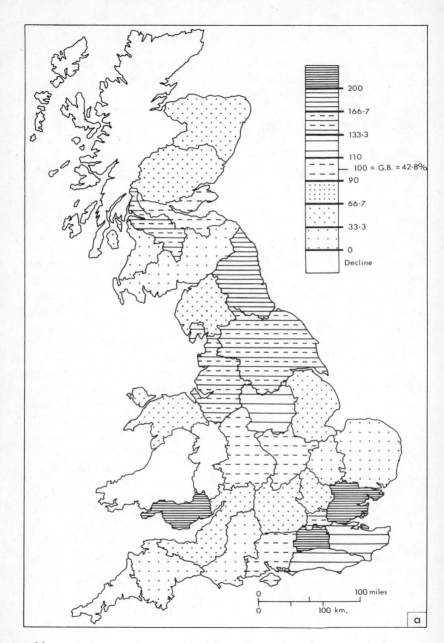

200

166·7

133·3

110

100 = G.B. = 42·8%

90

66·7

33·3

0

Decline

0   100 miles

0   100 km.

a

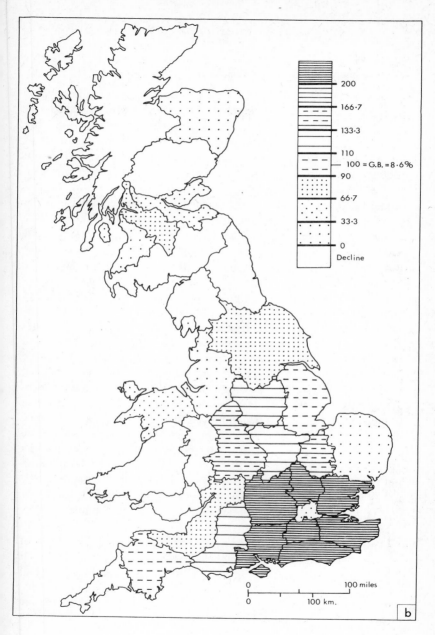

200
166·7
133·3
110
100 = G.B. = 8·6%
90
66·7
33·3
0
Decline

0   100 miles
0   100 km.

b

89

The Barlow Commission and its Report, 1937–40

In 1934 growing realization of the problem compelled the government to take action: the depressed areas were designated 'special areas', and commissioners were appointed for them – one for England, one for Scotland and one for Wales – with powers to spend public money to help invigorate the economy. From 1935 the English commissioner began to use his powers directly to stimulate the regional economy by the creation of 'trading estates' on the model of those successfully established by private enterprise in the South, like that at Slough: one of these in England, the Team Valley Estate on Tyneside, had assumed major proportions by 1939, and it was followed by another venture in South Wales, at Treforest near Pontypridd. But all this activity did little more than scratch at the surface of the problem.

Up to that point official thinking had been limited to the idea of positive government help for the special areas. But in his report to Parliament in 1936, the English Commissioner for the Special Areas, Sir Malcolm Stewart, made a radical suggestion. The growth of industry in London, he suggested, was due not to hard economic factors, but to purely psychological causes, which could be altered by government action. He suggested not merely an increased programme of government aid to the special areas, with positive inducement to industries which moved there, but an embargo on new factory building (with certain defined exceptions) for London. The idea stimulated great interest and controversy, and prompted the government into action. In 1937 it appointed a Royal Commission on the Geographical Distribution of the Industrial Population*, under the chairmanship of Sir Anderson Montague-Barlow (1868–1951), to investigate the problem comprehensively and make recommendations.

The importance of the Barlow Commission in the history of British urban and regional planning can never be overestimated. It was directly responsible, through a chain reaction that we shall

---

* When the report appeared in 1940, the reference to geography had been dropped.

26. Jarrow in the 1930s. Jarrow became known as 'the town that was murdered' after closure of its Tyne shipyard threw nearly half its male workers into unemployment in the early 1930s. Its plight contrasted strongly with the prosperity of towns like Slough.

27. *The Team Valley Trading Estate was modelled on the successful Slough estate; it brought new jobs to Tyneside. Treforest Trading Estate, near Pontypridd in Glamorgan, performed a similar function for South Wales.*

shortly trace, for the events that led up to the creation of the whole complex postwar planning machine during the years 1945–52. Together with the name of Howard, Barlow is the most important single name in tracing the evolution of the distinctive British planning policy in the years after 1945. But together with Barlow should be coupled the name of Patrick Abercrombie – a member of the Commission, a signatory of its influential minority report, and an architect (in every sense) of the postwar planning system.

In the British constitutional system the device of a Royal Commission permits a free-ranging, independent and deep-probing investigation of a particular problem; the commissioners need take nothing for granted. So it was with the Barlow commissioners. Their investigation was so exhaustive, and their report so authoritative and compelling in its arguments, that it actually represented a danger for later generations: the policies which were based on it became a kind of orthodoxy, very difficult to shake.

The particular contribution of the Barlow Commission to understanding and treating the problem was this: *it united the national/regional problem with another problem, the physical growth of the great conurbations, and presented them as two faces of the same problem.* In fact other observers had tended to do this before them: Sir Malcolm Stewart had done so, and indeed the coupling of the two problems was explicit in the Commission's terms of reference. These were, first, to inquire into the *causes* of the geographical distribution of industry and population, and possible changes in the causatory factors in the future; secondly, to consider the *disadvantages* – social, economic and strategic – of the concentration of industry and population into large centres; and thirdly, to report on *remedies* that were necessary in the national interest. Two things should be noted: first, that the national/regional distribution of industry and people was linked to the question of the concentration of population within regions – a rather different question; secondly, that the terms of reference were deliberately loaded, since it was assumed that disadvantages existed and that, implicitly, they far outweighed any possible advantages.

Given these terms, the findings of the Commission were perhaps predictable. On the first point, the report, when it emerged in 1940, confirmed the general impression that the growth of industry and population during the interwar period had been strikingly concentrated in the prosperous areas of the South and Midlands, and above all, around London. Table 1, taken from the Commission's analysis, shows that only in two areas of the country, London–Home Counties and the Midlands, was the growth of the insured employment greater in this period than in the nation as a whole; in London–Home Counties it was nearly double the national average. Another analysis of the same figures, also in Table 1, is perhaps even more striking: it shows that London and the Home Counties accounted for over two fifths of the growth of insured employment in this period, though they had less than one quarter of the employment at the start of it. Geographers testifying before the Commission argued for the existence of a main industrial axis, or 'coffin' area (the name referred to its shape) embracing the London region, the Midlands, Lancashire and Yorkshire, into which industry and people were concentrating; the commissioners found that this was not a very helpful framework of analysis because so much of the growth was at the southern end of the belt, virtually none of it at the northern end.

Table 1: Insured Workers, 1923 and 1937

	Insured workers (thousands)		Per cent increase	Per cent of national increase
	1923	1937	1923–37	1923–37
London and the Home Counties	2,421	3,453	42.6	42.7
Staffordshire, Warwickshire, Worcestershire, Leicestershire, Northamptonshire	1,212	1,554	28.2	14.1
Lancashire	1,697	1,826	7.6	5.3
West Riding, Nottinghamshire, Derbyshire	1,403	1,614	15.0	8.7
Northumberland and Durham	619	648	4.7	1.2
Mid-Scotland	792	868	9.6	3.1
Glamorgan and Monmouth	457	437	−4.4	−0.8
Rest of Great Britain	2,225	2,844	27.8	25.6
TOTAL	10,826	13,244	22.3	100.0

Source: Barlow Report, p. 24.

What were the causes of these trends? The Barlow Report found that the pattern of industrial growth – or the lack of it – was dominated by what has come to be called the 'structural effect'. This very important term – it will be discussed more fully in a later chapter – refers to the finding that the growth of the more prosperous areas can almost wholly be explained in terms of their more favourable industrial structure. In other words, their regional economy was so dominated by growth industries that by applying the national growth rates for these industries it was possible to predict the growth of the region; such industries were not, in most cases, expanding faster in these regions than anywhere else. For the depressed areas the conclusion was further depressing: their basic industries were declining so fast that they were running the whole regional economy downhill – it would be necessary to make superhuman efforts just to keep the economy in the same place.

Barlow's analysis of the causes of this locational pattern is still a classic: it has already been referred to, but it deserves a longer summary. Nineteenth-century industry, the analysis ran, had been diverted towards fuel and raw-material supplies and to navigable water, but twentieth-century industry needed these factors much less: their pull being weakened, industry would naturally gravitate to its main markets. But the market, that word used so casually in accounting for industrial location, is actually a complex thing: it includes sales to other industries, export agencies and a host of special sales facilities; and all these tend to be located in very big population centres. Such areas also tend to have a wide range of different labour skills and specialized services, which smaller industrial towns lack. Yet this pattern of forces, if it continued, would pull new industry away from the coalfields, which tended to be distant from the main marketing centres, leaving large concentrations of population and social capital stranded there. The Barlow Commission could find no good cause why the pattern of forces, left to itself, should start working in a different direction. So the question was: was there any reason for taking action to modify the natural course of events?

This led the Barlow Commission naturally to the second of the terms of reference: the analysis of disadvantages. Here, they were led into quite new and uncharted territory. Hardly anyone, anywhere in the world, had systematically considered questions like this before. And it should be remembered that then, very few economists were interested in urban affairs: there was no body of theory, no empirical research, to help the Commissioners. They looked systematically, and in detail, at records of public health, at housing, at traffic congestion, at the patterns of journeys to work, at land and property values. Then, *in camera*, sitting under the threat of imminent war, they heard the evidence of defence experts on the strategic dangers from bombing attacks on big cities – dangers which proved only too true in countless cases during the Second World War.

Some of the resulting analysis has been outdated by subsequent social changes; some of it, indeed, was tendentious and inconclusive at the time. For instance, the Commission concluded that, broadly, housing and public-health conditions tended to be worse in big cities (and in conurbations) than in small towns. But even then the evidence for that was contradictory: London, for instance, had better public-health records than the national average. And since then the position has changed out of recognition. As a result of general improvements in public health – better maternal and infant care, free national-health facilities, higher real incomes – indices like infant mortality have greatly improved, and the differences between one part of the country and another have been reduced. Some of the indices for poorer health, and for overcrowding of homes, are found in small towns. In an age when a nuclear holocaust could mean the virtual end of civilization, the strategic arguments against big cities have less force. Other arguments, though, continue to have force – sometimes, even greater force. Journeys to work have lengthened, though perhaps not so much if the measure used is time rather than miles; traffic congestion may have worsened (though it is very difficult to make comparisons over a long period, and some evidence for London indicates that the traffic has actually speeded up between the 1930s and the 1960s); land and property values have certainly escalated, especially near the centres of the biggest cities; some of the most serious housing problems, including homelessness, are certainly concentrated in the inner areas of the conurbations.

In the 1970s a Royal Commission would doubtless try to fit all this information within a theoretical economic framework, and to produce a cost-benefit analysis (see Chapter 10) of the advantages versus the disadvantages of life in big conurbations, all fully quantified in money terms for the sake of comparison. Such techniques were not open to Barlow, and indeed some would argue that they can be positively misleading, by giving a spurious impression of exactness. What the Barlow commissioners did was to sift the evidence as best they could. They concluded that the disadvantages in many, if not most of the great urban concentrations far outweighed any advantages and demanded specific government remedies. London, they thought, represented a particularly urgent problem which needed special attention.

So far the commissioners were agreed. When they came to discuss remedies – the third part of their terms of reference – they split. It was clear to all that, since no democratic government could direct people where to live, the controls would have to be applied to the location of new industry. In the conditions of the late 1930s such controls on the freedom of industry were considered radical, and even revolutionary. So the commissioners split into two groups. The more moderate majority suggested that in the first place there should be controls only on the location of new industry in and around London, to be imposed by a Board. The more radical minority – including the influential Professor Abercrombie – recommended more general controls on the location of industry throughout the whole country, to be administered by a new government department set up for the purpose.

In the event, as we shall see, when the government came to act on the Barlow recommendations – in 1945 – they opted for a modified version of the more radical variant. But in addition to this central investigation and set of recommendations the Barlow commissioners also studied a number of important related problems. Among these were the technical problems of controlling the physical growth of cities and conurbations, and of preserving agricultural land, through the establishment of a more effective system of town and country planning; and the linked problem of compensation and betterment in planning. On neither of these two questions could they reach definite recommendations: each was so complex, they concluded, that it needed further expert study. Similarly, though the Commission endorsed the general idea of building garden cities, or new towns, in association with controls on the growth of the conurbations, they thought that further investigation was needed of the ways in which this should be done.

These follow-up studies were made, and together with the Barlow Report itself they provide the intellectual foundation of Britain's postwar planning machinery. It will be convenient to consider the studies and resulting legislation together in the following chapter.

Further Reading

The best general source is the contemporary Barlow Report: *Report of the Royal Commission on the Distribution of the Industrial Population* (Cmd 6153, HMSO, 1940; reprinted 1960). It can be supplemented by the economic histories listed in the reading for Chapter 2, and more particularly by G. C. Allen, *British Industries and Their Organization* (Longman, fifth edition, 1970), Chapter 2. For a useful source on the implications of land use, see L. Dudley Stamp, *The Land of Britain: Its Use and Misuse* (Longman, second edition, 1962), Chapter 21.

5. The Creation of the Postwar Planning Machine, from 1940 to 1952

In Chapters 2 and 3 we traced the evolution of urban planning problems in Britain from 1880 to 1940, and of some proposed solutions to them; in Chapter 4 we traced the parallel evolution of the regional economic planning problem from about 1930 to 1940, and finally saw how the Barlow Report brought together the urban and the regional economic elements as two aspects of a single problem, proposing a common set of solutions to both. The Barlow Report was submitted to the government at the outbreak of war and was actually published in the middle of the so-called phoney-war period, a few months before Dunkirk, in February 1940. Shortly afterwards the war effort fully engaged most people's attention. But at the same time, in a remarkable mood of self-confidence about the future, the wartime government embarked on the follow-up studies which the Barlow Report had recommended.

The result was a remarkably concentrated burst of committee work and report writing, from 1941 to 1947. A whole succession of official reports, either from committees of experts or from planning teams, made recommendations to government on various specialized aspects of planning. These reports, known commonly after their chairman or team leader – Scott, Uthwatt, Abercrombie, Reith, Dower, Hobhouse – laid the foundations of the postwar urban and regional planning system in Britain. Then, in an equally remarkable burst of legislative activity from 1945 to 1952, postwar governments acted on the recommendations; not always following them in detail, they nevertheless enacted them in essence. A series of Acts – the Distribution of Industry Act 1945, the New Towns Act 1946, the Town and Country Planning Act 1947, the National Parks and Access to the Countryside Act 1949, and the Town Development Act 1952 – created the postwar planning system. Though since modified in many respects, its broad outlines have survived.

In this chapter we shall consider in sequence first the principal reports which provided the foundations of the system; then the legislation which brought it into being. Finally, we shall try to sum up the essential character of the system: its positive values and its limitations.

The Foundation Reports

(i) SCOTT AND UTHWATT

The first of the studies, the report of the Committee on Land Utilization in Rural Areas, was published in 1942. Though this committee is known after the name of its chairman, Sir Leslie Scott (1869–1950), the report bears the unmistakable imprint of the vice-chairman and chief author, the geographer Sir Laurence Dudley Stamp (1898–1966). The burden of this Report was that good agricultural land represented a literally priceless asset: unlike most other factors of production, once lost it was lost for good. Therefore, the report argued, the community should set up a planning system embracing the countryside as well as the town; and this system should regard it as a first duty to preserve agricultural land. In the case of first-class land – which Stamp's own land utilization survey in the 1930s had shown to be a very small part of the total land area of Britain (about 4 per cent) – there would be an automatic and invariable embargo on new development; this would prevent any recurrence of the process whereby west London expanded over the fertile market-garden lands of Middlesex. But even elsewhere the Scott report suggested the principle of the 'onus of proof': wherever development was proposed, it should be for the developer to show cause why his proposed scheme was in the public interest. Otherwise, the existing rural land use should have the benefit of the doubt.

It is easy to see the attraction of such an argument in 1942, when the blockade on the seas was making Britain more dependent on home foodstuffs than at any time since the early nineteenth century, and when British farmers made heroic efforts to increase production of basic cereals. And though the onus-of-proof rule has never been applied so rigidly in actual postwar planning, there is no doubt that the general sentiment behind the case has been very powerful in supporting the notions of urban containment and of encouraging higher-density urban development so as to save precious rural land. What is interesting is that even in 1942 the voice of an economist was heard to attack this view as lacking in economic sense. Stanley Dennison, a member of the committee, signed a minority report which suggested that the true criterion should be the value of the land to the community in different uses. In fact, Dennison was really calling for the application of cost-benefit analysis to urban planning decisions – a technique then hardly understood anywhere. Naturally, his voice went largely unheeded.

The Expert Committee on Compensation and Betterment, whose final report of 1942 is generally known after its chairman, Sir Augustus Andrewes Uthwatt (Lord Justice Uthwatt, 1879–1949) dealt with a perennial problem of urban development whose origins in English law can be traced back to 1427. It has two aspects, which are linked. The first is the problem of *compensation*: when a public body has to buy land compulsorily, for a new highway or a new school, for instance, what is the just rate of compensation to the dispossessed owner? At first, the answer might be simple: the public body should pay the current market value, since that will make the owner no worse off, nor better off, than if he sold in the market; furthermore, the public body ought to want the land enough to be willing to pay the going market price. But the complication is that the public body, unlike most private buyers, may have helped to create a large part of the land value it has to pay for. If, for instance, it announces a new motorway, land values might rise around the likely position of an interchange with the existing main road; if the community then had to pay this enhanced value, it would seem unfair.

The complication described here has a name in law: *betterment*. Originally this term was reserved for the case where the community took action which clearly made some people better off; the legal argument was that the community should then be able to claim a special tax from these people, reflecting the fact. (The 1427 case, mentioned above, referred to sea-defence works.) But then, it was seen that public actions may be more subtle, and yet make people better or worse off. Suppose the community takes the power to stop building on a fine piece of countryside. Some people – those who owned the land – will be worse off because they cannot enjoy the profit from development. Others – those who lived next to the area – will be directly better off, because they now have an unimpeded view which they expected to lose; they can now sell their land at a profit. Yet others – the general public who can come and enjoy the scenery – are indirectly better off. The third group are difficult to deal with, except perhaps by imposing a charge for entry to the area (as is done, for instance, in American, though not in British national parks). But with regard to the others, it would seem that in fairness the community should pay *compensation* to the first group and claim *betterment* from the others.

The Uthwatt Committee report went in great detail into the conceptual and technical aspects of this problem. Finally, they concluded that the complexities were such that the community would do best by a fairly simple, crude approach: cutting the Gordian Knot, as the committee described it. Land which was not developed – that is, all the rural land of the country – should in effect be nationalized: the State should acquire it, paying compensation to the owners on the basis of the value at some historic date in the recent past. But for the time being, and in some cases perhaps for all time – until such time as the land was needed for urban development – the owner could remain on the land. So his compensation would be limited to the loss of his right to develop the land. If and when the State needed the land for building, it would pay him additional compensation for expropriating him altogether. Then it could sell or lease the land to a developer. Within the built-up areas, on the other hand, the Committee recommended that any redevelopment of existing property should be carried out by the local authority, who would buy the land on the basis of its value at some recent date and carry out the redevelopment itself. Lastly, they proposed that all property owners should pay a regular betterment levy, calculated at the rate of 75 per cent of the increase of the value of the site alone (without the building) since the previous valuation; for this purpose, in addition to the usual valuation of property for rating, there would need to be a separate regular valuation of the site alone.

The Uthwatt Committee solution truly cut the Gordian Knot; and it could have been effective. Its most important feature was that in relation to the major problem – the development of rural land for urban purposes for the first time – it did not need the land market to work at all in the old way; the State would be the sole buyer. This was its technical strength, but its political weakness. Though the report was prepared by disinterested land experts, not by left-wing politicians, it generated immense controversy and opposition on the ground that it advocated land nationalization. The Coalition government of the time at first took no action on it, but then (in 1944) announced that after the war it would reform the law on another, less radical basis. But in the same year, in a Planning Act, it did provide an expedited procedure which allowed the blitzed cities to buy land for reconstruction on a quick and cheap basis.

(ii) ABERCROMBIE AND REITH

In 1944 the wartime government received – and early in 1945 it published – another major report – Patrick Abercrombie's *Greater London Plan*. Starting boldly from the position that the Barlow recommendations on industrial location controls would be accepted and acted upon, and that population growth in the country as a whole would be negligible – an assumption which corresponded to the best demographic forecasts of the time – Abercrombie worked on the basis that the population of London and its surrounding ring – a wide area stretching roughly 30 miles in any direction from London – could be held constant. The task he set himself was to achieve a massive decentralization of people from the inner, more congested part of this vast region to the outer rings. Within the inner part, the County of London Plan (on which Abercrombie had cooperated) had demonstrated that if the slum and blighted areas were to be redeveloped to adequate standards of open space, a planned overspill programme for over 600,000 people would be needed; outside the LCC area, Abercrombie now calculated that the corresponding overspill would amount to an additional 400,000, giving over 1 million in all. Up to 1939 the accommodation of these people would have been carried out in the most obvious way: by building peripheral estates at the edge of the conurbation, thus adding further to the urban sprawl.

Following the Barlow recommendations to the letter, Abercrombie proposed to end all this by a bold device. A green belt would be thrown around London, at the point where the conurbation happened to have stopped at the outbreak of war in 1939; five miles wide, on average, it would provide an effective barrier to growth and also act as a valuable recreational tract for Londoners.

Most importantly, the very width of the belt would fundamentally affect the treatment of the overspill problem. If the overspill were removed to the outer edge of the green belt, or even farther, that would put it well beyond the normal outer limit of commuting to London at that time. New communities could then be created to receive these 1 million people, which would be truly what Ebenezer Howard had intended: self-contained communities for living and working. Abercrombie thus seized the unique opportunity that had been offered to him: to produce a total regional plan as Geddes had advocated, and thus to carry out the principles that Ebenezer Howard had established nearly half a century before. Abercrombie, therefore, proposed that about 400,000 people be accommodated in 8 more or less completely new towns with an average size of about 50,000 each, to be built between 20 and 35 miles from London; another 600,000 should go to expansions of existing small country towns, mainly between 30 and 50 miles from London, but some even more distant than this.

All the other major conurbations of Britain were the subject of similar wide-ranging regional plans, either at the end of the war or shortly afterwards: Abercrombie himself prepared two of them, one for Glasgow and one (jointly) for the west Midlands. All made radical and far-reaching proposals for planned urban decentralization on the principles advocated by Ebenezer Howard, though in none, of course, was the scope so large as in London. Clearly, such large-scale population movements – to be carried out in a relatively short time – posed major problems of organization; the existing structure of local government appeared completely unsuited to deal with them. And apart from the experimental private new towns at Letchworth and Welwyn and the municipal venture by Manchester at Wythenshawe, there was no experience whatever in building new towns.

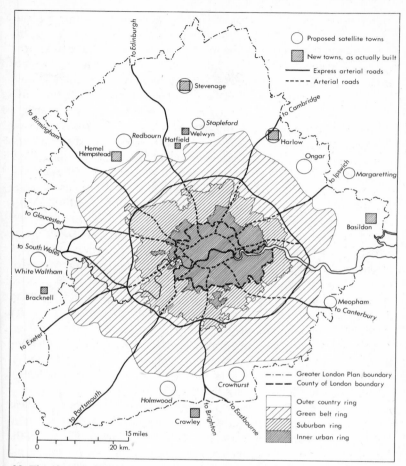

Legend (top right of map):

○ Proposed satellite towns
▨ New towns, as actually built
—— Express arterial roads
---- Arterial roads

Map labels:

to Edinburgh
to Cambridge
Stevenage
to Birmingham
Stapleford
Redbourn Welwyn
Hatfield
Hemel Hempstead
Harlow
Ongar
to Ipswich
Margaretting
to Gloucester
Basildon
to South Wales
White Waltham
Bracknell
Meopham
to Canterbury
to Exeter
Crowhurst
Holmwood
Crawley
to Portsmouth
to Brighton
to Eastbourne

-·-·- Greater London Plan boundary
---- County of London boundary

☐ Outer country ring
▨ Green belt ring
▨ Suburban ring
▨ Inner urban ring

0 ____ 15 miles
0 ____ 20 km.

28. *The Abercrombie Plan for Greater London, 1944. Patrick Abercrombie's bold regional plan involved the planned dispersal of over a million Londoners from the congested inner urban ring, across the new green belt which would limit the further growth of the conurbation, into planned satellite towns – the famous London new towns.*

Therefore, just after the end of the war, the incoming Labour government commissioned yet another major committee report. Dispelling some doubts on the matter, it announced that it supported the principle of planned decentralization to new towns, and appointed a committee to consider ways of building them, to be headed by the redoubtable Lord Reith (1889–1971) – creator of the BBC and the first Minister responsible for planning in the wartime Coalition government, until his enthusiasm and intransigence caused his abrupt dismissal. With his usual energy, Reith set his Committee on New Towns to work and quickly produced two reports – the second early in 1946. It recommended that new towns should normally be built very much as Howard had proposed them, with a size range of 30,000 to 50,000 or perhaps 60,000; though it had little to say about the Social City principle which Howard thought so important. As for organization, it confirmed that the existing local government structure was not suitable for the task. The new towns, it proposed, should each be built by a special development corporation set up for the purpose, generally responsible to Parliament, but free of detailed interference in its day-to-day management, and with direct Treasury funding. The formula, in other words, was rather like that of Reith's own beloved BBC.

Almost certainly, Reith's formula was the right one. In building the new towns, freedom for managerial enterprise and energy had to be given priority over the principle of democratic accountability; if the new towns had had to account for every step to a local authority, they could never have developed with the speed they did. This was particularly so, since almost by definition the existing local community tended to be opposed to the idea of any new town at all. When the new town was largely completed, the Reith Committee argued, that would be the appropriate time to hand it over to the local community for democratic management.

(iii) DOWER AND HOBHOUSE

With the publication of the Reith Committee's second and final report in January 1946, an extraordinary burst of official committee thinking had come almost to an end. Hardly anywhere, in any nation's history, can such sustained and detailed thought have been given to a set of interrelated and highly complex problems within a single field. Only two further reports, in a separate specialized area, remained to complete the list of recommendations. The Dower Report on National Parks, a one-man set of recommendations commissioned by the government from John Dower, a well-known advocate of the establishment of a national parks system, was published in 1945; it was followed in 1947 by the Hobhouse Committee Report on National Parks Administration with detailed recommendations about the organization of the proposed parks. Both reports agreed that the parks should be speedily established in areas of outstanding scenic and recreational importance, and that they should be fully national in character; further, that they should then be positively developed for the outdoor enjoyment of the people, as well as for purposes of conservation of resources. This suggested that the parks organization should be outside the normal framework of local government – there is a parallel here with the Reith Committee recommendations for the new towns. A National Parks Commission should be formed, with full executive powers, to plan and supervise the work of establishing the parks; it should then devolve its powers upon an executive committee in each park. The recommendations here, in fact, followed fairly closely the organization of the outstandingly successful and well-established National Parks Service in the United States, which are run by a bureau of a Federal government department – the Department of the Interior.

The period of committee sittings and report writing, therefore, was concentrated into a short period between 1937 and 1947, with the greatest activity actually in the wartime years of 1940–45. Together, shortly after the end of the war, the completed reports constituted an impressive set of blueprints for the creation of a powerful planning system. But the existence of these blueprints provided no guarantee that action would be forthcoming. In the event, the powerful reforming mood which swept over the country at the end of the war – and which expressed itself in the surprise victory of the Labour Party in the July 1945 general election – provided the impetus to turn recommendations into legislative action. The report writing period of 1940–47 was followed, with a momentary overlap, by the legislative burst from 1945 to 1952, which we must now

Urban and Regional Planning

follow. In doing so, we shall try to establish some sort of logical order, so as better to bring out the interrelationships between the different pieces of legislation. In one or two cases, this will mean important divergences from the chronological order of the different Acts of Parliament.

The Legislation

(i) THE 1945 DISTRIBUTION OF INDUSTRY ACT
The first in this great legislative series, both chronologically and in terms of the whole logical structure, was the Distribution of Industry Act of 1945, which was passed by the Coalition government just before the July election. Its great importance was that it provided for comprehensive government controls over the distribution of industry, of a negative as well as a positive kind. Upon the recommendation of the Barlow minority, these extended over the whole country. In future, any new industrial plant, or any factory extension, over a certain size (which was originally fixed at 10,000 feet and 10 per cent, but which was varied somewhat subsequently) must have an industrial development certificate (IDC) from the Board of Trade. The Board could refuse a certificate without any liability to pay compensation. Subsequently, in the 1947 Planning Act, the grant of permission to develop for industry was made contingent on the possession of the certificate, thus making its enforcement absolutely effective. With modifications in the lower exemption limit, and with varying degrees of toughness and gentleness, these controls have been operated by the Board of Trade (and its successor, the Department of Trade and Industry) throughout the period since 1945 to steer industry away from London and the Midlands, and towards the former special areas.

But the Act also contained new provisions for the positive encouragement of new industry in these areas – henceforth to be known as the development areas. (In 1945, they consisted of Merseyside, North-East England, West Cumberland, Central Scotland and South Wales.) Industrialists setting up plants in these areas would receive a variety of government inducements, including specially built factories, ready-built factories for occupation at low rents, investment grants for the installation of new equipment, and loans.

It seemed like an impressive combination of stick and carrot; but it contained three important limitations. The first was that the system of control applied to factory industry only; location controls were not applied to offices at all until nearly twenty years afterwards in November 1964, and they have never been applied at all to other forms of tertiary (service or non-manufacturing) industry. Probably the reason for this failure is to be found in the faulty analysis performed by the Barlow Commission; the employment figures available to the commissioners excluded a great deal of service industry, because of the incomplete national insurance coverage at that time, and so they underestimated the degree to which the rise in employment in London was the result of the tertiary sector. In any event, in their critical recommendations the whole Commission – majority and minority alike – seemed to confuse two meanings of the word 'industry': one, meaning *all* types of employment; the other meaning just *factory* employment. Their recommendations referred only to the second, limited definition; and the 1945 Act followed them. In the event, employment in manufacturing stagnated in Britain after 1945; the whole net growth of employment was in the service industries.

A second limitation – especially serious, in view of the stagnant state of factory employment – was that the incentives applied chiefly to provision of capital equipment. This meant, paradoxically, that a highly capital-intensive firm using a lot of machinery and very little labour could get generous grants to go to a development area, where it would do virtually nothing to reduce local unemployment. In fact, a firm could actually use the incentives to automate and reduce its labour force. Preposterous as this may seem, there are indications that in one or two cases it actually happened.

A third limitation was simply that the Act left many loopholes. Any firm that was frustrated in its attempts to get an IDC in London, or the Midlands, could easily do one of two things. Either it could extend its existing plant by just under 10 per cent (or 5 per cent, depending on the regulations at the time) a year, thus increasing by 50 or 100 per cent in a decade. It could supplement this by moving

out warehouse or office space into separate buildings, which did not
need a certificate, taking the space for factory production. Or it could
simply buy a 'second-hand' vacated factory in the open market.
There is plenty of evidence, therefore, that though the whole policy
did steer jobs to the development areas, the effect was far less
spectacular than many people hoped. Above all, contrary to expectations, the Act provided no sure machinery at all for curbing the
growth of employment in the South East or the Midlands.

(ii) THE 1946 NEW TOWNS ACT AND THE
1952 NEW DEVELOPMENT ACT
The New Towns Act of 1946 passed into law with remarkable speed
soon after the Reith Committee's final report in order to expedite the
designation of the first of the new communities. The Committee's
recommendations were faithfully followed. New towns were to be
designated formally by the Minister responsible for planning – a
Ministry of Town and Country Planning had been set up in 1943,
and this was one of its first important functions. The Minister would
then set up a development corporation, responsible for building
and managing the town until its construction period was finished.
The Act left open the critical question of what was to happen to each
town after that date, but it was generally expected (as the Reith
Committee had proposed) that it would revert to the local authority.
However in 1958 the government of the day finally decided instead
to hand them over to a special statutory authority, the Commission
for the New Towns. This aroused a great deal of controversy, but there
was an overpowering reason for it; as Ebenezer Howard had
prophesied, new town construction proved a very good investment
for the community because of the new property values that were created,
and it would seem inequitable to hand over all these values to the local
authority which happened to occupy the area. If the values belonged to
the community, they belonged to the whole community.

---

*29. The master plan for Stevenage, the first new town to be designated (in 1946)
Built for London overspill and sited thirty miles north of the metropolis, in
Hertfordshire, Stevenage is a good example of the 'Mark One' new town of the
1940s, designed on neighbourhood unit principles.*

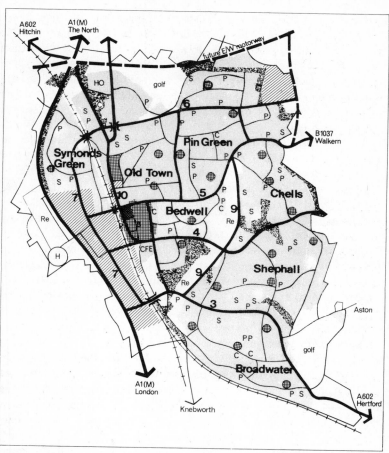

A602
Hitchin

A1(M)
The North

future E/W motorway

golf

HO

S

CFE

P

Symonds
Green

Pin Green

B1037
Walkern

Old Town

Chells

S

Bedwell

5

Re

9

4

CFE

Re

Shephall

9

Re

3

Aston

H

7

golf

Broadwater

A1(M)
London

Knebworth

A602
Hertford

Stevenage
Master Plan 1966

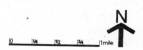

N

0   ¼   ½   ¾   1mile

Progress was rapid after the Act was passed: the first new town, Stevenage, was designated on 11 November 1946 — the very day the Act received the Royal Assent. Between 1946 and 1950, no less than 14 new towns were designated in England and Wales: 8 of them around London, to serve London overspill as proposed in the Abercrombie Plan of 1944 (though not always in the locations proposed in the plan, some of which were found to be unsuitable), 2 in North-East England to serve the development area, 1 in South Wales to serve a similar purpose (though it was actually just outside the development area), 2 in Central Scotland for the same reason (1 of which also received overspill from Glasgow), and lastly 1 attached to a prewar steel works. Then for a decade progress virtually ceased: from 1950 to 1961, only 1 new town — Cumbernauld in Scotland — was designated, and in 1957 there was an announcement that no more new towns would be started. But in 1961 there was an abrupt reversal of policy — for reasons which are analysed more fully in Chapter 7 — and between then and 1970 no less than 14 further new towns were designated in Great Britain. In 1971, a quarter of a century after the passage of the Act, Britain's new towns contained close to 1 million people, with over 180,000 new houses built since designation.

New towns were, however, only one arm of the policy which Abercrombie had proposed for Greater London; the other was the planned expansion of existing country towns, in order to serve the twin purposes of the development of the remoter rural areas and the reception of overspill. The notion here was fairly consistent: such towns would be more distant from the conurbations than the new towns; they would have an existing population and existing industry; and the new towns mechanism would not be suitable for their expansion. Rather, they should be aided in reaching voluntary agreements with the conurbation authorities, with a financial contribution from central government to cover necessary investments. The Town Development Act of 1952, prepared by the Labour government before the 1951 election but passed by the Conservatives after it, provided for this machinery. At that time, it was thought that the programme of new designations was substantially complete, and that further overspill could and should be provided for by the new Act.

30. Stevenage town centre. The Town Square was one of the first pedestrian precincts in a British town centre. Stevenage, like other Mark One towns, now has a full range of shops which rival older-established towns.

But in practice the financial inducements proved insufficient at first, and local authorities with housing problems in the conurbations found real difficulty in reaching agreements. By 1958, indeed, the whole procedure of the Act had provided a derisory total of less than 10,000 houses in England and Wales. Thereafter progress was more rapid, with some really big agreements reached by London for the large scale expansion of Basingstoke, Andover and Swindon; and by 1971, no less than 68,000 houses in England and Wales had been constructed under the provisions of the Act.

(iii) THE 1947 TOWN AND COUNTRY PLANNING ACT

Between them, the 1946 Act and the 1952 Act eventually provided effective mechanisms for the planned overspill of hundreds of thousands of people from the conurbations into new planned communities outside. It seems, from the statements of the time, that such planned developments were confidently expected to provide for the great majority of the whole new housing programme in the country in the postwar period. Between 1946 and 1950, the public sector – the local authorities and the new towns – built more than four in five of all new homes completed. It appears to have been thought that private speculative building for sale would never again achieve the role that it had played during the 1930s. Abercrombie, for instance, assumed in his 1944 plan that over 1 million people would move from London to new communities in planned overspill schemes, as against less than 250,000 moving by spontaneous migration. Between them, three types of public housing authority – city authorities building on slum clearance and renewal sites, new town development corporations and country towns (or the city authorities building in those towns at their invitation) – would provide for the great bulk of the people's housing needs; and these programmes would all proceed within the orderly framework of city regional plans.

This is important, because it provides the setting within which the 1947 Town and Country Planning Act was drawn up and passed. The 1947 Act, one of the largest and most complex pieces of legislation ever passed by a British Parliament, was indeed the corner-stone of the whole planning system created after the Second World War. Without it, effective control of land use and of new development would have been impossible. Green belts, for instance, could not have been drawn around the bigger urban areas in order to contain and regulate their growth; a plan like Abercrombie's would, therefore, not have been enforceable. The effectiveness of the powers is in fact remarkable by international standards since, though many countries have powers to limit development on paper, demonstrably they do not work in practice. But in seeing how this was achieved, it is worth remembering that the system was designed to deal with only a limited part of all the new development; the rest would be carried out in planned public developments like new towns. Such a system was nevertheless necessary, in order not to compromise the fairly radical public programmes.

The first important feature of the 1947 Act, and the key to all the rest, is that it nationalized the right to develop land. This was what the Uthwatt Report had recommended in 1942, in respect of rural land; the 1947 Act extended this to all land, but it did not provide for eventual State take-over when the land was needed for development (save, of course, in the case of compulsory purchase by public authorities for their own schemes). Apart from these last, the land market was still required in order for development to take place; private owners would sell directly to private developers.The Uthwatt proposal was really more consistent with the situation which seems to have been predicted for the postwar period; in a world where the great majority of all new development was in the public sector, it was surely logical to provide for outright State purchase of the land just before development took place, in the case of public and private schemes alike. But the government drew back from this extreme step.

At any rate, the nationalization of the right to develop was the minimum necessary to ensure effective public control over the development and use of land in accordance with a plan. The second feature of the 1947 Act, therefore, was the linkage of plan-making and development control through the creation of new local planning authorities charged with both functions. These were to be the largest available existing local authorities: the counties and the county boroughs in England and Wales, the counties and cities and large burghs in Scotland. At one step, the number of authorities responsible for planning was reduced from 1,441 to 145 in England and Wales. These authorities were charged with the responsibility of drawing up, and quinquennially revising, a development plan for their area, based on a survey and analysis (as recommended many years before by Patrick Geddes); the plan, to consist of a written statement and maps, was to show all important developments and intended changes in the use of the land over a twenty-year future period. This plan was to be submitted to the Minister responsible for planning, for his approval; thereafter, the local planning authority was to administer development control in accordance with the plan. Henceforth, anyone wanting to develop – the term was carefully defined in the Act, but basically meant changing the use of the land by creating structures on or in the land – must apply to the local authority for planning permission; the authority could refuse permission on the ground that the development was not in accord with the plan, or on other grounds, and though there was the right of appeal to the Minister (who might order a public inquiry at his discretion) the aggrieved owner had no other legal redress. This was only possible because of the nationalization of development rights embodied in the Act; these rights were then in effect presented by the State to the local planning authorities.

A third important feature of the Act was compensation. Just as the government at that time was nationalizing coal mines and railways, paying compensation to the shareholders for their interests, so here the government provided compensation to landowners for lost development rights. Many owners, after all, might have bought land expecting to develop it, and it seemed unjust to deny them this right without due compensation. The Act therefore provided a formula: all the development rights in the country were to be valued and added up, and then scaled down to allow for double counting. (This arose because round a city, only a certain percentage of the available plots were likely to be developed in any one period; but naturally, all owners thought that theirs would be the lucky plot, and valued it accordingly.) Then, on a day in the future, all scaled-down claims would be paid. Thereafter, the owners of land (who would continue in possession, retaining the right to enjoy the land in its existing use) would have no further claim to development rights; the State – or the local planning authority to which it had passed them – could exercise these rights freely.

The logic of this led to the next important feature of the Act. If development rights were nationalized, and if owners were compensated for losing them, they had no further claim to enjoy financial gains from any development: if, subsequently, the local planning authority gave them permission to develop, then the community should enjoy any profits that arose. The 1947 Act therefore provided that in the case of permission to develop being granted, owners should pay the State a 'development charge', representing the monetary gain arising; and under regulations made afterwards under the Act, this charge was fixed at 100 per cent of the gain in value. This was perfectly logical and equitable; the only difficulty was that it did not work. We saw above that in the Act, the government shied away from the radical Uthwatt solution of actually taking the land needed for development; in consequence, the private land market was still required to work. Yet the 100 per cent charge removed all incentive for it to work. By 1951 there was evidence that, to make the market move, buyers were paying over the odds for land: they paid the development charge twice over, once to the State and once to the seller.

This was inflationary; still more inflationary would be the once-for-all payment of compensation for lost development rights, amounting to £300 million, which was due in 1954. So in 1953 the new Conservative government to all intents and purposes scrapped the financial provision of the 1947 Act. They abolished the development charge (though many argued that the right course would have been to reduce it, not cut it out altogether). And they provided that compensation would be paid only as and when owners could show that they had actually applied for permission to develop and their application had been rejected. The end of the development charge, however, created an anomaly: landowners who could get development permission would enjoy the whole of the resulting speculative profit (though they now lost their claim on the £300 million); but if their land was compulsorily purchased by public authorities, as for a road or a school, they got only the existing use value. Under the 1947 Act this was logical (since the private seller got no more than this, after he had paid the development charge); now it was not. So in 1959, to restore equity, the government returned to full market value as the basis for compulsory purchase by public authorities. The one exception was where – as in the important case of a new town – the authority should not pay any value which resulted from its own actions on pieces of land around the land in question. In other words, a new town development corporation must pay the owner its assumed full market value in the event that no new town was being built. This completely artificial assumption was necessary to prevent the absurdity of a new town paying values which it had itself created.

One further attempt was made to grapple with the intractable related problems of compensation and betterment, which the financial provisions in the 1947 Act had attempted without success to resolve. This was the 1967 Land Commission Act, passed by the 1964–70 Labour government and repealed by the Conservative administration after the 1970 election. Though discussion of the Act logically comes later on, in Chapter 7, it is useful to discuss its compensation and betterment provisions here, to see how they relate to the 1947 solution.

The 1967 Act was a partial return to the Uthwatt solution of 1942. Originally the Labour government had thought to take the Uthwatt proposals more or less in their entirety, so that a Land Commission would be set up to buy any and all land when needed for development; but they drew back from this extreme step. Instead the Commission would progressively build up a land bank which it could release for development when needed. Additionally, the Act provided that a betterment levy should be charged whenever land changed hands (being payable by the seller), and at the point of development. This was similar to the levy proposed by Uthwatt, but it differed in two ways. First, it was a lower rate: 40 per cent rising to 50 per cent and perhaps more, as against Uthwatt's 75 per cent. Second and more fundamentally, it was not to be charged regularly whether or not the owner actually profited from the rise in value, as Uthwatt had proposed, but only when he realized the increase through sale or development. So it was a very watered-down version of the original Uthwatt idea. Nevertheless it did cut the Gordian Knot – in Uthwatt's phrase – by taking some betterment for the public purse, while hopefully leaving the owner with an incentive. And it did reduce the burden of land purchase for public authorities, since the Land Commission paid a sum net of levy when it bought either in the free market or compulsorily. Unfortunately, because of uncertainty whether the Act and the Commission would survive, the effect seems to have been inflationary, just as after 1947: sellers paid the levy to the Commission, but then added at least part of it again to the price they charged to buyers. And just as after 1951, this was one reason the incoming government gave in 1970 for rescinding the provisions altogether.

Despite these many changes in the financial provisions of the 1947 Act, the main body of the legislation has survived. (In fact all the 1947 provisions, together with subsequent amendments, were rolled up into a consolidating Act in 1962, and that in turn into an Act of 1971, so that the '1947 Act' as such does not exist.) However, in an Act of 1968, major changes were made in the way plans are prepared. We shall discuss those changes in the appropriate place, in Chapter 7.

(iv) THE 1949 NATIONAL PARKS AND ACCESS TO THE COUNTRYSIDE ACT

One further piece of legislation remained to complete the structure. The 1947 Act had at last given to local authorities strong powers to regulate the use of land in the countryside, and thus preserve fine landscape for the enjoyment of the community. But more positive action was thought to be needed on at least two fronts. First, certain especially fine areas needed to be planned in a special way for the enjoyment and recreation of the nation; and second, provision was needed to open up the countryside generally to the public, since (especially on many upland areas) they found themselves barred by sporting or other private interests.

Both the Dower and Hobhouse Reports, as we saw, assumed that national parks should be set up on the model already existing in America, with a strong national executive agency well provided with national funds to make large-scale investment for tourism and outdoor recreation – hostels, camp sites, trails and so on – and, most importantly, with the power to acquire land: the Hobhouse Report had assumed that about one tenth of the area of the parks should be acquired within ten years. But when the government established the parks, in the National Parks and Access to the Countryside Act of 1949, it fought shy of this radical step. In the 1947 Act it had just established local planning authorities based on the counties and county boroughs, it argued, and these were the appropriate bodies to plan the parks. In the case of parks overrunning county boundaries, provision could be made for joint boards. The only special

31. The London Green Belt, 1944–64. Earliest of the postwar green belts to be established around Britain's urban areas, the metropolitan green belt has increased in size since Abercrombie's original 1944 proposals. The green belt has several purposes – including urban containment, agricultural protection and the reservation of land for recreation.

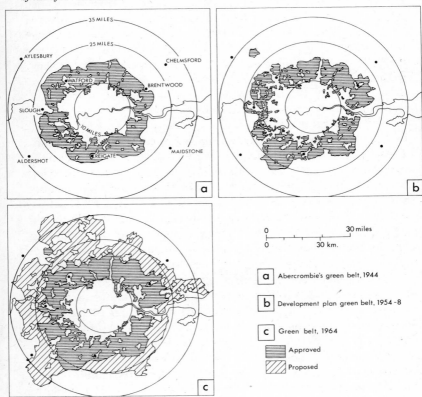

arrangements made for the parks were two. First, a National Parks Commission was set up, to be financed from central government funds, with the responsibility of planning the general programme for the establishment and management of the parks; but in relation to the local authorities, its functions were merely advisory. It did have the power to channel subsidies to these authorities for certain defined purposes of development in the parks, such as car parks or information centres, but only when local funds were forthcoming to match the grants. And secondly, the Act provided for minority membership of outside interests – recreationists, conservationists and amenity organizations – on the local planning committees responsible for the parks. But these committees, in turn, reported to their full councils, which did not contain the outsiders.

Critics at the time attacked the proposals for being weak and insufficiently positive: the local authorities, they argued, were not likely in most cases to support a positive programme of developing the parks for national use, especially when this involved a burden on local rates. This fear proved only too well grounded. In the two decades after the Act, expenditure was negligible, and most of it was concentrated in the two parks which happened to be managed by joint boards: the Peak District and the Lake District.

The 1949 Act also gave local planning authorities in general some additional powers and responsibilities. They were to negotiate with landowners for the development of long-distance footpaths across areas of fine scenery, such as the Pennines or the coasts of Cornwall; the National Parks Commission, again, was to take the lead in developing a plan for their establishment. The plan was quickly forthcoming, but again progress was very slow: in the twenty-three years to 1972 only five such paths were actually established and opened. Planning authorities were also enjoined to designate areas of outstanding natural beauty, which were areas not justifying the full national park treatment, but nevertheless requiring a very special degree of strict planning control to prevent obtrusive or alien development. Since this was the sort of negative control the local planning authorities were well capable of exercising under the 1947 Act, not requiring agreement of landowners or the expenditure of local funds, it proved to be one of the more successful provisions of the Act.

One further development at this time was important for the planning of the countryside. In 1948 the government responded to the promptings of scientists and conservationists, and set up the Nature Conservancy by Royal Charter. It was given the power, and a fairly generous budget, to set up national nature reserves for the conservation of natural habitats and of wildlife, either buying the land for the purpose or reaching agreements with the landowner which would preserve the land in its natural state. On these reserves, and elsewhere, it developed an ambitious research programme, both with its own scientists and through university contracts. In 1965 the Conservancy became one arm of the newly formed Natural Environment Research Council, charged with the coordination of all research in that field. The marked success of the Conservancy, compared with the relative weakness of the National Parks Commission, demonstrated to many observers the importance of creating a strong executive agency with adequate funding and the power to spend it – though in 1972–3 the research and management functions of the Conservancy were split.

A Tentative Verdict

A considered verdict on the '1947 system' – as it is convenient to call it, after its central piece of legislation – clearly has to wait until after a study of how it worked in practice, which we shall do in Chapters 6 and 7. But meanwhile it is helpful to point out a few important features.

Firstly, the system worked by giving strong *negative* powers of control to the new local planning authorities. Good *positive* planning, it seems to have been assumed, would mainly be carried out by public building agencies of various kinds – the local authorities and the new towns – in which close and virtually automatic union of planning and development would be the rule. They would be almost wholly responsible for the urban renewal programmes in the older parts of the cities and for the construction of new and expanded towns of all kinds in the countryside. The negative powers of control would be needed merely to control the minority of developments that would still be carried out by private agencies. In practice, we shall see in Chapter 7, it worked out very differently.

Secondly, the system clearly required some overall coordination. It was generally agreed that the right unit for spatial, or physical, planning was the urban region, as Geddes had suggested as long ago as 1915. There was not much empirical work at that time on the delimitation of the spheres of influence of cities; the first serious empirical work, by A. E. Smailes and F. H. W. Green, was published round about the time the system was being set up. But clearly it extended right outside the rather restrictive boundaries of the cities, into the surrounding countryside; and Abercrombie's plan for Greater London covered an area of over 2,000 square miles. Nevertheless, in the 1947 Act the government gave the local planning powers to the existing local authorities, not to bigger units. This was probably inevitable if planning was to be accountable to a local electorate; but in addition, despite considerable interest in the idea, the government attempted no fundamental reform of local government. The critical job of preparing plans for the orderly development of the great city regions – and in particular for the decentralization of population and jobs in them – was split between the country boroughs and the rural counties. Though there was provision for joint planning boards, these were not implemented save on an advisory basis, and although by 1948 regional plans existed for the areas around all the great conurbations, prepared either by outside consultants or by joint committees of the local authorities concerned, they were purely advisory in function.

In these circumstances some coordination from the top was clearly essential. The 1947 Act provided it, by the requirement that plans be submitted to the Minister for approval; he could amend them as he wished. Thus the various plans for any region could be coordinated. But for this to be done effectively, some kind of regional intelligence agency was clearly necessary to provide the Minister with advice. The original organization of the Ministry of Town and Country Planning, with strong regional offices in each of the main provincial cities, was specifically created to deal with this. But during the 1950s these offices were closed down for reasons of economy, and at this point the idea of coordinating the various local plans seems to have been more or less abandoned. The almost inevitable result was that the various local planning authorities, left to their own devices, pursued a defensive and negative policy. We shall trace some of the consequences in Chapter 7.

Further Reading

Stamp, already quoted in the reading to Chapter 4, provides an invaluable introduction. J. B. Cullingworth, *Town and Country Planning in England and Wales* (Allen & Unwin, third edition, 1970), is the standard text on the British planning system. The legislative base is set out in detail in Desmond Heap, *An Outline of Planning Law* (Sweet & Maxwell, 1973).

On new towns, see Frederic J. Osborn and Arnold Whittick, *The New Towns: the Answer to Megalopolis* (Leonard Hill, second edition, 1969); Frank Schaffer, *The New Town Story* (MacGibbon & Kee, 1970), and Pierre Merlin, *New Towns* (Methuen, 1971), which also deals with experiments in other countries. On urban containment, see David Thomas, *London's Green Belt* (Faber, 1970); and Peter Hall *et al., The Containment of Urban England* (Allen & Unwin, 1973).

6. National/Regional Planning from 1945 to 1972

In Chapter 5 we saw that the Distribution of Industry Act, 1945, effectively carried out the recommendations of the Barlow minority report: there was to be a strong policy of steering industrial growth from the more prosperous regions to the depressed areas of the 1930s, to be accomplished not only by positive inducements to locate in these latter areas, but also by negative controls over the location of new industry, and over extensions to existing industry, in the other areas. This control applied only to manufacturing industry, though limited evidence already existed from the interwar period that the more rapid growth was in the tertiary or service sector of employment; and this was not at all remedied until the control of office development in 1964.

In fact, little substantial change was made in the control mechanisms from 1945 to 1960, except for adjustments in the lower thresholds of size below which no industrial development certificate was needed. There is, however, clear evidence from the statistics of the Board of Trade that the whole policy of steering industry was operated rather more laxly in the 1950s than in the period from 1945 to 1950. This might be attributed to the fact that a Labour government was more enthusiastic about helping the development areas (where much of its voting support was concentrated) than a Conservative government; the more likely reason is simply that by the early 1950s it seemed clear that general economic management policies were keeping unemployment levels well below the levels of the 1930s, so that the case for strong regional policies seemed rather weaker than in 1945.

In this chapter, therefore, we will look first at the record of the controls, and their effects, from 1945 to about 1970. Then we shall turn to look in some detail at the rapid – and sometimes bewildering – policy shifts of the 1960s, and try in turn to sum up their effects.

The Pattern of Regional Change, 1945–70

An elementary point should first be made: that almost throughout the period from 1945 to 1970, the overwhelmingly most important aim of planning at the national/regional scale was to create employment. More precisely, it was to reduce unemployment rates and/or the rates of out-migration from the development areas. There are a number of possible aims of regional economic policy: they include improving the efficiency of industry, raising the level of gross regional product per worker or per head of total population, improving the distribution of regional income, and many other variants. Trying to keep employment up (or unemployment down) could in fact easily run counter to many of these other objectives. It could, for instance, lead to the retention or even the introduction of rather inefficient labour-intensive industries that paid poorly, thus keeping a large section of the population in low-income occupations and increasing the inequality of income within the region, as well as the inequality between that region and the rest of the country. Many economists would argue, indeed, that the obsession with employment as almost the sole criterion of British regional policy has been positively pernicious.

However, there are two obvious reasons why this objective has been so attractive. The first is that unemployment is much more visible than low income or inequality in income. People are less inclined to put up with it, and politicians are therefore more concerned about it. The second is that at least for much of this period the statistics with which to measure other criteria of regional performance were poor or non-existent. This particularly applies to figures about regional productivity, which were few in number and late to appear. In any case, calculations of productivity, unless they are accompanied by very full statistical information about some of the possible explanations – such as the amount and quality of capital and the training of the labour force – are notoriously dangerous to interpret.

We shall, therefore, concentrate on the employment criterion, as contemporaries did, with a sideways look at other possible indices. Table 2 shows the actual results of the Board of Trade's operation of the industrial development certificate machinery from 1956 to 1960 and from 1966 to 1970. It shows fairly clearly that while in the earlier period the machinery was not operated very actively on behalf of the development areas, in the later period there was a systematic diversion of new factory floorspace from the prosperous areas to the less prosperous areas. A measure of the amount of this diversion can be obtained by comparing the proportion of new floorspace in each region with the yardstick of the employment in that region at the beginning of the period. Thus the East and West Midlands, the South West and the South-East corner of England, consisting of the South East and East Anglia regions, had together 58.8 per cent of total national employment at the start of the 1966–70 period; but they obtained only 41.5 per cent of new floorspace in the following 4 years. Conversely the Northern region obtained no less than 10.9 per cent against the yardstick of 5.7 per cent; Scotland 14.0 per cent against 9.3 per cent; and Wales 8.6 per cent against 4.3 per cent. Dividing the whole country up into the 'more prosperous' regions of the South, Midlands, Lancashire and Yorkshire, and the 'less prosperous' regions of the North, Scotland and Wales (that is, the areas where the Development Areas were concentrated) the distinction is clear: the less prosperous regions got 58.8 per cent of new floorspace against a yardstick of 41.2 per cent. (In the 1956–60 period contrastingly, they got only 42.7 per cent against a yardstick of 43.2 per cent.) We can assume that the distribution of new factory jobs followed the distribution of new factory floorspace – though not precisely, since some at least of the new factory space was in capital-intensive, labour-saving types of production.

But the picture looks rather different when we turn to the right-hand column of Table 2. This shows the actual creation of employment in the regions – all employment, not just factory jobs. In the earlier period, when the south-east corner of England received only 30.9 per cent of new floorspace, it attracted 58.2 per cent of all new jobs. Between them, five less prosperous regions – the North West, Yorkshire, the North, Scotland and Wales – together got 42.7 per cent of new floorspace, but only 11.5 per cent of the new jobs: a derisory total. In the later period, the comparison is complicated by the fact that employment was almost everywhere falling. But the

Table 2: Industrial Building Completions and Employment Changes, 1956–60 and 1966–70

1956–60

Old standard region*	Employment at start of period		Industrial building completions		Employment changes	
	No. (thousands)	% total	million sq.ft	% total	No. (thousands)	% total gain
Northern	1279	5.9	13.2	5.6	+23	3.7
East & West Riding	1857	8.5	18.9	8.0	+17	2.7
North West	2983	14.4	32.4	13.7	+10	1.6
Wales	956	4.4	14.8	6.2	+13	2.1
Scotland	2163	10.0	21.7	9.2	+9	1.4
'Peripheral' Regions	*9238*	*43.2*	*101.0*	*42.7*	*+72*	*11.5*
London & South East, Eastern & Southern	7633	35.2	73.1	30.9	+365	58.2
South West	1189	5.5	11.6	4.9	+57	9.1
West Midland	2148	9.9	33.5	14.1	+83	13.2
North Midland	1485	6.8	17.9	7.6	+53	8.5
'Prosperous' Regions	*12455*	*57.4*	*136.1*	*57.5*	*+558*	*89.0*
Great Britain	*21706*	*100.0*	*236.9*	*100.0*	*+627*	*100.0*

* The 'old' standard regions, as explained above, were abolished in 1965 – a major statistical problem in comparison.

1966–70

New standard region	Employment at start of period		Industrial building completions		Employment changes	
	No. (thousands)	% total	million sq.ft	% total	No. (thousands)	% total loss
Northern	1335	5.7	20.7	10.9	−14	2.2
Yorks. & Humberside	2111	9.0	19.3	10.2	−87	13.9
North West	3034	12.9	28.6	15.1	−129	20.6
Wales	1007	4.3	16.3	8.6	−45	7.2
Scotland	2193	9.3	26.6	14.0	−41	6.5
'Peripheral' Regions	*9680*	*41.2*	*111.5*	*58.8*	*−316*	*50.4*
South East	8068	34.3	30.1	15.9	−212	33.9
East Anglia	615	2.6	7.9	4.2	+29	−4.6
South West	1355	5.7	10.7	5.6	−22	3.5
West Midland	2388	10.1	16.6	8.8	−95	15.2
East Midland	1437	6.1	13.3	7.0	−8	1.3
'Prosperous' Regions	*13863*	*58.8*	*78.6*	*41.5*	*−308*	*49.8*
Great Britain	*23554*	*100.0*	*189.5*	*100.0*	*−626*	*100.0*

Source: Abstracts of Regional Statistics. Total may not add due to rounding.

Table 3: Total Employment Changes by Industrial Orders: Great Britain, 1953–9, 1959–63, 1963–5.

Industrial order	Changes in estimated numbers of employees (total, male and female) in employment					
	1953–9 (six years)		1959–63 (four years)		1963–5 (two years)	
	Per cent	Order	Per cent	Order	Per cent	Order
Agriculture, forestry, fishing	−12.8	23	−13.6	21	−12.2	23
Mining and quarrying	−5.6	18	−17.8	22	−8.5	22
TOTAL: PRIMARY INDUSTRIES	−8.9		−16.0		−10.2	
Food, drink and tobacco	+6.5	9	+3.1	12	+0.6	14
Chemicals and allied industries	+10.7	7	−0.8	18	+0.7	13
Metal manufacture	+1.1	11	+3.2	13	+6.8	4
Engineering, electrical and metal goods	+11.3	6	+10.8	4	+6.6	5
Shipbuilding and marine engineering	−6.0	19	−20.7	23	−3.2	20
Vehicles	+10.4	8	+0.7	14	−0.5	15
Textiles	−12.8	22	−7.5	20	−1.2	16
Leather, leather goods and fur	−11.6	21	−1.9	19	−1.9	17
Clothing and footwear	−7.7	20	−0.6	17	−2.1	18
Bricks, pottery, glass, cement, etc.	−2.7	16	+4.3	11	+5.1	9
Timber, furniture, etc.	−1.1	14	+0.5	15	+5.6	7
Paper, printing and publishing	+15.0	3	+9.1	6	+2.0	11
Other manufacturing industries	+12.7	5	+10.4	5	+8.3	2
TOTAL: MANUFACTURING INDUSTRIES	+4.2		+3.3		+3.1	
Total: Construction	+4.5	10	+11.7	3	+7.5	3
Gas, electricity and water	+0.4	12	+6.1	9	+3.4	10
Transport and communication	−3.0	17	—	16	−3.2	21
Distributive trades	+14.5	4	+7.8	8	+2.0	12
Insurance, banking and finance	+18.9	2	+14.2	2	+5.6	8
Professional and scientific services	+19.6	1	+15.5	1	+8.8	1
Miscellaneous services	−0.2	13	+5.6	10	+5.9	6
Public administration	−1.3	15	+7.9	7	−2.7	19
TOTAL: SERVICE INDUSTRIES	+6.7		+7.8		+2.9	
GRAND TOTAL	+4.3		+4.7		+2.4	

Source: Department of Economic Affairs.

same conclusions apply; together the five less prosperous regions had 58.8 per cent of additional floorspace, yet more than half the total loss in jobs was concentrated here.

The simple reason, of course, is that most of the new jobs were not factory jobs. They were in services. Table 3 is a 'league table' of the 24 main orders of the Standard Industrial Classification in the period 1953–65, ordered in terms of the percentage increase in employment. During most of this period, the two fastest-growing employment groups were in the tertiary or service sector: professional and scientific services, and insurance, banking and finance. And these were not cases of big increases on small bases: both were among the more important industrial groups in the national economy. By and large, these jobs – together with some of the fastest-growing factory jobs – were particularly well represented in the more prosperous regions. Conversely, the development areas tended to have higher proportions of people in the stagnant or declining industries which occur at the foot of the league in Table 3. These tend to be the same older staple industries, like coalmining and textiles and shipbuilding, whose decline caused such acute distress in these areas in the 1930s. The problem of bad industrial structure, it seems, had not been eradicated.

This conclusion poses the question, first raised by Barlow: was the poorer performance of the problem regions, in terms of employment growth, wholly to be explained by this effect of industrial structure? Even a casual glance at detailed tables of regional industrial structure suggests that it is more complex than that: a region like the West Midlands has much-better-than-average growth, though apparently it has a lower-than-average representation of growth industry; conversely a region like Scotland has a poorer-than-average performance, though it has a better-than-average proportion of fast-growing industry. Several analyses by economists during the 1960s tried to calculate the importance of the structural effect, and have concluded that though in some regions it seemed to have dominated – especially in the poor performance of the problem regions – elsewhere it was quite unimportant. Illustration 32 shows one such set of results, published by Frank Stilwell in 1969. But this type of statistical analysis – it is called 'shift and share' analysis – is quite

Urban and Regional Planning

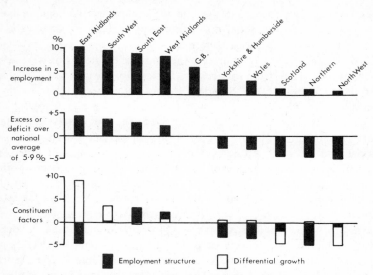

32. *The structural effect on regional employment change, 1957–67. Broadly, the regions of southern and midland England have had faster-than-average employment growth while the North, Wales and Scotland have lagged. Calculations by the economist Frank Stilwell show that in several cases – especially in the laggard regions – this can be explained largely in terms of the unfavourable economic structure, with a predominance of declining or static industry.*

abnormally sensitive to the classification of industry that is used. If the grouping of industry is very coarse, with a number of rather disparate industries having different location patterns lumped into one group, the structural effect is much less likely to show up than if the classification is a fine one; and the one used in the analysis described here was quite a coarse one.

The sluggish growth in employment in the less prosperous regions would not matter so much, of course, if it were in line with the demand for jobs. But there is clear evidence that it is not. In the first place, all these regions have continued to experience higher rates of unemployment, on average, than the rest of the country. The differential is much smaller than in the days of very high national unemployment rates during the 1930s; but it is there, and what is significant is

132

that whenever the national rate widens, then the differential of the less prosperous areas widens too. What is also evident, from Table 4, is that the unemployment rate does not measure the full extent of the true waste of labour. For in addition, *activity* or *participation rates* also tend to be lower in some of these regions, especially for women. These rates simply measure the proportion of adult men and women actually in the labour force (whether employed or unemployed). They show the extent to which the region is tapping its reserves of labour. Of course, female activity rates, in particular, can vary because of social customs: in some mining areas it has traditionally been thought that the woman belonged at home, not in the factory. But to a large extent, especially in recent years, they tend to reflect simply the availability of work: where the rate is low, it means that some people think there is no point looking for a job.

In many ways, the regional income per head is the best of all indices of economic health or the lack of it. It sums up many

Table 4: Regional relatives for unemployment, activity rates and incomes, 1961–6.

	Unemployment,* 1961–6 average	Activity rates 1961–6 average		Male earnings 1964/5– 1966/7 average	Weekly household income 1961–6 average
		Male	Female		
North	185	96	85	93	84
Yorks. & Humberside	75	104	100	94	95
North West	120	103	107	97	95
Wales	165	90	73	96	90
Scotland	205	100	99	92	94
South East	65 ⎱	102	106	⎰ 108	112
East Anglia	90 ⎰			⎱ 91	93
South West	100	85	81	92	92
West Midlands	65	106	109	102	109
East Midlands	65	99	96	95	98
Great Britain	100	100	100	100	100

* Wholly unemployed, excluding school-leavers.

Source: Department of Economic Affairs.

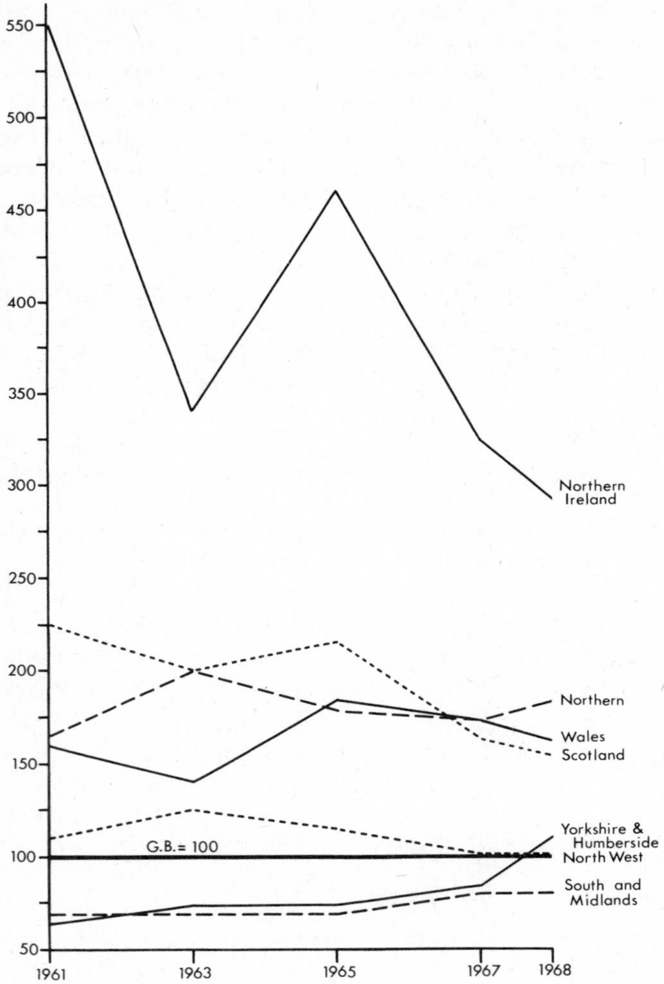
550
500
450
400
350
300
250
200
150
100
50
1961
1963
1965
1967
1968
Northern
Ireland
Northern
Wales
Scotland
Yorkshire &
Humberside
North West
G.B.= 100
South and
Midlands

33. Regional unemployment differentials, 1961–8. Generally, during the 1960s differentials narrowed, but there have been many perturbations and the less prosperous regions – the North, Wales, Scotland and Northern Ireland – are still noticeably worse off than the South and Midlands.

different causes working in conjunction: high unemployment, low activity rates, poor industrial structures with large proportions of low-paying jobs. Incomes can be presented in a number of different ways, from different sources. Table 4 shows two of them, and it is fairly clear from it that high unemployment and low activity rates are associated rather systematically with low personal and household incomes. Another source, the income tax returns, is mapped in Illustration 34 (a) and (b). It shows that in general the South and Midlands have a higher proportion of high and middle incomes — with middle incomes especially well represented in the Midlands — while the problem areas have larger numbers of really low incomes. Worst off of all, it seems, are the thinly populated upland rural areas such as Mid-Wales, which have large numbers of small-scale hill farmers subsisting on very low incomes.

Faced with the prospect of higher-than-average unemployment risk, fewer job opportunities for women, and lower incomes, it is small wonder that many people choose to leave the problem areas. But here again a word of caution should be entered. The *net* figures of inter-regional migration show very clearly that the broad drift is out of the problem areas and into the more prosperous South and Midlands. But these net figures are in fact relatively small differences between much larger *gross* flows (Table 5). The Northern region, for instance, lost 4,070 people between 1965 and 1966. But in this period there was a gross movement of 39,880 people into the region; it was, however, counteracted by an even larger movement of 43,950 in the reverse direction. Again it should be noted that the figures for the late 1950s and early 1960s, in particular, were distorted because they include movements into and out of the country altogether. One main reason why London and the South East seemed to be gaining so many migrants at that time was that they were a main area of attraction to immigrants from the Commonwealth. Since the restrictions on Commonwealth

---

34. (*a*) *Median net annual incomes* (*before tax*) *in the United Kingdom, 1969–70;*
(*b*) *Low income excess: areas where the percentage of net incomes* (*before tax*) *of less than £900 per annum is greater than national average* (*33.6 per cent*), *1970–71.*
Maps of regional income disparities reinforce the view that 'two nations' still exist in Britain. The most prosperous part of the country is the 'Megalopolis' stretching from London through the Midlands to Cheshire; the peripheral regions are noticeably poorer.

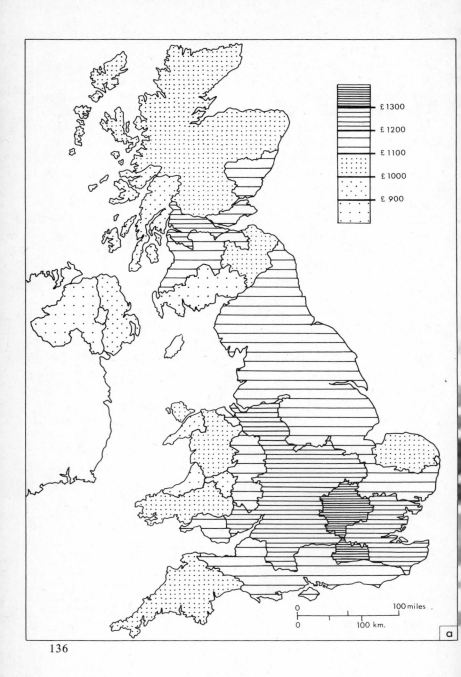

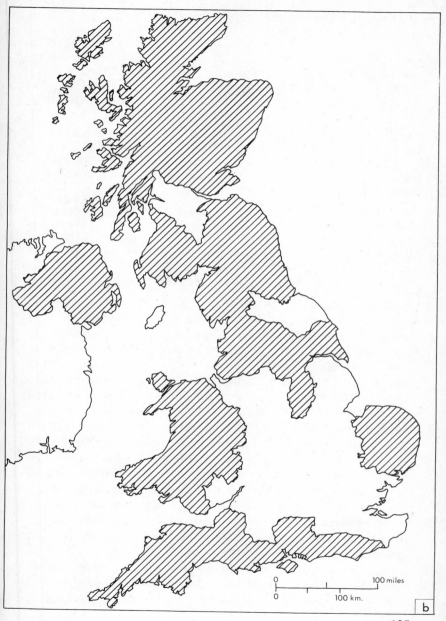

0   100 miles

0   100 km.

b

Urban and Regional Planning

immigration in 1962, the net gains in the South East have been sharply reduced; by the mid 1960s, indeed, as Table 5 shows, there was a net outflow from the South East to the rest of Britain.

Table 5: Migration, Gross and Net, 1965–6

Standard Region	Gross In-Migrants	Gross Out-Migrants	Net Migration
Northern	39,880	43,950	−4,070
Yorkshire and Humberside	61,680	62,640	−960
North West	63,810	69,120	−5,310
East Midlands	62,650	53,280	+9,370
West Midlands	60,560	67,760	−7,200
East Anglia	46,520	34,840	+11,680
South East	152,400	180,040	−27,640
South West	89,850	67,030	+22,820
Wales	35,540	34,240	+1,300
TOTAL – ENGLAND AND WALES	612,890	612,890	

Source: R. A. Hart, *Regional Studies* (1970), p. 290, based on 1966 census.

The conclusion that could be drawn concerning regional economic policy by the middle 1960s, then, was that it had worked hard to provide new jobs in the problem areas, but that it had made relatively little difference to the overall picture. Of course, it should be stressed that if the policy had not operated, matters would doubtless have been that much the worse. It was estimated that between 1945 and 1950, for instance, a gross total of 287,000 new jobs were created in the development areas. But the net increase was less than 200,000, because some 90,000 jobs disappeared in the same period. Had there been no policy, there would probably have been a net fall of 90,000 in employment, instead of a rise of 200,000. And this trend continues: it was estimated in the mid-1960s that Scotland needed 200,000 new jobs, and the North East 100,000 new jobs, between 1965 and 1975 to compensate for declines in basic industry.

At the same time, the bulk of new jobs was still being created outside the development areas. For this there were two reasons: growth in service-industry employment not subject to the IDC controls, and growth in factory industry which in one way or another fell outside the IDC net. A. E. Holmans, for instance, calculated in 1964 that of an increase of 577,000 factory jobs in South-East England

35. Aerial view of Port Talbot steel mill, Glamorgan, South Wales – an example of the new industry deliberately implanted in a development area. This picture also illustrates the attraction of deep water for heavy industry in postwar Britain.

(including East Anglia) in the 1950s, only 190,000 could be accounted for by the grant of IDCs; the rest had been created through small-scale extensions that escaped the controls, or through buying up existing factory buildings. In addition, Holmans pointed out, this area had the great bulk of all employment in two of the fastest-growing service industries, professional and scientific services and miscellaneous services: with 65 per cent of total national employment in these groups in 1959, it had 65 per cent of the subsequent growth from then to 1963. Though the rate of growth of these groups was no higher in the South East than elsewhere, they contributed importantly to its favourable overall growth record.

Urban and Regional Planning

36. Ford factory, Halewood, Merseyside. This modern plant outside Liverpool was located here in the 1960s, with government encouragement, to implant one of Britain's growth industries in a development area. Similar development took place on the opposite bank of the Mersey at Ellesmere Port (General Motors), Linwood in Scotland (Chrysler) and Bathwood in Scotland (British Leyland).

Policy Changes, 1960–72

During one part of the period just analysed, up to 1960, there was considerable stability in regional economic policy. Both the policies and the regions to which they related remained constant except in minor detail. The distinction between the development areas and the rest was quite fundamental, and it was maintained as the 1945 Distribution of Industry Act had determined. These development areas – Merseyside, the North East, West Cumberland, Central

140

Scotland and Dundee, and South Wales – had been fixed in the 1945 Act; they covered quite broad areas of territory, roughly the older heavy industrial areas based on the coalfields, which had been designated as special areas in 1934.

The first major policy shift, contained in the Local Employment Act of 1960, changed all this. It scrapped the development areas, and replaced them by the development districts, a more flexible concept defined as an area which had suffered a $4\frac{1}{2}$ per cent (or worse) unemployment rate over a sustained period of several months. The intention, laudable in principle, was to concentrate help on the distressed areas where it was most needed, and conversely to avoid helping those parts of the old development areas – especially the bigger commercial centres, which were seats of expanding service industries – that could well help themselves. But in practice the policy had all sorts of unfortunate effects. It proved to spread help very widely and thinly over sparsely populated rural areas, such as the Highlands of Scotland. This in itself might have been justified, because presumably such areas were in need of help. But by being applied rigidly to each and every local employment-exchange area which qualified on the unemployment criterion, it hindered the development of a concentrated strategy. Worse, by excluding the more prosperous local centres it frequently made it difficult to devise any strategy based on the natural point of growth in a region.

It was in fact just at this time – the early 1960s – that British economic planners and economic geographers began to show interest in the concept of the 'growth pole' (*pôle de croissance*) which had been developed in 1955 by the French economist François Perroux. They almost certainly mistranslated and misunderstood the concept: the 'pole' of Perroux was the sector of an economy rather than a geographical place or area, but in Britain it was interpreted in the latter sense. The result, naturally, was widespread professional criticism of the operation of the 1960 Act, on the ground that it inhibited the development of a 'growth pole' policy for the less prosperous regions. And, to make matters urgent, the winter of 1962–3 marked a serious recession in the national economy, which caused unemployment rates in these regions to swing up sharply.

The outcome, in November 1963, was the publication of govern-

37. *Reconstruction in central Glasgow. To clear the backlog of obsolescence in Scotland's biggest city is a herculean task. Government policies have deliberately diverted funds into the city's ambitious urban motorway programme, seen here; the objective is to give a new image to the city and to Scotland.*

ment plans for two of the most seriously hit regions: the North East and Central Scotland. Both plans, in effect, represented partial abandonment of the 1960 development district policy, and its replacement by the concept of the growth pole – or, as it was translated, growth zone. The idea was to identify those parts of the region which had the best prospects of rapid industrial growth and to concentrate help – especially public investments in infrastructure

38. *Cumbernauld new town, Dunbartonshire, Scotland. Designed in the mid-1950s, this is a celebrated example of a compact new town built at higher densities than the 'Mark One' examples, with an extensive network of high-capacity roads. The town is intended to house overspill arising from Glasgow's slum clearance programme, and to serve development in central Scotland by attracting new industry.*

(transport, communications, power lines and the like) – on them. The other areas, in effect, would be treated as virtually beyond help. But since they would normally be quite near the growth zones, their populations could quite easily readjust over time either by short-distance migration or by commuting to work there. In effect this neatly reversed the 1960 policy. For instance, in the North East the 1960 Act had concentrated help on the struggling western industrial districts of County Durham, west of the Great North Road; the 1963 Plan concentrated most of the help east of it.

At the same time, there was widespread criticism of the continuing disparity between the distress in the problem areas and the continuing rapid growth of the more prosperous areas — above all London and the South East. The 1961 census revealed that the area embracing London and the ring 50 miles around had added 500,000 to its population in the 1950s. Much of this, in fact, represented either natural increase or immigration from the Commonwealth; but that was not generally noticed, and it was widely assumed that London's prosperity was somehow connected with the North's distress. Particular criticism was directed at the office building boom in London, which was adding 3.5 million square feet of floorspace a year in the late 1950s, and which was certainly instrumental in the continuing increase of employment in the South East.

Prodded, the government began to take action. It sealed an absurd loop-hole in the planning regulations, which had allowed office developers to put back much more on a site than they demolished. Then in 1963 it set up the Location of Offices Bureau (LOB) to act as an information and publicity centre to encourage office firms to move voluntarily out of London. LOB's vigorous and compelling propaganda campaign, which seldom missed a topical opportunity, brought results: 10,000 jobs were being exported from the capital in this way each year during the late 1960s, most of them, however, to locations within 40 or 50 miles. And there was nothing to stop other users taking the offices they left.

The *South East Study* (HMSO, March 1964) added to the voices of the critics. An official study based on three years' work, it revealed that between 1961 and 1981 the region within 50 miles of London was likely to add $3\frac{1}{2}$ million to its population, and suggested a further series of new towns to cope with the growth. The Labour party, in particular, were highly critical of the situation, and on return to office in October 1964, they immediately began to review the *Study*. Meanwhile, as of midnight on 4 November 1964, they imposed a ban on further office building in London and the region around it. In 1965, they formalized this emergency control in the Control of Office Employment Act, which at last put the creation of new office space on the same basis as the building of new factory floorspace. This gave them power to regulate new office building by the requirement that prospective builders apply for an office development permit (ODP). The controls applied initially to the London and Birmingham areas, and they were operated strictly. However, no powers at all were taken to cover any of the other fast-expanding sectors of tertiary industry, such as retailing or higher education. Much of the latter, ironically, was growing very rapidly in the South East, including the centre of London, as part of publicly approved and financed programmes.

During 1965, the new Labour government created a totally new organization for promoting and coordinating national/regional planning, as they had promised to do before the 1964 election. This, however, was less a party political platform (though the Labour Party was historically committed to helping the less prosperous areas) than the reflection of a general movement of thought among economists and planners. There was at this time an intense interest in the French system of economic planning, which had been in operation since 1946, and which had come to contain a very strong regional element. The French system was well adapted to a mixed economy with both public and private sectors, such as that of France itself or Britain. Called *indicative* planning (as distinct from regulatory planning), it relied heavily on the coordination of public and private investment programmes through a complex structure of councils and committees. (It is explained in more detail in Chapter 8.) In the system as it existed in the early 1960s, when British observers were studying it intensively, there were basically two sorts of coordination: by industrial group, and by region. For the latter purpose, the country was divided up into 21 planning regions, consisting of groups of *départements* (the basic system of French government in the provinces, though not 'local government' in the British sense), each under a Director, or *Super Préfet*.

The 1965 reform was in essence an attempt to apply this system to Britain. Immediately on entering office the Labour government had set up a Department of Economic Affairs, which set to work on the preparation of a National Plan of an indicative type. To provide the necessary element of regional coordination, they set up a series of *economic planning councils*, consisting of members appointed by the government to represent different groups in each region (industrialists, trades unionists, traders, transport men, academics), and *economic planning boards* of civil servants seconded from their London departments to work together in the regions; each of the regions had a council charged with the preparation of a regional study and plan, assisted by the professional board members. The regions used for the purpose in England were basically the old standard regions which had been used for statistical purposes ever since the Second World War, with some detailed modifications in the South East and on Humberside. Wales and Scotland each constituted a region by itself.

In practice the record of the councils and boards was a mixed and not always a happy one: one council chairman resigned after disagreement with the government, at least one other threatened to do so, and many expressed private frustration over the relative powerlessness of the councils. The original National Plan was published before it could contain any contribution from the councils and boards. Subsequently every council published a regional study and most published a plan for economic development, but in many cases the government rejected their recommendations. More seriously, the Department of Economic Affairs (DEA) – which coordinated the work of the councils – became weaker after the departure of George Brown as its political head: and in 1969 it was formally abolished, its long-term economic planning functions passing to the Treasury and its regional responsibilities passing to the Ministry of Housing and Local Government.

In part, this can be attributed to inter-Ministerial warfare: from the start, the Treasury disliked the idea of a rival economic department, and the Ministry of Housing was worried that physical planning would be subordinated to the new Department. But more basically, the new structure had real difficulties. On the economic side it proved difficult to divide up economic planning – the short-term work staying with the Treasury, the longer-term plans going to the new DEA – as the government had thought possible in 1964. On the regional side it transpired that in many cases – especially in the more buoyant, faster-growing regions of the country – the work of the councils and boards had an extremely strong element of physical planning. After all, in a region like the South East, the main responsibility of economic planning must be to prepare a plan for the orderly decentralization of employment and population, which is taking place anyway; and this is a spatial or physical plan. One result was a demarcation dispute between the council and the existing physical planners, which is discussed in Chapter 7. The outcome was that by 1969 it seemed natural that the work of the councils and boards should be coordinated by the Ministry of Housing and Local Government – reflecting the fact that the main work in future would be in overall spatial planning of the regional/local variety, rather than as part of a national/regional planning exercise which seemed to have come to a sad end.

This story has taken us some way ahead of chronology, to which we should now return. Between 1966 and 1967 the Labour government made a major shift in the structure of incentives to firms moving to the problem areas. In the 1966 White Paper on Investment Incentives, and the resulting Industrial Development Act of 1966, they scrapped the development districts and replaced them again by development areas – though defined more widely than in the 1945–60 period. Indeed, they were defined so widely that they could be criticized on almost the same grounds as the development districts: that they offered the prospect of help to areas beyond help. However, they were an improvement in that (with one or two glaring exceptions) they did not exclude the growth centres in the regions from the possibility of aid. The new development areas took in the whole of northern England, north of a line from Morecambe Bay to Scarborough; all Scotland, save Edinburgh; all Wales, save the Cardiff and Newport areas and Flintshire; north Devon plus north Cornwall; and Merseyside. (Shortly after special development areas were defined for declining coal-mining regions such as Lancashire, West Cumberland and the Welsh valleys.) There was much detailed criticism of the boundaries, as was perhaps to be expected: it was pointed out that the exclusion of Cardiff made it difficult to prepare a rational regional plan for South Wales (and later – a more glaring anomaly – a new town was proposed at Llantrisant, north of Cardiff, on a site that was half inside the development area, half out); that Merseyside was really no worse off than the depressed cotton towns

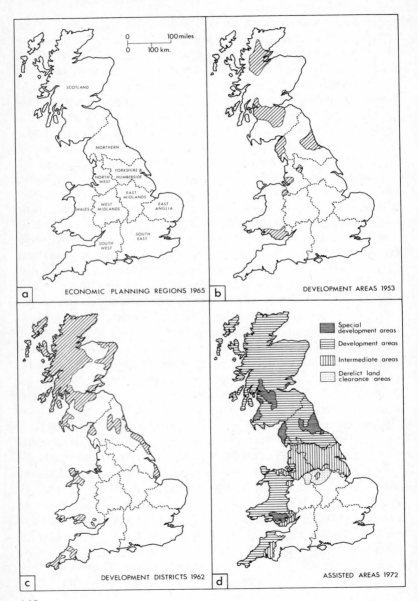

0		100 miles	
0		100 km.	

SCOTLAND

NORTHERN

YORKSHIRE &
HUMBERSIDE
NORTH
WEST

EAST
MIDLANDS

WALES   WEST
MIDLANDS

EAST
ANGLIA

SOUTH
EAST

SOUTH
WEST

a ECONOMIC PLANNING REGIONS 1965

b DEVELOPMENT AREAS 1953

Special
development areas

Development areas

Intermediate areas

Derelict land
clearance areas

c DEVELOPMENT DISTRICTS 1962

d ASSISTED AREAS 1972

of north-east Lancashire, which got no aid at all; that it was wrong to treat the struggling coalfield towns of south Yorkshire on the same basis as the prosperous Home Counties; and so on. These criticisms caused the government to appoint a Committee of Inquiry on the Intermediate Areas – the areas like Lancashire and Yorkshire, which were more prosperous than most development areas but decidedly less prosperous than the South or Midlands, as many of the tables and diagrams earlier in this chapter show. We will consider its recommendations shortly.

Meanwhile, the 1966 Act stipulated that firms moving to the development areas, as now redefined, should receive a cash grant amounting to 40 per cent of the value of any investments in plant and machinery (as against 20 per cent elsewhere). This provision provoked some criticism on the ground that it would attract capital-intensive industry which would bring very little employment into the development areas; it was even argued that the result could be to diminish employment, since the grant would be used to install automatic machinery. Responding to this charge, the government in 1967 proposed a radical new departure. The year previously they had introduced the Selective Employment Tax (SET), with the aim of diverting labour from service industry to manufacturing by means of a tax on all establishments in the tertiary sector. This tax originally did not have a regional component: it was nationally uniform, and its stated aim was to increase the productivity of labour, since economic experts argued that bigger productivity gains could be made in manufacturing (with efficient machinery and management) than in the often under-organized, under-capitalized service sector. But in 1967, the government proposed (and then introduced) an important modification: the Regional Employment Premium (REP). From then

39. *The pattern of regional development in Britain, 1945–72. (a) The whole country is now covered by economic planning regions, created in 1965, with Councils (in England, with Welsh and Scottish equivalents) advising the government on economic development matters. (b) The original postwar scheme of closely defined development areas was replaced in 1960 by (c) development districts based on a criterion of persistent unemployment, and then in 1966 by (d) more generously defined development areas; later, special development areas were designated within these, qualifying for more generous State aid.*

on, not only would manufacturing industry in the development areas not have to pay the tax; it would also receive money grants, amounting to nearly £100 per annum per worker in the case of male adults. This meant that the difference in status between development areas and non-development areas (and between manufacturing and service industries in the development areas) was very large; and it broadened further when in 1968, in a financial crisis, the government announced that all firms in non-development areas – even in manufacturing – would pay SET. At that point, in fact, SET–REP became a completely regional device to attract industry into the development areas – and a very powerful one.

This of course added to the complaints from the less prosperous areas outside the development areas – the grey areas, or as they were called in the official report on the problem in 1969, the intermediate areas. This report, commonly known as the Hunt Report after its chairman (Sir Joseph Hunt), recommended substantial additional help to Lancashire and Yorkshire, in the form of building grants and an end to all IDC restrictions in those areas; it also recommended withdrawing Merseyside's status as a development area, which it claimed was no longer justified. The government gave only limited help to the intermediate areas in its 1970 Act; and the considerable difference in status between the development areas (including Merseyside) and the rest persisted.

In 1970 the incoming Conservative government soon made it clear that it intended to scrap many of the policies of its predecessor with regard to regional incentives. It announced a phasing-out of SET and REP altogether from 1974 and therefore an end to any differential applied to labour costs. It also announced an end to investment grants, replacing them by tax allowances on new investment. It estimated that the end of REP would save some £100 million a year in government expenditure, despite loss of the revenue from SET; ending investment grants would save £400 million a year in 1972–3, offset by £200 million a year for the new allowances. Later, though in the 1972 Industry Act it re-introduced investment grants (entitled regional development grants) in the development areas, special development areas and intermediate areas, the government made it clear that much of its industrial policy would be directed at the modernization of industrial plant everywhere in the country through investment allowances, free depreciation for plant, and a high initial allowance for buildings – even where no notable increase in employment was in prospect. Creation of jobs in the development areas clearly was no longer the overriding aim; even the regional development grants would not depend on this criterion.

A Verdict on Regional Economic Policies, 1960–72

The account above has consisted of a kaleidoscopic, often abrupt, series of changes and even reversals in policy. It may have bewildered the reader; certainly the events themselves seemed to bewilder many of those affected by them. Perhaps only one consistent element appears: there has been much more concern about regional problems, and a much more energetic attempt to find regional solutions, than in the 1950s. The question is how much all this has affected the broad picture of regional trends we gave for that earlier period, at the beginning of this chapter.

The analysis in the Hunt Committee report, published in 1969, contains a detailed analysis of trends in the 1960s, which admirably serves this purpose. It shows that during the period 1961–6, total employment in Britain in manufacturing and services rose 4 per cent, and male employment rose 2 per cent; but in the development areas there was a very slow rise in total employment and a fall in male employment. Incomes, too, rose by less than the national average in Scotland and the Northern region, while in the South East and Midlands they rose more rapidly than the average: the differential was growing. But some of the so-called intermediate areas were hardly in a better position than the development areas: Lancashire had slower growth in employment than the national average, and so did the west Yorkshire woollen area; Lancashire and Yorkshire as a whole had a slower-than-average growth in income.

Unemployment, too, remained stubbornly concentrated in the development areas. From 1961 to 1968, unemployment rates that were persistently and substantially above the national average were almost confined to those areas. With one fifth of the country's population, they accounted for more than one third of the number of wholly unemployed. Migration, too, continued out of the development areas. Between 1961 and 1966 the censuses showed widespread net migration from the Scottish, Northern and Welsh development areas; but there were also losses outside these areas, as from north-east Lancashire or from west or south Yorkshire. Here, as on other indices, the intermediate areas frequently resemble the development areas. High unemployment is the one criterion that really distinguishes the development areas from all the rest.

Overall, the Hunt Committee found that the major contrast was between the rapid growth in the South East and the West Midlands, together with large parts of East Anglia, the South West and the East Midlands, as against sluggish growth in the older industrial areas. But with the latter group the problems of the development areas were still more severe, especially with regard to unemployment. Save for unemployment, the symptoms of economic difficulty that gave most concern were in the North West (basically Lancashire) and in Yorkshire.

Nevertheless, there were distinct signs of improvement over time. The Board of Trade's own detailed analysis of the trends shows that between 1952–9 and 1960–65, the development areas' share of employment from new mobile industry rose from 29 per cent of the national total to 55 per cent. The IDC statistics show that between 1956–8 and 1965–7, the development areas' share of approvals rose from 16 per cent to 24 per cent by number, and from 22 per cent to 53 per cent in terms of estimated employment. The figures of industrial building contracts for 1965–7 showed that the Northern region, Scotland and Wales together obtained about one quarter of new orders, though they had only one fifth of the manufacturing employment. The investment grant statistics from 1966 onwards indicate that between one quarter and one third of investment in plant and machinery has been in these areas. Overall, it was estimated that in 1966 there were some 438,000 jobs in the development areas in plants that had been opened there since 1946. Of these, 175,000 were in projects that had originated in the South East, 68,000 in the West Midlands and 77,000 abroad.

These developments had had significant results. For instance, whereas for most of the 1960s total unemployment in the development areas as a whole was double the national rate or more, by the end of 1968 it was 4.1 per cent, compared with 2.3 per cent for Great Britain as a whole. At that point, too, 1,000 IDCs had been approved in the year 1968, which were expected to provide 72,000 more jobs in coming years. The difficulty was that these would do barely more than keep pace with the decline of the basic industries there. The Northern Economic Planning Council had estimated that between 1966 and 1971, over 80,000 jobs would disappear in its region alone in mining, shipbuilding, metal manufacture and transport: one job in every fifteen.

To offset this, and also reduce unemployment and net migration, would need the creation of well over 100,000 jobs. Though many of these jobs would be in services it was significant that the total was well above the entire movement of new factory jobs into the region from 1945 to 1965.

The position of the development areas was therefore in many ways as Barlow had described it almost thirty years before. They had to run to keep still. Despite great efforts to change the industrial structure since the Second World War, too many jobs were still concentrated in declining sectors of the economy. In important parts of these declining sectors, especially in coal mining, the 1960s saw even more rapid contraction than had been previously feared. However, the Hunt Committee concluded that this process would have a limit. The long process of attrition of the old industries, which by 1970 had been taking place for about half a century, would exhaust itself – hopefully, by the mid-1970s.

Meanwhile the basic system of controls and incentives, which Britain introduced on the basis of the Barlow recommendations in 1945, survives. On one hand, there is the IDC–ODP policy; on the other, a varying battery of financial inducements to firms going to the development areas, including investment allowances, ready-built factories to rent, building grants and loans, training facilities and transfer payments. In addition, throughout the 1960s – ever since the regional reports of 1963 – public infrastructure investments in the development areas, especially on transport and communications, have deliberately been kept at a higher level (in relation to population) than elsewhere in the country. This basic bundle of incentives and controls looks like surviving well into the 1970s, though there have been proposals, including one from a Labour Party study group in 1970, that the control system should gradually be supplemented – and, conceivably, in the long run replaced – by a varied system of payroll taxes and incentive payments: an SET–REP system on a wider scale. If this is to happen, it is still some years ahead. Meanwhile the more certain prospect from a Conservative government is a move towards greater encouragement of investment for industrial modernization rather than support for job creation, supplemented by selective help to industry to be administered by decentralized regional organizations. This, however, marks a detailed modification of traditional post-1945 policies; not a breach.

Further Reading

Gavin McCrone, *Regional Policy in Britain* (Allen & Unwin, 1969), Harry W. Richardson, *Elements of Regional Economics* (Penguin, 1969) and A. J. Brown, *The Framework of Regional Economics in the United Kingdom* (Cambridge University Press, 1972) are standard sources. They can usefully be supplemented by: A. E. Holmans, 'Industrial Development Certificates and the Control of Employment in South East England', *Urban Studies*, 1 (1964), 138–52; R. S. Howard, *The Movement of Manufacturing Industry in the United Kingdom 1945–65* (HMSO, 1968); Frank Stilwell, 'Regional Growth and Structural Adaptation', *Urban Studies*, 6 (1969), pp. 162–78, and D. E. C. Eversley, 'Population Changes and Regional Policies since the War', *Regional Studies*, 5 (1971), pp. 211–28.

7. Planning for Cities and City Regions from 1945 to 1972

At the end of Chapter 5 we summarized some of the chief features of the elaborate planning system set up in Britain just after the Second World War. We saw that, essentially, the system was designed for an economy where the bulk of urban development and redevelopment would be carried out by public agencies. We saw too that an essential function of the system was to control and regulate the pace and direction of change – social, economic and physical. It was assumed that control of change was both feasible and desirable: feasible, because the pace of population growth and of economic development was expected to be slow, and also because new and effective powers would be taken to control the regional balance of new industrial employment; desirable, because decision-makers generally shared the Barlow hypothesis that uncontrolled change before the Second World War had produced undesirable results. Furthermore we noticed that the administrative responsibility for operating the new system was not lodged in central government but in the existing units of local government with a degree of central monitoring. The system thus created was from the beginning more powerful on its negative side than on the side of positive initiative.

These features were of course interrelated. Because the pace of change was expected to be slow, it seemed possible to control it. Because the positive role in development would be taken by public agencies, the remaining negative powers could safely be vested in the local authorities. The danger was that if any one of the basic assumptions proved wrong, the logical interrelationships would also go wrong. And in fact the postwar reality proved very different from the assumptions of those who created the planning system between 1945 and 1952.

The Reality of Change in Postwar Britain

The story of postwar Britain has been one of rapid change, unparalleled in some respects during any other era, save that of the Industrial Revolution. Partly because of the speed of change, partly because of shifts in political philosophy, a much larger part of the resulting physical development has been undertaken by private enterprise than was expected in 1945 or 1947.

Firstly and most basically of all, the postwar era has been one of unprecedented population growth – unprecedented, at any rate, by the standards of interwar Britain. Immediately after the war there was a sudden 'baby boom': a rise in the birth rate resulting from delayed marriages and delayed decisions to have children. Demographic experts predicted both this boom, in 1945–7, and its subsequent waning, from 1948 to about 1954. By the latter date the crude birth rate (numbers of babies born per thousand people) was sinking towards the level of the 1930s. The experts, who were advising the planning officers that they should plan for an almost static national population total in the near future, seemed to be vindicated. But from 1955 to 1964 they were plunged into disarray by an unexpected and continuous rise in the national birth rate; by the mid-1960s the crude birth rate – 18.7 per thousand in 1964 – was threatening to approach that at the outset of the First World War. As a result the official national projections of future population had continually to be revised upwards. Whereas in 1960 the population at the end of the century was expected to be 64 million, by 1965 the projection had been raised to no less than 75 million. From this point the birth rate fell again, to 15.0 per thousand in 1972, and the projection was scaled down to 66 million. Illustration 40 shows these fluctuations.

This change was of critical importance to planners everywhere in the country: as will be seen in detail in later chapters, population

40. (a) Birth rates in England and Wales, 1871–2004. The long secular decline in birth rates was halted at the end of the Second World War and again by an upswing from 1955 to 1964; but afterwards births again declined. (b) Population growth in Great Britain, 1871–2004. As a result of fluctuations in birth rate, projections of future population have changed markedly in recent years.

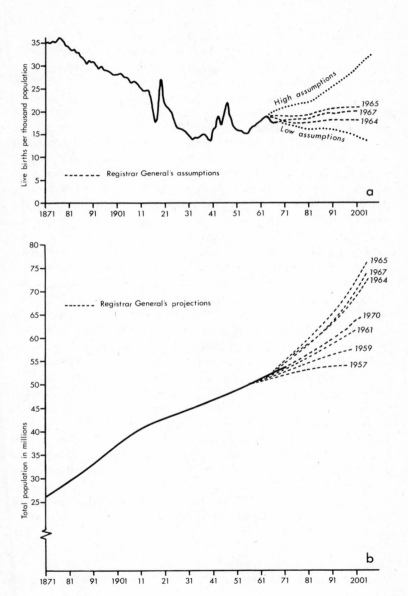

157

forecasts influence almost every other forecast the planner has to make. Housebuilding programmes, projections of car ownership and demands for road-space, forecasts of recreational demands and their impact on the countryside – all were automatically revised upwards. By the mid-1960s the population of Britain was rising by $\frac{1}{2}$ million a year and the expectation was that for the future this total would be augmented. It would be necessary, leading planners were saying, to reckon on building the equivalent of one Bristol a year for the remainder of the century. In the event these predictions, too, came to be falsified: after 1964 the birth rate turned down again, falling nearly to mid-1950s levels by the early 1970s, while simultaneously the restrictions on Commonwealth immigration reduced the total of arrivals from outside. By the late 1960s the average increase of the population was about 300,000 – still the equivalent of a Bradford a year, but only about half the expectation of a few years earlier.

This growing population, furthermore, proved to be splitting itself up into an ever-increasing number of smaller and smaller households – the product of social changes such as earlier marriages, the tendency of many young people to leave home in search of educational or job opportunities, and the increasing trend for retired people to live by themselves in seaside colonies. As a result, while the average size of a home in Britain remained roughly constant, the average size of the household living in it fell sharply: in England and Wales the average household had 3.7 members in 1931, 3.2 members in 1951, but only 3.0 members in 1961 and 2.9 members in 1971. Thus people were enjoying more space within their homes, but an ever-increasing number of homes was needed to accommodate any given number of people. Reinforcing the rise in population, this trend meant that the total housing programme, and the consequent demands on space, were much greater than had been comfortably assumed in the late 1940s.

At the same time, as we saw in Chapter 6, the population proved to be much more mobile than the planners had been assuming when they made their original local development plans after 1947. The Barlow Commission seems to have assumed, and the professional planners followed them without serious question, that it would be possible after the war largely to control inter-regional migration through effective controls on new industrial location. But as we saw, this belief was totally unjustified: there were no controls on the dynamic service sector of employment, and even the controls on factory industry could be largely circumvented by repeated small-scale extensions or by buying up existing factory space. The result was a continued and strong net drift, on the lines of the movement that had so alarmed the Barlow Commission, from Scotland and Wales and Northern England towards the Midlands and South. After 1960, as we shall see, this continuing trend came in for much attention and criticism. But it is worth noting that even when it was stemmed – as in the South East after about 1966 – rapid population growth continued to take place because of the strong underlying trend in natural growth within the region itself.

Coming together, these trends could only mean continuing, and even increasing, pressure for new urban development in and around the big urban areas, especially in the Midlands and South. It was in these areas, above all around London and Birmingham, that planning authorities were most taken by surprise by growth in the late 1950s and early 1960s. At the same time the natural increase of population in the development areas created a potential demand for even more employment than had been expected, increasing the scale of the problem of economic development there; though a generally expand-ing economy provided a steady total of mobile industry to move into these areas. In general, the pace of change created great problems for a generation of planners schooled to believe that change in itself was not particularly desirable.

Lastly, rising prosperity after 1955 resulted in rapid buying of durable consumer goods which created demands for more useable space in and around the home. Above all, it was the rise in mass car ownership that perhaps took planners most by surprise. When local authorities and the first new towns drew up their development plans, austerity was still the rule of the day and car ownership levels were barely above those of the 1930s; only about one in ten households owned a car, and new town planners felt safe in fixing one garage to four houses as a generous norm. But by the 1966 census, half the families in the country owned one or more cars, and one garage per family (with additional space in reserve) had become the standard almost everywhere. Not only, however, did the new cars need house-room in the residential areas; they put increasing strain on the country's road system, the most congested in the world, and this resulted in a constantly increasing road-building programme from the mid-1950s on. Rising car ownership was in part a response to the increasing decentralization of populations from the cores to the suburban fringes of the major urban areas, a development which was already observable in the 1930s but which gained momentum in the 1960s. But since employment and urban services (above all retailing) did not decentralize so rapidly, mass motorization created tremendous pressures for urban reconstruction in the form of urban motorways and multi-storey car parks, threatening the existing urban fabric as never before in history.

In any event, changes of this magnitude would probably have compelled a massive readjustment in the objectives, methods and machinery of planning. In particular, it is hard to see how public programmes could have adapted themselves quickly to the challenges of rising population, continuing mobility and greater affluence; private enterprise, almost inevitably, would have had to undertake a greater role than was foreseen in 1947. As a coincidence, the onset of the period of change came with the arrival of a Conservative government in 1951, heavily committed to reliance on the private sector. Very rapidly thereafter, the balance of the housing programme shifted from an emphasis on the public sector to approximate equality between the public and the private programmes. But it is significant that after its return in 1964, the Labour government did not significantly change this relationship. The mixed economy in urban development is one of the facts of life in postwar Britain.

This, in turn, had serious implications for the administrative machinery of planning. Far heavier responsibilities came to rest upon the local planning authorities, who were required to deal with a much larger amount of complex change than had ever been anticipated. And because the fundamental trends of the interwar period continued after all – population moving *into* the great urban regions, and simultaneously *out of* their congested inner areas and *into* their suburban fringes – the emphasis on local private initiative exposed the failure, in and just after the 1947 Planning Act, to grapple with

41. Suburban development at Heswall, Cheshire. Though after the Second World War it was at first throught that most urban development would be in comprehensively planned new towns, the unexpected population growth of the late 1950s and early 1960s – plus a changed political climate – led to a big private building programme on more conventional lines.

the problem of fundamental local government reform. By lodging responsibility for plan-making and development control with the separate county-borough and county authorities, the Act divided cities from their hinterlands, and made effective planning of entire urban regions a virtual impossibility.

Planning in the 1950s: Cities versus Counties

It took some time for this lesson to emerge. Contemplating a more leisurely pace of change, the architects of the 1947 Act had believed that effective coordination of the different local plans could be achieved through Whitehall vetting, first in the light of the major regional advisory plans (such as Abercrombie's for London), and then with the aid of monitoring and updating by regional offices of the Ministry of Town and Country Planning. Ironically, soon after coming to power in 1951 the Conservatives abolished these regional offices as an economy measure. Henceforth there was no machinery for effective regional coordination, save such as could be provided from London; the various local authorities were left to stand up for themselves. At the same time, and in much the same spirit, the new government made it clear that though the existing new towns would be completed, the emphasis in future would be on voluntary agreements between local authorities to expand existing towns, within the framework of the 1952 Town Development Act.

Furthermore, the government made it clear that it favoured a very negative attitude towards urban growth. Encouraged by the falling birth rates of the early 1950s, in a famous Circular of 1955 it actively encouraged the county authorities to make plans for green belts around the major conurbations and freestanding cities; and subsequently the Minister indicated that even if it was neither green nor particularly attractive scenically, the major function of the green belt was simply to stop further urban development. But since there

42. Major restraints to development in Great Britain. Altogether national parks, green belts and other specially designated areas exclude more than 40 per cent of Britain's land area from the prospect of large-scale urban development of any kind. Little of this land had any protection before the Second World War.

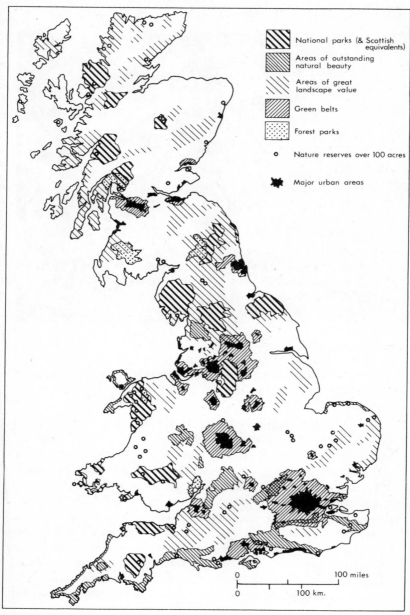

National parks (& Scottish equivalents)

Areas of outstanding natural beauty

Areas of great landscape value

Green belts

Forest parks

○ Nature reserves over 100 acres

Major urban areas

0 _____ 100 miles

0 _____ 100 km.

163

43. A view of the London Green Belt at Cockfosters, North London. The
effectiveness of the green belt is well illustrated by the sudden stop to London's urban
area. Most of the land in this picture would almost certainly have been developed but
for the postwar planning controls. Trent Park, on the right of the picture, is a country
park designated under the 1968 Countryside Act.

was no effective machinery for coordinated regional planning, and
since the 1952 Act was proving ineffectual because of weak financial
provisions, these strong negative powers were not accompanied by
any positive machinery for accommodating the resulting decentralization of people from the cities and the conurbations.

The result, in the late 1950s, was a series of epic planning battles
between the great conurbations and their neighbouring counties,
culminating in a number of major planning inquiries – notably those
on the proposals of Manchester to build new towns at Lymm and at
Mobberley near Knutsford in Cheshire, and on the proposals of
Birmingham to develop at Wythall in the Worcestershire green belt.
In a series of contests on both these cases, the cities lost and the

44. Reconstruction in London's East End. Formerly the scene of some of London's worst slums, the East End has been largely reconstructed since the Second World War. The old terrace houses have been replaced by mixed development including tall blocks of flats – now criticized, here as elsewhere, on social and aesthetic grounds. Rebuilding could not house all the former population, so some have left London in planned dispersion under the 1944 Abercrombie Plan.

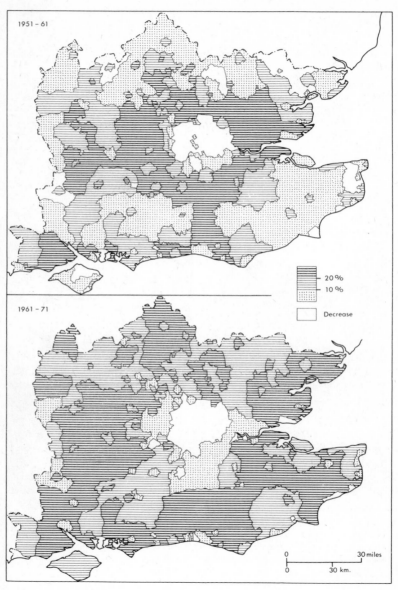

1951 – 61

1961 – 71

20 %
10 %

Decrease

0   30 miles
0   30 km.

166

counties preserved their rural acres. In every case, the overriding need to conserve agricultural land was quoted, echoing the words of the 1942 Scott report. But in the 1958 Lymm inquiry, the agricultural economist Gerald Wibberley produced powerful evidence to indicate that the agricultural value of the land involved was fairly low compared with the extra costs which might be involved in high-density redevelopment within the cities. At about the same time another economist, Peter Stone, was beginning to demonstrate just how great these additional costs of high-density redevelopment could be. Yet government subsidies continued to encourage such high-density schemes.

By the end of the 1950s, the position was becoming desperate for the cities. They had been encouraged in 1955 to start again on their big slum-clearance programmes, which had been interrupted at the start of the war in 1939; but ironically, this came at just the point when the birth-rate rise began. Adding together the demands from rising population, household fission, slum clearance and over-crowded families, and reporting on their virtual failure to get substantial agreements under the 1952 Act, city after city by 1960 was simply running out of land for its essential housing programme. The plight of the cities was underlined in this year in an influential book by Barry Cullingworth, *Housing Needs and Planning Policy*. In the same year Geoffrey Powell, a government official, pointed out publicly the rapid rate of population growth in the ring of Home Counties around London – an increase that no one, official or otherwise, would have thought likely ten years earlier. A year later, the census showed that population growth in this ring during the 1950s had amounted to 800,000 people – one third of the net growth of population in Britain. And contrary to the expectations of the architects of the 1947 system, the vast majority had been housed not in planned new or expanded towns, but in privately built suburban

---

45. Population growth in the London region, 1951–61 and 1961–71. Since the Second World War Greater London has become a zone of widespread population loss, surrounded by a belt of rapid gain which has moved steadily outwards. By the 1960s the fastest gains were being recorded 40 and more miles from London. Similar patterns of urban decentralization were recorded around other conurbations, though on a smaller scale.

estates on the familiar interwar model. The only change was that the green belt had been held; the developers had therefore leapfrogged it, pushing the zone of rapid population growth into a wide band up to 50 miles from the centre of London (Illustration 45).

The changed situation could not be ignored. In 1961 the government, reversing its previously declared policy, announced the designation of the first new town in England for twelve years – Skelmersdale near Wigan in Lancashire, designed to relieve the pressing needs for housing of the Merseyside conurbation, which had the most concentrated slum clearance problem in England. In the same year, in an even more fundamental reversal, the government began once again to embark on a series of major regional planning studies, intended to provide guidelines for the plans of the individual local planning offices. A new era for planning had begun.

The Major Regional Studies of the 1960s

Shortly after the government had embarked on the first of these studies, focused on the South East, regional planning received a sharp impetus from a different source: the recession of 1962–3, which – as we already saw in Chapter 6 – led to the production of stop-gap regional development plans, on what was virtually an emergency basis, for the distressed regions of the North East and Central Scotland. As at the time of the Barlow report in 1940, two main strands in British regional policy again fused: one, the objective of more rapid economic development in the Development Areas; the other, the attempt to control and channel the rapid growth around the more prosperous major conurbations, such as London and the West Midlands. The first of these strands has already been discussed in Chapter 6, where we saw the evolution of a much stronger policy of regional controls and incentives during the 1960s. It is the second that is relevant here.

The *South East Study*, published in March 1964, caused considerable surprise and even political controversy by its major conclusions: that even with some measures to restrain the further growth of the region around London, the pressures for continued expansion were such that provision must be made to house a further $3\frac{1}{2}$ million people in the whole region during the twenty-year period 1961–81. The main justification for this, which few critics seemed to realize at the time, was that even then, the main reason for the population growth of the region was not the much publicized 'drift south' of able-bodied workers from the North and from Scotland; the reasons were the natural growth of the region's own population, migration from abroad (much of which had been cut off by the Commonwealth Immigration Act of 1962) and migration of retired people to the South Coast resorts. To channel the pressures for growth, and to avoid the problems of congestion and long commuting journeys focused on central London, the report recommended a strategy based on a second round of new towns for London at greater distances than the first round, well outside London's commuter range: Milton Keynes in northern Buckinghamshire, 49 miles from London; Northampton, 70 miles from London; Peterborough, 81 miles from London; and Southampton–Portsmouth, 77 miles from London, were among the more important projects which finally went ahead in one form or another (see Illustration 46). Significantly, only Milton Keynes among these was a green field new town on the old model, albeit with a bigger population target than any previously designated town; the others all represented a new departure in being new towns attached to major existing towns or cities. To cope with the development nearer London which might still depend to some degree on commuting, the *Study* was much less clear; this, it implied, was a matter for local planners. The Labour Party, returned to office in October 1964, at first demanded a second look at the *Study*'s conclusions; later, it accepted them in large measure.

Meanwhile, in 1965, further regional studies, produced in the same way by official *ad hoc* teams, appeared for two other major urban regions: the West Midlands and the North West. Recognizing the changed situation brought about by population growth and by the continuing slum clearance programme, both studies calculated that the problems of accommodating planned overspill from the conurbations were greater than had earlier been appreciated – even though the North West was an area of net out-migration. To accommodate the growth, the reports called for an accelerated programme of new town building in each region, neither of which had received any new towns before 1961. By 1965 two new towns had already been designated in the Midlands: Dawley (1963) and Redditch (1964); later (1968), as the result of the *Study*'s conclusions, Dawley was further expanded and renamed Telford. In the North West, Skelmersdale (1961) and Runcorn (1964) had been established to receive Merseyside overspill; the report suggested that similar developments were needed for Manchester, and this need was eventually met by designations at Warrington (1968) and Central Lancashire (Preston–Leyland, 1970). In Central Scotland, further overspill pressures from the Central Clydeside conurbation (Greater Glasgow) resulted in the designation of Livingston (1962) and Irvine (1967). And lastly, south of Newcastle the new town of Washington (1964) was designated to receive overspill from the Tyneside and Wearside areas. Thus, in addition to the new towns for London, the major conurbations outside the capital had no less than 9 new towns designated between 1961 and 1970 to aid with their overspill problems (see Illustration 46). Significantly, as with the London towns, several of these – notably Warrington and Central Lancashire – worked on the formula of attaching a new town to an old-established existing town possessing a full range of urban services.

These reports of 1963–5 mark an important stage in the evolution of British postwar urban planning. They recognize officially that the fact of continued population growth demanded positive regional strategies, covering areas that embraced the conurbations and a wide area around them; the reports themselves make it clear that this wider area extends much farther than the conventional 'sphere of influence' defined by geographers in terms of commuting or shopping patterns, and may even in some cases approximate to the area of the wider region used for purposes of economic development planning. These strategies, involving new and expanded towns, were required

---

46. New towns in Britain, 1946–70. Over thirty new towns have been started in Great Britain and Northern Ireland under the 1946 New Towns Act and its Ulster equivalent. They fall naturally into two groups: Mark One new towns of the 1946– 50 period, concentrated around London and in the Development Areas, and a second wave started in the 1960s to serve the needs of the major conurbations.

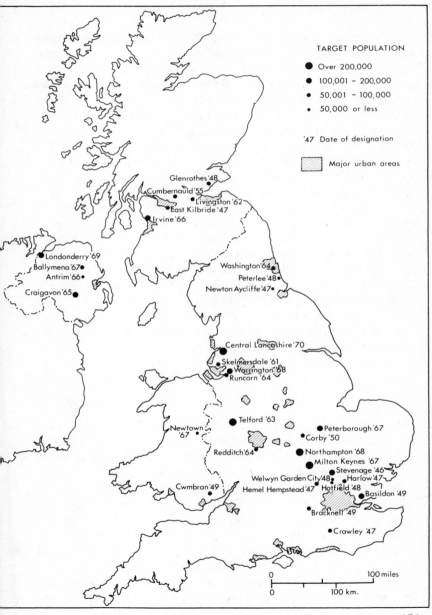

TARGET POPULATION

● Over 200,000
● 100,001 – 200,000
• 50,001 – 100,000
• 50,000 or less

'47 Date of designation

▨ Major urban areas

Glenrothes '48
Cumbernauld '55
Livingston '62
East Kilbride '47
Irvine '66

Londonderry '69
Ballymena '67
Antrim '66
Craigavon '65

Washington '64
Peterlee '48
Newton Aycliffe '47

Central Lancashire '70
Skelmersdale '61
Warrington '68
Runcorn '64

Telford '63
Peterborough '67
Corby '50
Newtown '67
Northampton '68
Redditch '64
Milton Keynes '67
Stevenage '46
Welwyn Garden City '48
Harlow '47
Cwmbran '49
Hemel Hempstead '47
Hatfield '48
Basildon '49
Bracknell '49
Crawley '47

0   100 miles

0   100 km.

171

even for those conurbations in the development areas; there, despite continued out-migration, slum clearance and natural growth necessitated a positive overspill policy. Essentially, what these reports represent is an application to the major urban regions around London of the standard Howard–Barlow–Abercrombie formula: planned decentralization of the conurbations, coupled with green belt restrictions and new communities placed in general outside the commuting range of the conurbations. Save for an emphasis on the housing problem, there is little attention to social policy planning; these are still physical plans in a traditional British mould.

Lastly, it is significant that these regional reports were the work of *ad hoc* teams of central government officials. This was because there was no other machinery to produce them. In 1965 the regional organization of the central government planning ministry had not been restored. (This took until the early 1970s, when a regional organization was announced for the new Department of the Environment.) Nor was there a general tradition of cooperation among the local planning authorities in each region, though some areas, notably London and the surrounding authorities, had taken a lead in the Standing Conference on London and South-East Regional Planning.

The New Regional Structure and Local Government Reform, 1965–72

During 1965–6 this gap in the formal machinery was partially filled. We have already seen, in Chapter 6, that the economic planning regional councils and boards were originally intended specifically to work at a rather different sort of planning: economic development planning in its relation to the national economic plan. But almost as soon as they were set up, the councils found themselves immersed in spatial planning at the scale of the city region, using that last term in its broadest sense. The logic should have been evident. Even in the development areas it was impossible to produce a development strategy for an area like the North East of England without a physical component including elements like main roads, major new industrial areas and associated housing schemes, ports and airports.

And in the more prosperous and rapidly growing areas, such as the South East or the West Midlands, economic planning would largely consist of a physical plan to control and guide the spatial directions of economic expansion. Thus, though they were partially concerned with broad overall totals of regional investments in relation to national programmes, the councils and boards found their main concern to be the internal disposition of these investments within the region – in other words, spatial planning.

This emphasis was already clear in many of the preliminary studies published by the councils in 1966 and 1967. It came to a head in the publication of one of the first positive strategies from one of the councils: the South-East Planning Council's report, published in November 1967. This report, which recommended a strategy for future development based on broad sectors following the main concentrations of radial transportation lines from London, ran into predictable opposition from the regional standing conference of local authorities, which was concerned that local autonomy in planning matters was being undermined by an outside body with a purely advisory remit to central government. Clearly, here was a point of great importance once the case for positive regional planning was generally accepted – as by this time it was. Given that such planning involved the cooperation of central and local government, how was this best to be assured? The regional councils had a wide remit but no power – as their members were by this time discovering. The local authorities had the power but were unlikely to agree on a strong regional strategy.

In 1968 the government resolved the problem, at least for the South East: yet another *ad hoc* team was set up, commissioned jointly by the Standing Conference and the Planning Council, and including both central and local government officials. This formula proved successful, at any rate in this instance: the team's 1970 report, which evaluated two alternative strategies (one of them the one contained in the Planning Council's 1967 report) and emerged with yet a third, based on developing a number of growth centres at varying distances from London, was generally accepted by central and local governments alike as a future framework for regional development (see Illustration 47). (It marked a significant change in

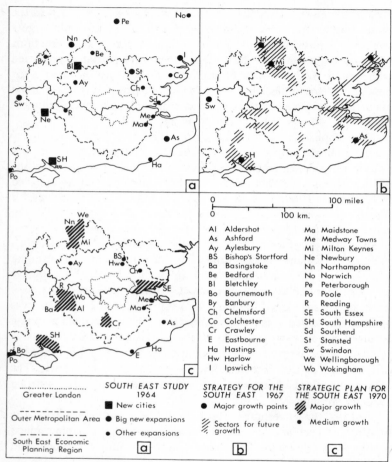

Al	Aldershot	Ma	Maidstone
As	Ashford	Me	Medway Towns
Ay	Aylesbury	Mi	Milton Keynes
BS	Bishop's Stortford	Ne	Newbury
Ba	Basingstoke	Nn	Northampton
Be	Bedford	No	Norwich
Bl	Bletchley	Pe	Peterborough
Bo	Bournemouth	Po	Poole
By	Banbury	R	Reading
Ch	Chelmsford	SE	South Essex
Co	Colchester	SH	South Hampshire
Cr	Crawley	Sd	Southend
E	Eastbourne	St	Stansted
Ha	Hastings	Sw	Swindon
Hw	Harlow	We	Wellingborough
I	Ipswich	Wo	Wokingham

·············· Greater London	SOUTH EAST STUDY 1964	STRATEGY FOR THE SOUTH EAST 1967	STRATEGIC PLAN FOR THE SOUTH EAST 1970
	■ New cities	● Major growth points	▨ Major growth
− − − − Outer Metropolitan Area	● Big new expansions	▨ Sectors for future growth	● Medium growth
−·−·−·− South East Economic Planning Region	· Other expansions		
	[a]	[b]	[c]

47. *Plans for expansion in the South East, 1964–70: (a) The* South East Study *(1964) proposed new towns and cities outside London's then commuting range, 50 and more miles away. (b) The* Strategy for the South East *(1967), from the Economic Planning Council, proposed connecting these to London by urbanized sectors, which would not however be continuously built up. (c) The* Strategic Plan for the South East *(1970), which was accepted as the basis for further planning, groups much of the growth into five major growth areas, some of which incorporate new towns or cities from the 1964* Study.

British planning philosophy: the new-town concept, having grown from a community of 60,000 in Reith's 1945 report to one of 250,000 in the 1964 *South East Study*, became dramatically enlarged into a multi-centred growth zone of between $\frac{1}{2}$ million and $1\frac{1}{2}$ million people.) By 1971, therefore, the joint plan team formula was being applied again to another heavily urbanized region, the North West; while local government officials, aided and encouraged by regional officers of the central government, were just completing a similar plan for the West Midlands.

Some voices argued that this level of plan-making, which essentially involved very broadly based city regions approximating to the scale of the economic planning regions, demanded an appropriate new scale of regional or provincial government in Britain, with a democratic basis; and in 1969 the government appointed a Royal Commission on constitutional arrangements, to consider the merits of this proposal among others. (It reported in 1973, but was divided in its recommendations: all members rejected a federal solution, but some wanted legislative authority for Scottish and Welsh councils, others a merely executive devolution which might extend to the English regions.) Certainly the idea had a long ancestry, going back at least to the publication of the geographer C. B. Fawcett's book *The Provinces of England* in 1919. But the difficulty in its actual implementation was that it was very clearly related to the question of fundamental local government reform, which was being considered by other royal commissions at the same time. To understand the matter in its wider perspective, we must now turn to consider the problem of local government.

City Region Planning and Local Government, 1965–72

The 1961 census showed that despite strict policies of urban containment, the population of the conurbations was rapidly overspilling beyond the green belts into much more widely spread urban regions; population in the so-called rural districts, during the 1950s and 1960s, was increasing faster than that in urban England (see Illustration 48). Even during the earlier decade many of the conur-

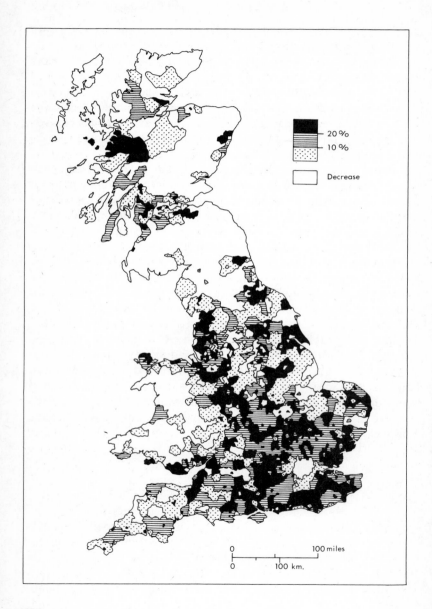

bations – including Greater London and Greater Manchester – were actually losing population, while the rings all around them, stretching in the case of London up to 50 miles, were gaining rapidly. Employment decentralized more slowly, and during the 1950s many cities and conurbations were actually gaining new concentrations of tertiary (service) industry in their central areas; but during the 1960s, there was clear evidence that this process too was being reversed. Nevertheless, in general the result of urban decentralization was increasing long-distance interdependence of the different parts of the big urban regions. Journeys to work or to shop increased in average length. The new-towns programme and the expanded-towns programme between them did not contribute more than about 3 per cent of the total housing programme, so the fond hope of Ebenezer Howard and the 1945 Reith Committee – that urban populations would decentralize towards self-contained communities – was never fulfilled. But as car ownership produced greater personal mobility, this seemed less necessary. Nevertheless the resulting pattern of movement created unprecedented new problems – above all for transportation planning.

By the early 1960s, it was already being realized that the realities of long-term transportation planning, to accommodate projected future traffic movement, could only be handled within the framework of a wide urban region, so defined as to include both the origins and the destinations of the great majority of all the traffic movement. Following the pattern of the pioneer American transportation studies, wide-area studies began to be commissioned in Britain, first in 1961 for London, then for other major urban areas such as the West Midlands, Merseyside, south-east Lancashire–north-east Cheshire (Greater Manchester) and Greater Glasgow. But because there was no framework of local government at this level, like the major regional studies they had to be set up on a purely *ad hoc* basis.

---

48. Population growth in Great Britain, 1961–71. Most areas of Britain, save the thinly populated rural peripheries, have gained population. But particularly clear is the loss from the major conurbations to their suburban fringes, especially around London. Rapid population growth characterized wide rural areas in southern and midland England.

Even the reform of London local government in an Act of 1963, which created the Greater London Council, failed to encompass the entire area needed for meaningful transportation planning. (It excluded, for instance, the line of the planned orbital motorway for London.) As the various studies proceeded from fact-gathering to analysis and projection and then to proposals, the inadequacies of the existing fragmented local government structure became more and more evident. More and more *ad hoc* arrangements proved to be necessary – for instance, the passenger transport executives for the major conurbations and their fringe areas, set up under the 1968 Transport Act. The case for fundamental reform became more urgent.

It was given a further impetus in 1965 by the publication of an important report of an official advisory committee, the Planning Advisory Group (PAG). This concluded that the style of development planning set up under the 1947 Act, with its emphasis on detailed statements of future land-use proposals, did not suit the rapidly changing situation of the 1960s. Instead, there should be a new two-tier system of plan-making: first, structure plans containing main policy proposals in broad outline for a wide stretch of territory; second, local plans for smaller areas which would be prepared within the framework of the structure plans as occasion arose, including action-area plans for specific developments. (The structure plans still would be submitted for detailed vetting to the central planning ministry; the local plans in general would not.) The logic of this argument, which was generally accepted and embodied in a Planning Act of 1968, made the case for local government reform even more compelling. For the structure plans could by definition be prepared only for large areas encompassing the whole extended sphere of influence of a city or a conurbation. From 1966 onwards, some local authorities began to cooperate on an *ad hoc* basis to produce early experiments in such planning for areas like Leicester city and Leicestershire, Derby–Nottingham–Derbyshire–Nottinghamshire, Coventry–Solihull–Warwickshire, and south Hampshire. And by 1970–71, following this lead and anticipating local government reform, most local authorities in the country were beginning to band together on city regional lines to work on the new structure plans.

In 1966 the government recognized the logic of the new situation.

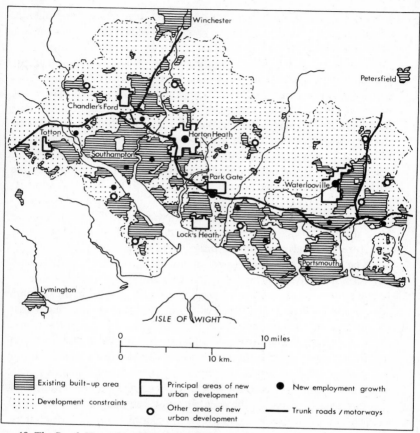

*49. The South Hampshire Plan, 1972. In this early example of structure planning
for a whole city region, major growth is grouped in a number of new communities of
different sizes, close to existing urban areas and well served by public transport.
Employment growth will occur both in these new areas and in the cores of the
existing cities and towns.*

They set up Royal Commissions on Local Government for England, under Sir John Redcliffe Maud (later Lord Redcliffe Maud) and for Scotland, under Mr Justice Wheatley, with a separate inquiry for Wales. Unlike a previous Commission on Local Government for England, whose terms of reference had been narrowly circumscribed, the new inquiries were specifically charged to take a fresh look at the problem. From the beginning, it was generally accepted by their members, and by the informed public, that something loosely called the city region – that is, the city or conurbation plus its sphere of influence – would be the right basis for local government reform. This indeed was the burden of the evidence submitted in 1967 by the Ministry of Housing and Local Government to the English commissioners.

The difficulty was that in practice it was more difficult than had been thought to define the city-region concept. Essentially, the new structure of local government units must possess four attributes. It must be able to form local government services *efficiently* (that is to say economically, in terms of resources) and *effectively* (in terms of reaching the clients who need the services). It should express some *communal consciousness*; that is, it should take in an area which people recognize that they belong to. And it should take in the whole area whose *planning problems* need to be analysed and resolved together. Unfortunately, these four requirements by no means lead to a common solution. In thinly populated rural areas, efficiency may suggest big units, effectiveness small ones. The unit of communal consciousness – broadly, the area within which people travel to work or shop – may be much smaller than the planning region, which may have to take in distant sites for potential new towns.

Faced with these contradictions, the commissioners came up with two entirely different solutions when they reported, almost simultaneously, in the summer of 1969. The first was subscribed to by all except one of the English commissioners. It held that efficiency was most important; that effectiveness and community demanded the same set of units for all services; and that planning problems required to be solved by rather large units. Some compromise between these principles had to be made; the English commissioners settled on a pattern of *unitary authorities* capable of running all local services, covering the whole of provincial England except for the three biggest conurbations of Greater Manchester, Greater Liverpool and Greater Birmingham. Here, there would be a two-tier structure with a metropolitan authority responsible for overall physical and transport planning, and metropolitan districts for the more personal services (Illustration 50a). This was the structure already adopted in the 1963 Act for London, which was left outside the English commissioners' terms of reference.

The opposite view was expressed by one English commissioner (Mr Senior) and by a majority of the Scottish commissioners. It started from the premise that planning demanded a quite different scale from the personal services. Thus there should be a two-tier system over the whole country, based on large city regions (in the Scottish report called provinces) at the top level and on small districts at the lower level. The English majority admitted the force of this argument, but thought that the claim of simplicity in the structure, with only one level, was overriding.

In 1970 the Labour government accepted the different prescriptions for the two countries, with minor modifications; in 1971 the Conservative government reaffirmed its broad acceptance of the Wheatley recommendations for Scotland, but replaced the English proposals by a two-tier system over the whole country. This, however, was not Mr Senior's minority prescription, but a reform based on the existing county structure at the top-tier level (with some modifications to take account of the city regional principle) and on amalgamations of existing county district authorities at the lower level (Illustration 50b). In the conurbations the reform retained the metropolitan principle, and extended it to west and south Yorkshire, but it cut back the boundaries approximately to the physical limits of the built-up area; the green belts, and the growing suburbs beyond them, were generally left under non-metropolitan county control.

From the point of view of planning, this reorganization – which was implemented in an Act for England in 1972, and introduces the new system in 1973–4 – only underlines the fundamental problem of coordinating the structure-planning process over a wide area. The Redcliffe Maud proposals, by giving overall planning powers to very broadly based metropolitan authorities, might just have coped with

50. Local government reform proposals, 1969 and 1972. (a) The English Royal Commission (Redcliffe Maud) proposals of 1969 suggested single-tier, unitary authorities for most of the country, with a two-tier solution reserved for three metropolitan areas based on the conurbations.

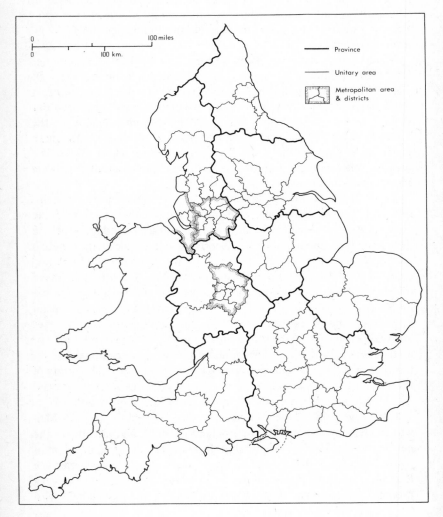

(b) *The 1972 Local Government Act, in contrast, introduced a two-tier system everywhere, but with a different distribution of functions in the Metropolitan Counties — now increased to six — as compared with elsewhere.*

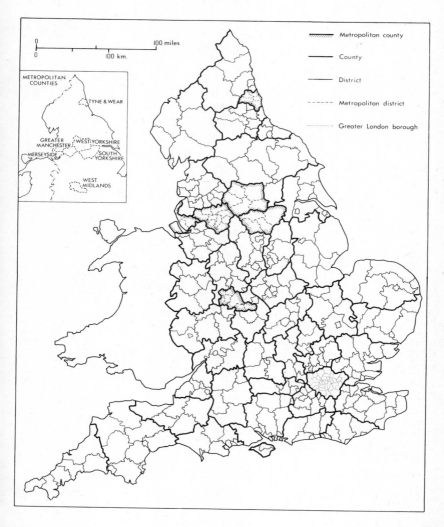

(c) In Scotland the Royal Commission (Wheatley) proposals of 1969 envisaged a two-tier system different from anything proposed in England, with top-tier authorities covering wide regions; this proposal, with minor amendments, is being implemented.

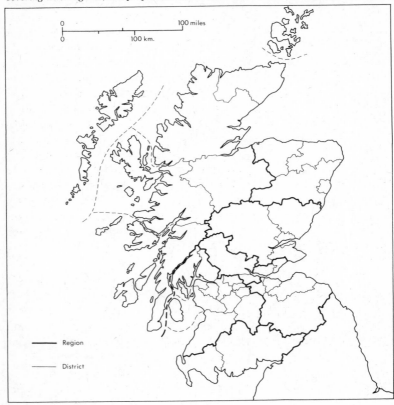

this problem. But even they failed to take in the whole area which needed to be planned as a unit around the biggest conurbations; indeed, in the extreme case – that of London – such a unit would take in the whole of the economic planning region. The 1972 changes certainly do not even aim to do this, and they merely underline the need for some intermediate level of regional planning between the reformed structure of local government and Whitehall. Indeed, it is clear that in many critical cases around the conurbations – in the fast-growing Coventry area or the Reading–Aldershot–Basingstoke area west of London, designated as one of the major future growth areas in the 1970 South East Plan – the new local government units will immediately have to come together on an *ad hoc* basis for city-region planning, as well as being involved in a cooperative planning process for the wider West Midlands or South-East region. The Redcliffe Maud report had recommended a structure of provincial units for England, above the unitary and metropolitan authorities, for just this purpose; it may well be that after the report of the Commission on the Constitution, something along these lines will prove necessary.

The Changing Content of Planning

Not merely the geographical basis of planning, but also the content of the plans themselves, showed great changes during the 1960s. The reasons were essentially the same as those we have listed in considering the question of geographical boundaries: the new emphasis on broad-based plans stressing basic policies rather than on detailed land-use allocations; the new importance of transportation planning as perhaps the central element of physical planning at this scale; the link between city-region planning and economic planning. But there were other forces no less important, both in the intellectual underpinnings of planning and in the wider socio-economic framework within which planning takes place. Among these were the potentialities released by the use of the computer, especially in transportation planning; the new emphasis on economic rationale in planning; the stress on environmental quality; the growing concern with social

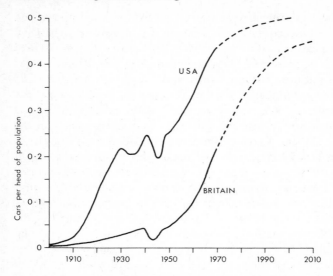

51. Car ownership in Great Britain and the USA, 1900–2010. The growth of car ownership in Britain has closely paralleled that in the USA with a lag of about twenty-five years. By 1990 levels of ownership should equal the American levels of 1965.

planning; and the increasing infusion of management techniques into local authorities. Nearly all these were individually so important, and so complex, that ideally they should have chapters to themselves. In the final chapter of this book, we shall try to discuss some of them in more detail. But at this stage, their influence must at least be outlined.

Chronologically, we already noticed that the first of these impacts – the increased emphasis on transportation, and the associated use of computers in analysis and prediction – occurred in the early 1960s, with the setting up of the first wide-area transportation studies in Britain. Essentially, the techniques for these early studies – and often, too, the personnel – were imported from the United States, where they had been developed in early exercises like the Detroit and Chicago area transportation studies. They depended on establishing statistical relationships between travel patterns and the underlying patterns of land use or economic activity, so that by then predicting changes in these underlying patterns in the future, it would be possible to predict the resulting traffic flows. The main use of the results, which explained the urgency of the exercise both in Britain and in North America, was to develop advance highway-construction plans to meet the expected growth of travel by private car.

As the transportation planning exercises grew in number and complexity during the 1960s, both in Britain and in the United States, they developed in two important ways. In the first place, it soon came to be realized that the prediction of the underlying patterns of land use and economic activity was not the relatively simple matter that traffic engineers had at first naïvely thought. It was possible to postulate alternative patterns of growth for a region, with different consequences for traffic flows and investments. By a process

52. The transportation planning structure. To accommodate the growth of car ownership most major urban areas had to develop increasingly complex transportation planning processes during the 1960s. The need for better-integrated transportation planning was a powerful stimulus to local government reform.

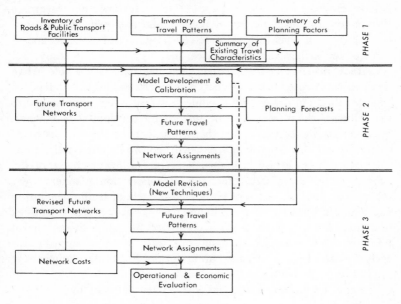

of feedback, different patterns of investment would affect the pattern of urban growth. As spatial planners became increasingly involved in the process, they developed techniques of modelling simultaneously the patterns of urban growth and travel in interaction with each other. The early work on such combined urban growth and travel models was done in the United States, by such workers as Ira Lowry of the Rand Corporation and Stuart Chapin of the University of North Carolina. But after the setting up of the Centre for Environmental Studies in London in 1966, with joint funding from the British government and the Ford Foundation, an intensive pro-gramme of development began, both in the Centre itself under its Assistant Director, Alan Wilson, and at the Universities of Reading and Cambridge. Certain pioneer local authorities, such as Bedfordshire, were already using models by the mid-1960s; their number grew at the end of the decade with the rapid switch to the new structure planning.

Simultaneously, the second related change was occurring in the transportation planning process: the focus was shifting from an ex-clusive emphasis on highway investments towards an integrated programme of development in both public and private transport. This shift had not yet fully occurred even by the end of the decade, in some of the earliest major exercises, such as the London study. But as it took place, it began to affect thinking about the whole urban modelling process. For different investment patterns will tend to generate different urban forms, while conversely the urban structure will influence the range of options open to the transportation planner. High-density concentrations, either of residential populations or of economic activities in urban areas, will tend to favour public trans-port, while low-density scatter will favour widespread use of the private car. Increasingly, therefore, transportation planners were inclined to work in terms of combined models of traffic generation and public/private transport split, and to try to relate these to options in future urban growth. Such a combined model, with options in terms of urban form and of modal split, was not yet developed in the early 1970s. But it represented an important line of development for the future.

Another important intellectual development in planning also came during the 1960s via transportation planning: the increased emphasis on economic evaluation. Planning in general, up to the early 1960s, had to a remarkable degree avoided the exercise of generating or evaluating alternative future plans; the recommended method which dated from Patrick Geddes (survey–analysis–plan) seemed to assume that the planner would proceed logically to discover a single correct answer. But the techniques of transportation planning, as they evolved more or less independently of traditional planning in the late 1950s, from the beginning stressed a technique which allied engineering and economics: the attempt to measure the costs and benefits of alternative plans. In planning the line of a major new motorway, as in planning alternative ways of providing for a city's water supply, it was logical to quantify the costs of construction and of subsequent operation, and also the more obvious benefits that could be measured. Practically, the early exercises of this kind in England – such as the well-known studies of the M1 motorway by Beesley and others, or that of the Victoria underground line in London by Beesley and Foster – stressed the very large time-savings that construction of the new facility would bring. They tended to make a strong case for such major investments, even where – as in the case of the Victoria Line – they could not be justified on conventional accounting criteria.

Such pioneer exercises were little concerned with some of the less tractable elements of evaluation – above all, the controversial issue of amenity, or the quality of environment. But at the same time, a quite separate study commissioned by the British government – the famous report on *Traffic in Towns*, by a team headed by Colin Buchanan, published in 1963 – took the stand that in reaching planning decisions, it was necessary to quantify the environmental costs and to reckon them in. This suggested that investment in urban roads should be governed not by the costs necessary to reduce congestion to a defined level, but by the higher level of costs necessary to reduce congestion while maintaining some defined environmental standards; if the community was unwilling to pay these costs, then the level of traffic in towns should be restrained by various means until environmentally acceptable limits were reached. The report, which generated immense public attention and approval, took

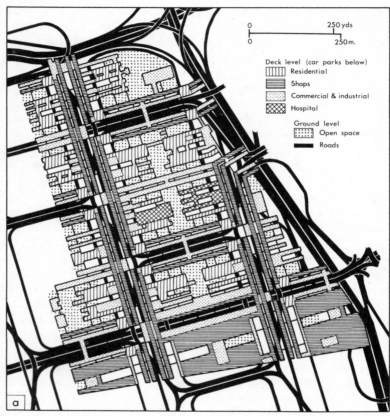

0   250 yds
0   250 m.

Deck level (car parks below)
Residential
Shops
Commercial & industrial
Hospital

Ground level
Open space
Roads

53. Alternative levels of urban redevelopment in part of London's West End, from the Buchanan report: (a) Maximal; (b) Minimal. The report Traffic in Towns *(1963), by a group under Sir Colin Buchanan, argued that the traffic capacity of a town should be fixed at an environmentally acceptable level. More traffic could be accommodated by complex reconstruction of the urban fabric, but this would be expensive; the alternative would be traffic restraint.*

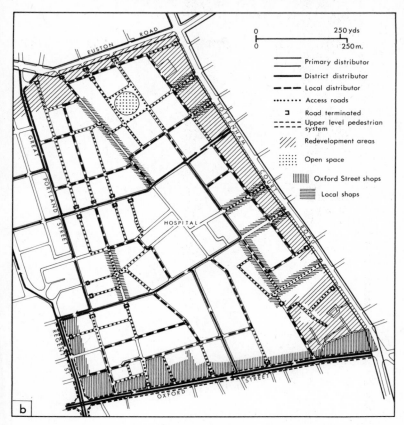

an approach which proved extremely difficult to fit into the new cost-benefit framework of the economists. When at last a major cost benefit study was undertaken for an official inquiry which depended centrally on the evaluation of environmental quality – the study of the location of London's third airport, in 1968–70 – the result was widespread public criticism and controversy. By the start of the 1970s, this was yet another important area where the techniques of planning still urgently awaited development, though at central government level the creation in 1970 of the Department of the Environment – at last integrating urban and transport planning in

191

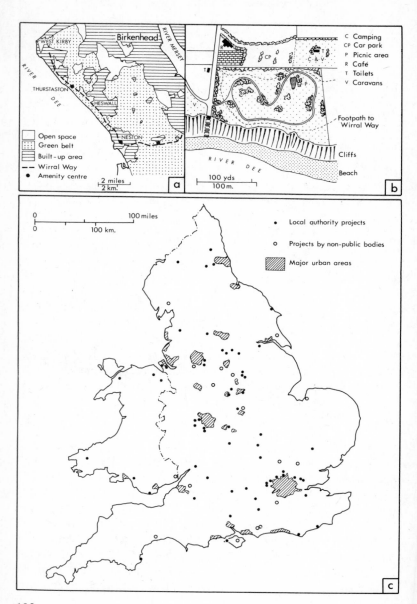

West Kirby | Birkenhead | RIVER MERSEY
RIVER DEE
THURSTASTON
HESWALL
NESTON

Open space
Green belt
Built-up area
Wirral Way
Amenity centre

2 miles
2 km.

a

C Camping
CP Car park
P Picnic area
R Café
T Toilets
V Caravans

Footpath to
Wirral Way

Cliffs
Beach

RIVER DEE

100 yds
100 m.

b

0 ——— 100 miles
0 ——— 100 km.

Local authority projects
Projects by non-public bodies
Major urban areas

c

192

one organization – provided a better framework for the incorporation of environmental factors into decisions on transport investments.

Increasing concern with the quality of environment expressed itself in other ways too. In 1968 the Countryside Act marked an important stage in the evolution of planning for outdoor recreation. It replaced the National Parks Commission, which had been created by the 1949 Act (Chapter 5), by a Countryside Commission with wider responsibilities and greater financial powers. It promised more money to the new Commission to back up these powers, though the sums still remained puny in comparison with other spending programmes. And it empowered local authorities or private agencies to create country parks near major centres of population, with subsidies from the Commission, so as to act as 'honeypots' relieving pressure on the national parks. Later on, in the 1972 reform of English local government, an important change was made in the administration of national parks; though they would still be managed by the county councils, or by joint boards of county councils, henceforth there must be a separate committee and planning officer for each park. Here the government was recognizing the weighty criticism that in many of the parks, the local administration had shown little enthusiasm for positive planning and hardly any willingness to spend money. The consequences were becoming serious, as increasing car ownership and motorway extensions brought floods of motor traffic into the heart of the parks at peak holiday periods.

At the time of the 1972 United Nations Stockholm Conference on the Human Environment, environmental quality became a major political issue throughout the world. Britain took a number of important steps at this time. It followed up the highly successful 1956 Clean Air Act – whereby local authorities, with central government financial aid, were empowered to introduce clean-air zones in Britain's towns and cities – with a radical reorganization of water-

---

54. Country parks: (a) Wirral Way Country Park, Cheshire; (b) A picnic place on Wirral Way; (c) Location of country parks in England and Wales, 1972. The country park concept, introduced in the Countryside Act 1968, allows local authorities and other bodies to develop sites for intensive outdoor recreation close to the major urban areas.

55. Elvaston Castle, Derbyshire. This country house and grounds, standing between Derby and Nottingham in open countryside, was one of the first local authority country parks designated under the 1968 Act.

supply and sewage-disposal services, coupled with a programme that promised to clean up the country's more grossly polluted industrial rivers by the early 1980s. And, following recommendations by official committees, it reorganized compensation and road-building procedures so as to give better guarantees of environmental quality to those living alongside new highways. It provided grants for double-glazing and similar measures – a scheme already operated for householders around London's Heathrow airport; it provided more generous compensation for those wishing to move away from high-way construction; and it provided for more environmentally sensitive, and more expensive, designs for new urban roads.

All this represented an answer to a very evident demand on the part of the public – or at least the vocal section of the public. Controversies like the location of London's third airport, or London's proposed motorway system, or new roads in places like Winchester and the Lake District all demonstrated that substantial numbers of people were now very sensitive to any threat to their own environment. Their interest gave added point to the problem of incorporating environmental assessments into the evaluation of alternative plans. But at the same time it emphasized the point that in any planning decision there were likely to be winners and losers. If better-informed, better-organized groups campaigned successfully in their own environmental interests, the real risk was that the decision would go against the less informed and the less organized – who, in general, were also the poorer members of the community.

Meanwhile, two quite separate but related developments had been occurring in other fields, whose consequences for planning seemed likely to be momentous. The first was the growing concern – first evident, in the late 1960s, in American city planning but then increasingly imported into Britain – for the social objectives of planning. Essentially the argument, as developed in the United States, was that physical or spatial planning had failed many of the people that it ought to have helped, because it had not started from sufficiently clear and explicitly social objectives. In particular, critics pointed to the many examples where American urban renewal had simply displaced low-income residents from inner urban areas without providing alternative housing, leaving them worse off than before; and to the way in which public programmes, such as the Interstate Highway Program, had contributed to suburban dispersal of people and employment, leaving low-income inner city residents increasingly separated from job opportunities. Great concern developed all over the United States, during the 1960s, at the increasing polarization of the metropolitan areas, whereby higher-income residents and their associated services and jobs migrated to far-flung suburbs, while the older central cities were left to cater for low-income residents with a constantly declining local tax base. By the early 1970s, in the inquiry on the Greater London Development Plan, fears were being expressed that a similar fate was overtaking London — and, by extension, perhaps other British cities as well.

Some of the conclusions to be drawn from such analyses were purely in terms of changed machinery: larger units of local government uniting cities and suburbs, for instance, or new sources of local revenue for cities, or revenue-sharing between central (or regional) and local governments. But more deeply, the debate seemed likely to shift the central focus of what spatial planners did. While the injection of transportation planning in the early and mid-1960s had led to an emphasis on economic efficiency as the central objective of planning, the injection of social planning in the late 1960s and early 1970s seemed certain to lead to an emphasis on equity in distribution. Planning, some sociologists were increasingly arguing, essentially distributed public goods (i.e. goods which could not be bought and sold in the market, such as clean air or quiet residential areas) to different groups of the population. It could be progressive in its social consequences, by distributing more of these goods to the lower-income groups, or the reverse. Too often, certainly in the United States but perhaps also in Britain, it had been regressive. The question that needed to be asked now was: who benefited from planning policies like urban containment, or green belts, or high-rise urban renewal? And who, conversely, suffered the disbenefits? The conclusions could be disturbing. But again, this was an item on the agenda for future development at the beginning of the 1970s.

Lastly, but relatedly, the late 1960s saw an increasing influence on British local authorities generally of modern management techniques originally developed within private profit-making industry. The critical events here were first the publication in 1967 of the Maud Committee report (not to be confused with the Redcliffe Maud Commission report) on local authority management, which recommended a new structure for local government based on a few major committees covering wide policy areas, together with a central policy-making committee; and secondly the parallel reform of the personal social services of local government during 1969–70, which created new combined social services departments embracing public health and child care. But intellectually the new movement was associated with the influence of the new techniques of Planning–Programming–Budgeting Systems (PPBS) imported from the United States, and originally developed for a very different area of public enterprise: Robert McNamara's Department of Defense. Essentially, PPBS demanded that management of public enterprises should be re-structured on the basis of *objectives* rather than of traditional departmental responsibilities. Applied to American defence problems, it asked for instance how to achieve a specific objective – for instance, how to provide for defence against surprise attack – rather than how to develop specific programmes for the army or the air force. Applied to the very different world of British local government, it would again ask how to achieve an objective – for instance, preventing the break-up of families – rather than emphasizing separate programmes of housing or child care.

Again, the influence on planning seemed likely to be profound. Many of the central objectives which local government seemed certain to develop for itself under the new PPBS framework would be social objectives: objectives in terms of people and their needs, rather than in terms of physical policies. Management by objectives, therefore, seemed likely to shift planning further away from its old emphasis on physical policies, and towards a style in which policies had to be developed, and then defended, in terms of their specific implications for the welfare of the people involved. But this was yet another item where, in the early 1970s, a great deal of hard thinking needed to be done.

Only one thing seemed certain – that the traditional professional structure of planning in Britain, organized around membership of a Town Planning Institute which in turn was devoted to the principle of a generally trained, physically focused planner, could not survive the new changes without adaptation. The Town Planning Institute (which became the Royal Town Planning Institute in 1971) had been founded in 1914, at a time when town planning was largely concerned with small-scale problems of civic design. It had translated itself after 1945 to the larger scale of planning implied by the 1947 Planning Act, with the creation of the new county planning authorities in the countryside; and after 1950, following the well-argued recommendations of the Schuster Committee on the training of planners, it had broadened the base of its membership to take in increasing numbers of people whose first training had not been in the traditional areas of architecture and engineering, but rather in the social sciences, such as geography, economics and sociology. By the early 1960s it was already clear that in one important area – transportation planning – the general basis of training favoured by the Institute was already inadequate; by the late 1960s there were increasing doubts whether it would cater for the needs of the new structure planning. But the simultaneous injection into local government of management by objectives, and the closely related area of social planning, brought further doubts. By 1971 the President of the Institute was publicly stating his view that in future there would be at least three types of professionals, all calling themselves planners: spatial planners embracing various specialities, social planners and management planners.

Planning, in other words, was in a state of intellectual flux such as had never before been witnessed. But this, perhaps, was only characteristic of professionalism in general at the beginning of the 1970s – the result of the explosive growth of applied higher education and research during the 1960s, a process which had originated in North America, but which had increasingly been exported to Britain. It left a set of key questions for planning, on which further research and debate would be needed: the clarification of the objectives of planning; the improvement of the techniques of prediction and forecasting, especially for the longer term; the further development of techniques of evaluation of alternative plans; the study of decision-making in conditions where even the best forecasts, because of their interdependency, were apt to prove unreliable and uncertain. These are some of the questions that must be addressed in the final chapter of this book.

Further Reading

Cullingworth, 1970 (see reading list, Chapter 5), and Eversley (reading list, Chapter 6) are useful sources here.

On the pattern of urban decentralization, see Peter Hall, 'The Spatial

Structure of Metropolitan England and Wales', in Michael Chisholm and Gerald Manners (eds.), *Spatial Policy Problems of the British Economy* (Cambridge University Press, 1971), pp. 96–125; on land use implications, see Peter Hall, 'Land Use – the Spread of Towns into the Country', in Michael Young (ed.), *Forecasting and the Social Sciences* (Heinemann, 1968), pp. 95–117; on the impact on landscape, Nan Fairbrother, *New Lives, New Landscapes* (Penguin, 1972).

For a fuller treatment of urban growth, see Peter Hall, Ray Thomas, Harry Gracey, Roy Drewett, *The Containment of Urban England* (Allen & Unwin, 1973). Useful for long-term population trends, with a forward look, is *Long Term Population Distribution in Great Britain: A Study* (HMSO, 1971). Peter Cowan (ed.), *Developing Patterns of Urbanisation* (Oliver & Boyd, 1970), has useful essays on contemporary society and economy; it can be supplemented at a more popular level by Michael Chisholm (ed.), *Resources in Britain's Future* (Penguin, 1972).

On the social content of planning, see J. B. Cullingworth, *Problems of an Urban Society*, 3 vols. (Allen & Unwin, 1973), especially Vol. 2.

8. Planning in Western Europe since 1945

The six western European countries which formed the original European Economic Community of 1957, together with their Scandinavian neighbours to the north, offer some instructive comparisons for the planner – both with each other, and still more so with the experience of Britain as it has been outlined in the preceding chapters. These are all highly industrialized countries; but in general, with the possible exception of Belgium, their industrialization took place later than Britain's, it took rather different forms and had rather different spatial effects, while in the 1970s it was still less complete. Whereas Britain by this time had only some 3 per cent of, its labour force in agriculture, and the percentage of its total population which was urban had remained almost unchanged at about 80 per cent since the beginning of the twentieth century, the EEC countries still had about 14 per cent of their workers in agriculture, and in general a higher proportion of their people lived in villages and small towns. With rare exceptions, such as the Ruhr coalfield in Germany and the nearby coalfield of southern Belgium, continental western Europe has avoided the rapid industrialization which produced the sordid industrial landscapes of the Midlands and northern England; coming much later, after the advent of railways and even of electric power, the industrial revolution in these countries affected the existing older cities, so that its effect both on social patterns and on the landscape was less profound.

But these differences should not be exaggerated. The major economic and social trends are as unmistakable in all the Continental Western European countries as in Britain. Despite strongly protectionist agricultural policies which result from the historic strength of the farm vote, workers – especially younger workers – have been leaving the family farms in huge numbers since 1945; the system of peasant farming, which was typical in most of these countries, would not guarantee them the standard of living they expected, so they moved to the cities. There have been big long-distance migrations of farm workers from the poorer parts of the countryside, especially from southern Italy, to the major industrial areas of Europe. In these reception areas, cities have grown to form the equivalents of the great British conurbations – the *agglomerations* of France, the *Ballungsräume* of Germany. A stark contrast has appeared, in all these countries, between the backwardness and stagnation of the remoter rural areas and the dynamic growth – too often accompanied by familiar problems of congestion, high land prices, poor living conditions and pollution – of the agglomerations.

These trends are producing a new geography of Europe – a geography of stagnation and growth, of 'have' regions and 'have-not' regions. This geography appears to ignore international boundaries. The major agglomerations tend noticeably to have a central location within the European Community; most of them are found within a giant 'Golden Triangle' whose corners are Birmingham, Dortmund and Milan, and a significant proportion are even found within a much smaller triangle whose corners are Paris, Birmingham and Dortmund. Conversely, regarding either of these triangles as the new European heartland, the major problem areas are all noticeably on Western Europe's periphery: they include much of northern England, all of Scotland and most of Wales (and, of course, all Ireland); the north-eastern Netherlands; most of the eastern districts of the German Federal Republic, against the border with the Democratic Republic; southern Italy, the so-called 'Mezzogiorno' south of Rome; and virtually all of southern and western France, below the diagonal line from Le Havre on the Normandy coast down to Marseilles.

There are very good economic reasons for this situation. The *raison d'être* of the agglomerations – Greater London and its surrounding towns, the Randstad of Holland, the Rhine–Ruhr and Rhine–Main areas of Germany, the Paris region – is manufacture and, increasingly, tertiary industry. Both these industries seek locations with large markets and large, skilled labour forces; tertiary industry and its modern outgrowth, decision-making quarternary

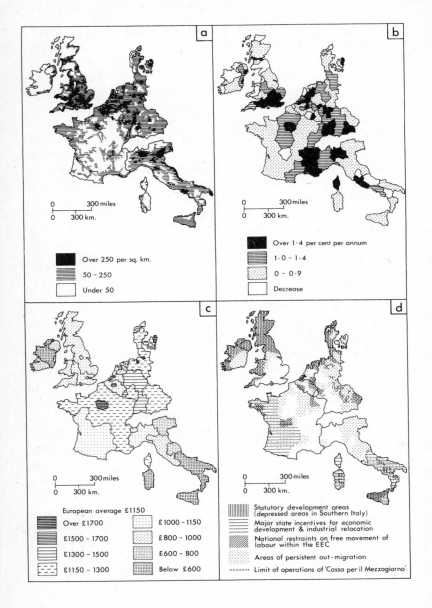

a

0 — 300 miles
0 — 300 km.

■ Over 250 per sq. km.
▤ 50 – 250
□ Under 50

b

0 — 300 miles
0 — 300 km.

■ Over 1·4 per cent per annum
▤ 1·0 – 1·4
▨ 0 – 0·9
□ Decrease

c

0 — 300 miles
0 — 300 km.

European average £1150
▤ Over £1700
▤ £1500 – 1700
▤ £1300 – 1500
▤ £1150 – 1300

▨ £1000 – 1150
▨ £800 – 1000
▨ £600 – 800
▨ Below £600

d

0 — 300 miles
0 — 300 km.

▥ Statutory development areas
(depressed areas in Southern Italy)
▤ Major state incentives for economic
development & industrial relocation
▨ National restraints on free movement of
labour within the EEC
▨ Areas of persistent out-migration
------ Limit of operations of 'Cassa per il Mezzogiorno'

industry, demand specialized transportation and marketing services and increasingly form a complex in order to exploit economies of agglomeration and scale. Goods and also non-material intelligence are increasingly exchanged between these areas. Because powerful forces of inertia work in the location of such activities, they tend to grow where they have been traditionally located: in the old-established trading and governmental centres, which in turn are related to historic trade routes. In the twentieth century as in the middle ages, these are heavily concentrated in a relatively small zone of northern France, the Netherlands, western Germany and south-east England, spreading in a line southwards up the Rhine and across the Alps to northern Italy. The stagnant rural areas, in contrast, are without exception well away from these major lines of force in European geography. The existence of the European Economic Community, with the associated growth in trade in industrial goods among its member nations, can only reinforce the trend, unless corrective action is taken.

The difficulty is that the process is not without costs. On the one hand, large tracts of countryside run the danger of virtual depopulation, if trends continue, by the 1980s; for the out-migration of young people, if continued long enough, will result in a rapid ageing of the population and a reduction in the natural increase. Already, across large tracts of France and Italy, it is evident that the population is too thin and scattered to support modern services, and the many market towns are working at much less than the scale for which they were intended. On the other hand, from all the agglomerations come similar stories of housing shortages – despite often draconian measures of control; traffic congestion and increasingly long journeys to work; rising land prices and land shortages; public services that cannot cope; and increasing pollution of air and water. Though they have seldom been precisely quantified in relation to the

56. *The European Economic Community in maps: (a) Density of population, mid-1960s; (b) Population change, 1958–68; (c) Gross Regional Product per capita, 1971; (d) Development programmes and problem areas. The nine nations of the enlarged EEC encompass great variations in the level of economic and urban development, highlighting the search for Community regional development programmes in the early 1970s.*

private advantages that bring people and industry to the agglomerations, there can be little doubt that the public costs of the process are very large.

Thus the problems are similar, whether in south-east England or the Paris region, the Randstad of Holland, the Rhine–Ruhr, or the plain of Lombardy. The solutions, however, have been different. Despite the elaborate provisions in the Rome Treaty for coordination of regional policies, the administrative traditions and the political outlooks of the major western European countries have remained sharply differentiated in the postwar period. The strongly centralist tradition of the French public administration has been contrasted with the Federal system of postwar West Germany. The social-democratic tradition in Scandinavia, with its emphasis on State intervention, is contrasted with the market economy which for most of the postwar period has characterized the German economy. Controls over land use have been more effective in north European countries, such as Scandinavia, Germany and the Netherlands, than in Italy.

Because these countries each show at least some unique features, their problems are best discussed separately, with a general summing-up at the end.

French Postwar Planning

There are many reasons for starting with France. The country shows an extreme version of the centre–periphery contrast, resulting in an acute problem of planning at what we have called, throughout this book, the national/regional scale. But the very size of the Paris agglomeration throws up additional questions of planning at the scale of the city region: the regional/local scale. At both scales, the French have shown remarkable inventiveness in developing new organizations and new techniques of planning. Indeed, at the national/ regional scale they have developed a planning apparatus which is unparalleled, in its comprehensiveness and its sophistication, in the developed world.

The geographical and historic background to the problem is a highly individual one. In the nineteenth century, France never experienced the rapid population growth typical of other advanced countries. Large-scale industry, with the exception of a concentration in the north, near the Belgian frontier, failed to develop on any scale. Instead, because of the strong tradition of centralization in French life, Paris grew apace while other parts of the country stagnated and even declined. Paris came to dominate the economic and social life of the country to an unusual degree.

Since the Second World War, the demographic situation has been revolutionized; population has rapidly grown, but in the process it has concentrated further in the urban areas and above all in Paris. Two thirds of the population was urban in the 1960s, as opposed to only one quarter a century before. An undue part of this urban population, and of the total population growth, was concentrated in the northern and eastern parts of France; south and west of the critical line from Le Havre to Marseilles, there was a contrasted rural landscape of stagnation and decay. In the early 1960s the Paris region, occupying 2 per cent of the area of France, had 19 per cent of its population and 29 per cent of its industrial jobs; an even smaller area, Paris proper, had one quarter of the nation's civil servants, one third of the higher education students and nearly two thirds of all the commercial headquarters. In contrast, the rural west, with 55 per cent of the area, had 37 per cent of the population and only 24 per cent of the industrial jobs.

A remarkable book published in 1947, right at the beginning of the postwar reconstruction period, first drew attention to the problem. *Paris et le désert français*, published by a young geographer, Jean-François Gravier, argued that the contrast was rooted in an accident of history and not in economics; technological innovations, such as widespread electric power and motor vehicles, Gravier argued, could promote dispersed industrial development in the countryside and reverse the trend.

Gravier's book had immense influence and soon brought practical results, for in 1946 France had embarked on an ambitious experiment; under the direction of Jean Monnet, the country tried to develop a system of economic planning based not on State ownership of all resources (as in Soviet Russia during the 1920s), but on a mixed economy where about half the total investment was in private hands. In the early years of the plan, there was little interest in questions of the geographical distribution of investment or of economic activity generally. But from the mid-1950s, as economists took an interest in these questions, the regional element became an increasingly important part of the plan. Already in the early 1950s special state funds were created for regional development, though these were outside the plan process; from 1955 the central plan agency (the Commissariat général au plan) was given regional responsibilities. In the same year, a decree established that government approval would be necessary for new factory building or reconstruction in the Paris region; and thereafter the capital's proportion of new industrial building did fall. Appropriately, at the smaller scale of the city region, a 1960 plan for Paris (the so-called PADOG) proposed a stop on the future physical growth of the agglomeration.

By this time the process of integrating regional and national planning was becoming increasingly sophisticated. The resulting

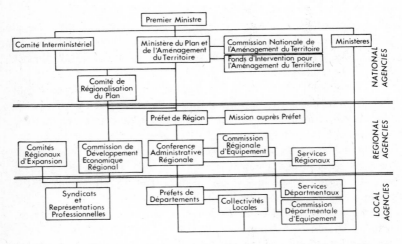

57. *The administrative structure of French regional planning. To integrate national and regional planning, the French had to develop a complex structure during the 1960s. The English economic planning councils and boards, dating from 1965, were developed after a study of the French system.*

structure, as fully evolved in the mid-1960s, was a highly complex one – too complex to explain in detail here (see Illustration 57). Essentially, the Commissariat général au plan (CGP) worked through a regional arm, the Delegation à l'aménagement du territoire et l'action régionale (DATAR) which coordinated regional agencies and administered regional development funds, and which was responsible directly to the Prime Minister. The country was divided into 21 economic planning regions (Illustration 54), consisting of groups of the *départements*, the basic administrative units of France; each region had a regional *préfet*, an official of the central government, assisted by a regional conference of officials and a regional commission of appointed experts from areas like industry, trade unions and universities. Together the regional and the central planning machine prepared regional sections (*tranches opératoires*) of the plan, through an elaborate process of refinement conducted between centre and region. In fact, as Illustration 57 demonstrates, the relationship and responsibilities – especially at the centre – were far from clear; they resulted only partially from the rational thought for which the French are renowned, and rather more from interdepartmental rivalries and suspicions. That is why there are so many parallel bodies, and so few vertical responsibilities in the chart.

Yet another system exists to promote and coordinate plans at city region level. In 1966, metropolitan plan organizations (each known as an OREAM) were set up for the six major urban regions of Lille–Dunkerque, Rouen–le Havre, Nantes–Saint Lazaire, Lyon–Saint Étienne, Marseille–Aix and Nancy–Metz; while a central planning group in Paris, set up two years earlier (known as GCPU, for Groupe central de planification urbaine), advises ministers on planning questions at this level. The organization for the Paris region is of course rather special; set up in 1961, it has provided a model for the other regions. Here, there is a full-time regional *préfet* assisted by a team of civil servants; he is chairman of a board consisting of local government representatives from the region. There is also a research association, corresponding to the OREAM in the other major urban areas; called the Institut d'aménagement et d'urbanisme de la région parisienne (IAURP), it has acquired a considerable international reputation for the quality of its studies. At the same time, in order to bring the government of the Paris region into line with the realities of its great size and complexity, the number of *départements* within the region was increased from 3 — out of an old total of 90 for the whole country — to 8.

Elaborate machinery — sometimes confusingly elaborate — is then one of the outstanding features of French regional planning at both national/regional and regional/local scales. The critical question must be what this machinery has achieved. At the major scale of the relationship of the regions to the national economy, the policy of trying to restrict the growth of Paris has been retained; but it has been modified. In contrast to the 1960 plan which tried to put an absolute stop on the physical growth of Paris, a later 1965 plan (the so-called Schéma directeur) assumes a continuing high rate of growth of population (4 per cent per annum, giving more than a doubling of population in 20 years), but slows down the planned rate somewhat in the interests of the other major urban regions. The objective has been to slow down the rate of migration to the Paris region, first by careful localization of government investment, and then by guiding private investment through the provision of public infrastructure. Especially important here has been the designation, in 1965, of 8 *métropoles d'équilibre* ('balancing metropolitan areas') designed deliberately as counterweights to the capital. Carefully selected on the basis of the major provincial centres of population, they are designed to act as centres of economic development for their respective regions. The first, based on the northern cities of Lille, Roubaix and Tourcoing, will help the regeneration of an old industrial area based on coal and textiles. The second, Nancy–Metz in Lorraine, and the third, Strasbourg in Alsace, are based on quite prosperous eastern industrial areas. The fourth, Lyon–Saint Étienne, includes a problematic coalfield area and will serve the poor marginal hill-farming area of the Massif central. The fifth, Marseille–Aix, includes both the rapidly developing industrial area of the Lower Rhône and the southern slopes of the problematic Massif. The sixth, Toulouse, is a very important centre of industrial development in the south west, best known for its aircraft-building complex which built the first Concorde. Not very far away on the west coast is the seventh centre, Bordeaux; the eighth, Nantes–Saint Lazaire, is farther north on the

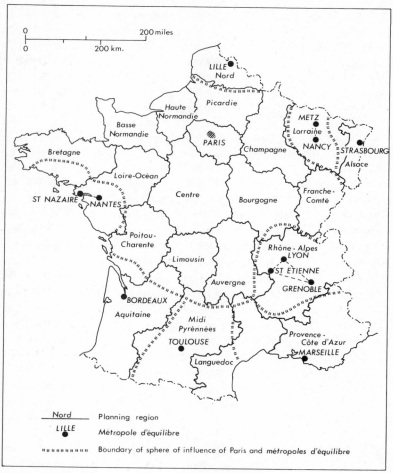

Map labels:

0 — 200 miles
0 — 200 km.

LILLE
Nord

Picardie

Haute
Normandie

Basse
Normandie

METZ
Lorraine
NANCY
STRASBOURG
Alsace

Bretagne

PARIS

Champagne

Loire-Océan

Centre

Bourgogne

Franche-
Comté

ST NAZAIRE — NANTES

Poitou-
Charente

Limousin

Rhône - Alpes
LYON
ST ÉTIENNE
GRENOBLE

Auvergne

BORDEAUX

Aquitaine

Midi
Pyrénnées
TOULOUSE

Provence -
Côte d'Azur
MARSEILLE

Languedoc

Legend:

Nord — Planning region
LILLE — Métropole d'équilibre
"""""""""" — Boundary of sphere of influence of Paris and métropoles d'équilibre

58. *French planning regions and the* métropoles d'équilibre. *French regional planning is carried out through 21 planning regions which are aggregations of* départements. *To try to achieve more balanced growth and avoid over-concentration on Paris, the objective is to concentrate investment in 'balancing metropolises' based on the major provincial cities.*

same west coast and is intended as the spring-board for the development of Brittany.

This is a dramatic and bold policy, which corresponds fairly well to the realities of French geography; outside the Paris region, France is less urbanized than Britain or Germany and the urban population is heavily concentrated into the 8 regional centres, so that these are the logical places from which to generate regional economic development. But there are two snags. One is that all the regions contain large (and often thinly populated) rural areas which are well outside the sphere of influence of these centres; to help them it would also be necessary to develop other 'poles of growth' based on smaller centres, but that runs the risk of spreading investment too thinly. The other problem is that investment in the *métropoles* also has to compete with investment in Paris. Though to many provincial Frenchmen Paris seems to have a disproportionate share of everything, the fact is that for many decades the capital city's infrastructure has been running down through under-investment. After the great burst of investment under Haussmann in the 1850s and 1860s, there was relatively little new house-building; after the construction of the new boulevards by Haussmann at that time and the building of the Métro in the early years of the twentieth century, the transport system also suffered the effects of low investment. To make the city more efficient and more liveable also requires a massive dose of investment. So a delicate balance is involved.

This is underlined when one looks more closely at the problems of planning at the regional/local scale within Paris itself. To try to make up for the backlog of investment, the 1965 plan suggests the creation of 8 new cities, strung out along two parallel axes on either side of the Seine, east and west of Paris: the first, 55 miles long, south of the river from Melun to Mantes, the second, 45 miles long, north of it from Meaux to Pontoise. These would nearly double the size of the existing built-up area within a 35-year period up to the end of the century. To service all this would demand 540 miles of new highways and 156 miles of an entirely new regional express Métro system (the first parts of which were opened in 1971). Also involved is the expensive renovation of existing centres within the urban fabric of Paris, such as those at La Défense and Nanterre (the first to be begun, and largely completed by the early 1970s), Saint Denis, Bobigny, Creteil, Versailles, and Choissy-le-Roi/Rungis (the site of the new markets of les Halles, close to Orly airport). All this is necessary, of course, not only to make up for the deficiencies of the past, but to cater for a population growth that may take the population of the region from 9 to 14 million within 35 years.

Both scales of planning have a common theme – the attempt to break the concentration of economic life at the centre, by developing a full range of economic opportunities, and of social and cultural

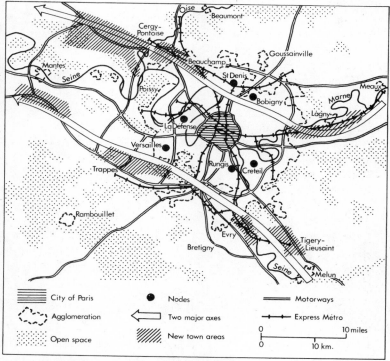

59. The Paris regional plan of 1965. To provide for the projected growth of the metropolis from 9 to 14 million by the year 2000, the plan provides for a number of major new cities grouped along two major axes of development, one north and one south of the river Seine. New motorways and express rail links will serve the new developments.

211

60. *Reconstruction of La Défense, Paris. Located just outside the limits of the historic city of Paris, La Défense is one of the biggest pieces of reconstruction in Europe in the 1960s and 1970s. It contains offices, homes, a station on the new Métro and a new highway interchange.*

facilities, in a number of urban counter-magnets. From this view-point the new cities of the Paris region, some of which may have up to 1 million inhabitants by the year 2000, will perform essentially the same role as the *métropoles d'équilibre* in the provinces. Both policies may well prove successful, but neither is likely to modify the strong underlying trend in the French economy: the increasing con-centration of population and of economic life in the major urban regions. Outside their sphere of influence, stagnation and decay are still likely to be the rule. And the dream of Gravier, to spread economic advantage fairly evenly across France, is unlikely to be realized.

The German Experience

In the Federal Republic of Germany, as in France, the same contrast is evident. A large and increasing proportion of the whole population lives in a limited number of major urban agglomerations and their wider spheres of influence which extend outwards into those parts of the surrounding rural areas which are within commuter range. The population living in these large concentrations has risen from $\frac{1}{2}$ million in 1870 to nearly 20 million in 1970, when one third of the population of the Federal Republic was living in only 3 per cent of its area. Taking in the wider spheres of influence, 13 per cent of the total area accommodated 43 per cent of the population, 51 per cent of the industrial employment and 62 per cent of the industrial production. Furthermore these areas are themselves highly concen-trated within the Federal Republic; they tend to occur in two parallel north–south axes (one from Hamburg through Kassel to Munich, the other from Bremen through the Ruhr to Frankfurt, Stuttgart and Basel) with short east–west cross links between them. These axes clearly extend into other neighbouring countries; thus the cross-link from Aachen and Cologne to Hannover and Braunschweig extends westwards into Belgium and eastwards into the German Democratic Republic. And though no part of the Federal Republic is more than 200 km (120 miles) from one of the agglomerations, there are large tracts which to all intents and purposes are outside their spheres of influence. Most of them tend to be upland plateau areas with bleak climates and rather poor agriculture; most tend to be frontier areas, against Belgium in the west or Denmark in the north, or against the Democratic Republic and Czechoslavakia in the east. They include areas like the lowland Emsland in the north-west, Schleswig–Holstein in the north, the Eifel in the far west, the Böhmer Wald and Bayerischer Wald in the south-east.

The contrast between the great agglomerations on the one hand, and the remoter rural areas on the other, is the outstanding feature of the geography of Germany. But Germany shares with Britain the feature that not all her major urban areas are equally prosperous. Since the late 1950s the greatest of them all – the Rhine–Ruhr district, with over 10 million people concentrated into an area measuring 70 miles by 50 – has suffered badly from the decline in demand for coal. Conversely the more consistently prosperous urban areas have been those in the southern half of the country, such as Frankfurt–Wiesbaden–Mainz, Mannheim–Ludwigshafen, Stuttgart, and Munich, where faster-growing newer industries, many of them displaced from the east at the end of the war, have tended to gather. Because the major agglomerations of Germany tend to be much smaller than London or Paris, they do not have the same problems of congestion and overloaded services; in this sense, Germany has been lucky in its decentralized pattern of urban growth. But in the Ruhr above all, there are acute problems of regional/local planning. The decline of basic industry there makes it more difficult to provide the revenue to grapple with questions of traffic congestion, long work-journeys, lack of green space and above all, air and water pollution. The poisonous state of the river Rhine has become an international problem, since the Netherlands must draw much of their water supply from it. Air pollution from the heavy concentration of chemical and metal plants is a problem not only in the Ruhr – where postwar developments have often been badly sited in relation to residential areas – but also in the low-lying Rhine–Main industrial area between Frankfurt, Wiesbaden and Mainz.

The problems, therefore, are similar to those of France, though the different geography of the countries means that they express themselves differently. A more important difference lies in the administrative tradition, which determines the way the problems are treated. France is a highly centralized country in which the provinces are administered from the capital through a system of civil servants (*préfets*) established in each administrative division. Postwar West Germany has been a federal republic, in which basic administrative responsibility for most aspects of home affairs is given to the constituent states, or *Länder*. (There are 10 of these, which vary greatly in area and population from the city states of Bremen and Hamburg, at one end, to the state of Nordrhein-Westfalen with its 15 million people and the state of Bavaria with one quarter the total area of the republic.) Regional planning is no exception; under the Federal Law on the subject, passed on 8 April 1965, the Federal government lays it down that a fundamental aim is to develop and organize the nation so that equal conditions exist everywhere, but the major responsibility to ensure this is given to the *Länder*.

The difficulty is that, as so often, administrative boundaries do not conform to the realities of administrative problems. Most of the *Länder*, it is true, are large and are based reasonably clearly on one or more urban regions. Thus the *Land* of Hessen focuses quite naturally on the Rhine–Main urban area; Baden-Württemberg has a natural focus in the Stuttgart–Heilbronn region; Nordrhein-Westfalen has a heartland in the great Rhine–Ruhr industrial area. But other *Land* boundaries are by no means as convenient. The most anomalous is around Hamburg, where the tightly drawn boundaries of the city state put the suburbs north of the Elbe in the *Land* of Schleswig–Holstein, and those to the south in the *Land* of Niedersachsen (Lower Saxony). And on a wider scale the anomalies multiply. Thus the planning of the Emsland, a thinly populated lowland zone near the Dutch border west of Bremen, needs to be related to the influence of the Ruhr region to the south; but the Emsland is in Niedersachsen and the *Ruhrgebiet* is in Nordrhein-Westfalen. In France, similar anomalies in the structure of *départements* around Paris were rectified by a stroke of the ministerial pen. But in Germany, a change would mean modification of the constitution – an unlikely event.

For good reasons, most of the effort in planning at the national/ regional level has been directed at the problems of the remoter rural areas. Despite efforts to maintain agriculture through restructuring,

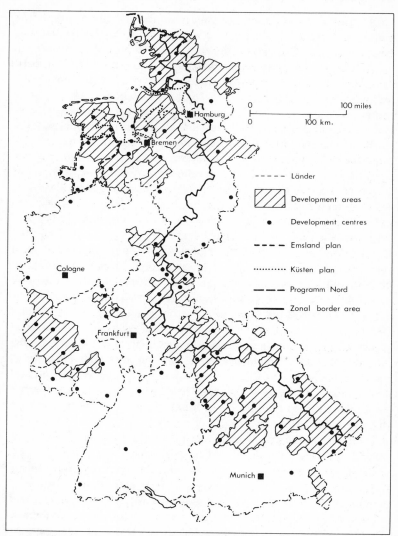

61. Development areas in the German Federal Republic. As in Britain, German postwar economic development has been strongly concentrated into a corridor in the western and northern parts of the country. The objective of regional policy is to steer growth into the peripheral areas outside this zone of rapid growth.

Map legend:
- - - - - Länder
- Development areas
- • Development centres
- - - - Emsland plan
- .... Küsten plan
- – – Programm Nord
- ——— Zonal border area

0   100 miles
0   100 km.

Hamburg
Bremen
Cologne
Frankfurt
Munich

the agricultural population has fallen by nearly half between 1950 and 1970; and it tends to be the younger, more active people who have left, especially from those areas where industrial and other job opportunities were thin on the ground. As it had evolved by the late 1960s, the system recognized three main types of area requiring assistance: development areas (*Bundesbaugebiete*), development centres (*Bundesbauorte*), and the frontier zone (*Zonenrandgebiet*). It also recognized four special areas, all of them peripheral: the Emsland against the North Sea in the north-west, northern Schleswig–Holstein in the far north, the North Sea coast itself, and the Alps in the far south. In fact all the development areas were themselves frontier zones, and a large proportion of them lay against the zonal border with the Democratic Republic; in all they included Schleswig–Holstein, Eastern and Western Lower Saxony, Eastern Hessen and Northern Bavaria, the Bavarian Forest (Bayerischer Wald) and the Eifel. All these areas were distinguished by a poor basis in natural resources and a weakly developed infrastructure; they were helped by agricultural reform, tourist development and industry. Most of the development centres have been in the development areas or the Frontier Zone (62 out of 81 of those designated between 1959 and 1969). And, though the development areas as a whole have been rather conspicuously unsuccessful in attracting new industry, by the late 1960s the development centres were proving their capacity to bring in industry: 23,000 new jobs were created between 1963 and 1967, with 40,000 more planned. Even here, though, success has not been uniform: centres in the south have been more successful than those in the north and west.

In all the development areas the policies are similar, and indeed they closely resemble those that have been applied in France. One element is the provision of a better infrastructure, especially in the form of improved communications; this is important because by definition these areas tend to be away from the main lines of rapid transportation, which run along the major industrial and urban axes. Another is the granting of financial incentives, either as loans or grants, to help private investment, especially in industry. The frontier areas with the Democratic Republic have received two other forms of help: special tax benefits and the placing of special Federal contracts. (These would normally not be permissible under the Common Market agreement, but when Germany signed the Treaty of Rome in 1957, it was allowed to maintain these special arrangements for the border areas.) The development centres have some similarity in principle to the *métropoles d'équilibre* in France, but in detailed practice they are completely different; as against the eight *métropoles* there were, in the late 1960s, 81 such centres in the Federal Republic. And far from being major urban centres which formed the natural focuses of major provinces of the country, the German centres were in general quite small market towns with some advantages in the form of transport services, cultural and social facilities, and some existing industry. They were nearly all in the development areas or near them, away from the main currents of economic life. This reflected the fact that in Germany, unlike France, the main regional cities were themselves highly buoyant.

The four special areas are all being helped under particular schemes. That for the Emsland, which is run by a specially-created development company, for instance, is mainly concerned with agricultural development, and has been criticized for being too narrowly conceived. It ought, critics suggested, to have been seen in conjunction with the development of the Bremen area to the north and the Ruhr to the south. But administrative divisions hindered this.

Help to these areas is given by the Federal government but is then mainly administered through the *Länder*. But in the case of the problem of structural adaptation in the Ruhr coalfield, a supernational authority – the European Coal and Steel Community (ECSC) – has a responsibility for giving re-adaptation grants to displaced miners. In so far as this problem is geographically concentrated in the bituminous coalfields of the belt from the Ruhr westwards into southern Belgium and northern France, this is a particularly striking example of action by the European Community in the interests of a particular region which stretches across international frontiers.

At regional/local level, planning is once again circumscribed by administrative divisions. The basic unit for physical planning is the municipality, or *Gemeinde* – and in much of the country, these can be very small. Advisory planning associations, called

Urban and Regional Planning

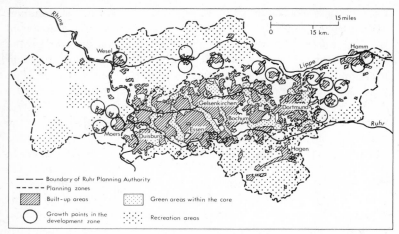

62. The development plan for the Ruhr. The Ruhr regional plan authority pioneered the idea of planning for an entire city region as early as the 1920s. Its 1966 plan aims to steer development into the open areas in the north of the region, while preserving green barriers between the major cities in the central part. Wide recreation areas will be preserved on the northern and southern peripheries.

Landschaftsverbände, provide some measure of coordination over larger areas, roughly corresponding to city regions. Only in the Ruhr coalfield, ever since the early 1920s, has there been an effective executive authority exercising real power over a whole urban agglomeration. This unique organization, the Ruhr Coalfield Settlement Association (Siedlungsverband Ruhrkohlenbezirk), has developed a very imaginative and thorough plan for the region, which involves an attempt to preserve the separate character of the cities which make up the area (Illustration 62). By this means, it will maintain the limited green spaces which divide one city from its neighbour, and which are so important in limiting the spread of air pollution in this region of 5 million people. Since in general the cities of the Ruhr are aligned on an east–west line – the line of a medieval trade route – and since also the higher land to the south is important as water-gathering grounds and as a recreational area, this means that future growth will be to the north, where open land is available. Until the decline of the coal industry, this made good sense in terms of

220

economic development, because the zone of main coal extraction was tending to move progressively northwards. And though this is now in doubt, the logic of the emphasis on movement towards the north is irresistible. Apart from anything else, this means an extension of the urban zone and its sphere of influence towards the development area of the Emsland, so that here regional/local planning arguments are reinforced by national/regional ones.

Regional Development in Italy

Postwar Italy presents acute problems of planning both at the national/ regional scale and the regional/local scale: the contrast between the dynamic industrial economy of the north and the stagnant agricultural society of the south is paralleled by the uncontrolled – and apparently uncontrollable – development of the major city regions, such as Milan–Turin, Rome or Naples. But in all fairness, it must be said that Italy's main innovations, and its main interest for the rest of the world, are at the broad scale of national/regional relationships rather than at the local scale of physical planning controls. As even the most casual visitor to the large Italian cities must notice, the planning machinery does not seem to have been equal to the problems it had to face. Again and again the same features recur: massive traffic congestion due to failure to control the use of the private car in densely built-up cities; a huge stock of obsolescent older housing, seriously deficient in basic facilities; new housing areas which are poorly conceived and poorly located, often without elementary social provision in the form of parks, clinics or shops. It is true that efforts have been made to remedy these deficiencies: Milan and Rome have built underground railways, Milan has pioneered the development of priority for bus traffic on the streets, and most cities have some attractive suburban areas. And due to the facts of history, solutions are often difficult to find: in few cities can it be said, as it is in Rome, that every few yards the underground railway builder finds a precious historic relic in his path. Nevertheless it is logical that this summary account should concentrate on the larger regional scale.

Urban and Regional Planning

The centre-periphery contrast is observable in other European countries; but nowhere, perhaps, as acutely as in Italy. For nowhere else in the Common Market can it be said that one substantial region of the nation is, in effect, an underdeveloped country; nowhere else is the contrast between the different regions, in the stage and in the speed of their economic development, so great. The Italian south – the so-called Mezzogiorno – comprises approximately one third of the entire country, including most of the area south of Rome. In 1950, just after the Second World War, its *per capita* income was only 40 per cent of that in the prosperous north-western part of the country – the heavily industrialized Plain of Lombardy, including Milan and Turin; by 1967 the figure had climbed only to 48 per cent. Some 40 per cent of the total labour force of the south remains in agriculture, while conversely 40 per cent of the total national industrial labour force is found in the industrial north-west. During the 1950s and the 1960s the south has increased its non-agricultural labour force more slowly than it ought to have done, on the criterion of its share of the total national population; and in absolute terms this increase was smaller than the net out-migration from the area, which actually exceeded the above-average birth rate. Two thirds of all births in Italy occur in the south; but if it were not for this massive drift to the north, the modest growth in *per capita* income that has occurred would almost certainly have become a decline.

The roots of the problem in the Mezzogiorno are both physical and historical. On the one hand, the south lacks natural resources in the form of coal or hydro-electric power, though oil is found in Sicily; its land surface is mountainous and arid, and the agricultural possibilities are limited; because of the terrain, communications are poor and to improve them is an expensive job. History has exacerbated the problem: up to unification in the 1860s the Kingdom of Naples remained basically feudal, and thereafter the policy of protection encouraged the maintenance of inefficient agriculture at the same time as it permitted the infant industry of the north to grow. In the postwar period, too, the south's loss has been the north's gain: the constant flow of new labour northwards allowed northern industry to increase its productivity faster than the average wage rate. But the south itself remained massively under-represented in modern

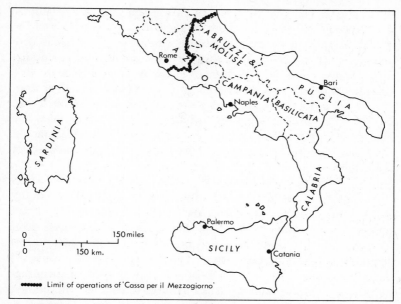

63. The Mezzogiorno. The southern half of Italy is one of the great problem regions of Europe. With income levels well below those of northern Italy and a poor economic structure based on subsistence agriculture, this has been a zone of out-migration to the northern cities and the rest of Europe. But the Mezzogiorno has witnessed an ambitious development programme since the Second World War.

industry, especially the critical growth sectors of engineering and chemicals. Most disturbingly, the Mezzogiorno failed to develop concentrations of large-scale industry that could exploit economies of scale and inter-industry linkages. The disequilibrium between Italy's own 'Golden Triangle' (Milan–Turin–Genoa, itself part of the wider European Golden Triangle) and the remainder of the country, but above all the south, became steadily more marked.

To try to remedy this imbalance, early in the postwar period Italy took a pioneer step in regional development. The Cassa per il Mezzogiorno, set up in 1950, originally had a heavily agricultural emphasis associated with the land-reform movement; it was to help the break-up of the traditional large estates of the region, and their

223

distribution among the peasants, by investment both in agricultural improvement and in better transportation. But in the course of the 1950s it became apparent that a broader-based strategy was needed, and emphasis shifted to industrial development through industrial credit at low rates (partly through specially created State funds), subsidies for industrial investment in buildings and plants, tax concessions, and even the taking of a share in the equity of private firms. By the late 1960s these forms of help together represented the highest level of total regional aid available in the Common Market, though still less than those given to firms in the development areas of the United Kingdom.

There were, however, quite severe limitations on the effectiveness of the policy. It was not accompanied, as in the United Kingdom, by negative controls on industrial growth in the prosperous north; all that was done was to establish that a certain fixed share of investment by public firms (40 per cent, and 60 per cent of new investment) should be in the south. Furthermore, since most of the help consisted of subsidies to investment, it had the paradoxical result of encouraging capital-intensive industry (such as large-scale power generation or oil refining) in an area where labour surpluses were the problem. Relatively late in the 1960s, some attempt was made to correct this by offering remission of social security payments on behalf of their employees to firms establishing themselves in the south – an incentive similar to the regional employment premium introduced in Britain at the same time.

The other limitation was a geographical one. Partly by deliberate intention – from 1957 the attempt was made to concentrate the provision of infrastructure, so as to encourage poles of growth – the main effects of the programme were seen on the western side of the mainland and in eastern and southern Sicily. As a result the eastern part of the mainland – the so-called heel of Italy – benefited relatively little, apart from the creation of a petro-chemical complex in the Bari–Brindisi–Taranto area. In this policy the planners were concerned to develop linked industries of a more labour-intensive kind, which would naturally associate themselves with the capital-intensive chemical and electrical plants already established in a few of the more developed urban areas of the Mezzogiorno. But it has been argued that such linkages are relatively unimportant in so under-developed an area as the south.

As in France, regional policy in Italy has exposed the dilemma of investment priorities. In the growing cities of the north and centre, there is an acute demand for investment in new infrastructure; the better economic conditions create the resources necessary for the purpose, especially in the private sector. But at the same time, this programme draws further construction workers from the south; it is done at a high cost, as such urban re-structuring always must; and it generates further problems of congestion in the long run. The answer may be a policy of developing counter-magnets in the south, along the lines of the French *métropoles d'équilibre*. Yet, apart from Naples and perhaps Palermo, the Mezzogiorno lacks the existing urban concentrations to provide the basis for such developments. They would have to be painstakingly built up, through the growth pole policy. And the question would remain whether such centres could really spread their effect widely enough to help the bulk of the rural population of the south. As in France and Germany, the question of the size and number of these centres, and their relation to the areas of greatest distress, is a crucial one.

Overall the record of postwar regional planning in Italy is far from encouraging. The south has failed to develop manufacturing industry on any scale, and still accounted for less than one fifth of the total national value-added-by-manufacture in the late 1960s; its *per capita* income was still less than half that of the industrial north-west. What industrial development had occurred was mainly in the capital-intensive sectors such as power, water and oil-refining rather than in modern, labour-intensive industry with capacity to develop linkages with other industry (such as chemicals or engineering). This in turn reflected the predominance of State public utility corporations in the development of the region. There had been a failure to develop large-scale industry. The agricultural policy had largely been a failure, with a remaining agricultural surplus population working for low incomes, with inadequate equipment, on poor land. Thus the experience of the Mezzogiorno seems to demonstrate that reliance on providing public infrastructure, plus investment by capital-intensive State corporations, is not enough to promote regional development;

either the available incentives to private industry to locate in the south were too weak or inertia was too strong, or both. A stronger policy, with some negative controls on industrial growth in the more prosperous regions closer to the heart of the Common Market, would seem to be necessary. Additionally, the geographical benefits of the development did not spread themselves widely enough through the south; to achieve that, it would have been necessary to couple the wider extension of the public infrastructure (particularly the new motorways) through the region with some planned coordination of private industrial investment. Perhaps the application of French methods of indicative planning, which was beginning at the end of the 1960s, will achieve this by involving private industry and public infrastructure planning in a common process. Such a policy might achieve the unquestioned main objective of planning in the Mezzogiorno: the provision of new industrial jobs for agricultural workers widely across the whole of the region.

Scandinavian City Region Planning

At the opposite end of Europe, the main interest for the planner is at the more local scale. Scandinavia as a whole is distinguished by having a remarkable degree of concentration of its population within a few major urban regions; about a quarter of the population of Denmark live in the Greater Copenhagen region, and about 40 per cent of the people of Sweden live in the three main urban areas of Greater Stockholm, Malmö–Hälsingborg, and Göteborg. This is a reflection of economic conditions that are almost precisely the reverse of those in southern Italy: agriculture is prosperous and highly capitalized, surplus agricultural labour has long since deserted the land for the cities, and the major urban regions have developed as centres of advanced industry, international trading nodes, and seats of administration. This development, however, has been relatively recent; the industrial revolution in these countries occurred much later than in Britain, so that (as in Germany) the development took place in the existing commercial cities rather than in newly developed coalfield towns. Because urban growth came so late – at the end of the nineteenth century and in the twentieth – these cities were able to develop effective town planning controls almost from the start. Soon after 1900, when it was still a small city of 100,000 people, the city of Stockholm began to buy the land all around, so as to guarantee properly planned development. By 1970, with a population of $1\frac{1}{2}$ million, Stockholm had the most comprehensively planned suburbs in the whole of western Europe.

Together with postwar Britain, these cities have thus contributed quite disproportionately to modern ideas about planning at the scale of the city region – regional/local planning, as we have called it throughout this book. Soon after Abercrombie's famous 1944 plan for Greater London (Chapter 5) with its emphasis on green belt controls on the growth of the city region and the development of new towns outside it, both Copenhagen and Stockholm produced plans based on different solutions to the problem of urban growth. Just as in London, the available controls were strong enough to guarantee that, in essentials, the plans were implemented.

Specifically, Copenhagen produced its now celebrated Finger Plan in 1948, four years after Abercrombie. The scale of the problem was much smaller: against 8 million in the Greater London conurbation and 10 million in the wider region, Greater Copenhagen at that time contained just over 1 million people. But the character of the problem was the same: like London, Copenhagen had grown in annular strips around a single core containing much of the employment, and a radial pattern of roads and public transport routes had reinforced the pattern. (With Copenhagen, however, the city took a semi-circular and not a circular form, because of the existence of a stretch of water – the Öresund – which separates Denmark from southern Sweden.) By 1948 development had reached a critical stage: the outer terminals of the public transport routes were already about 45 minutes from central Copenhagen, about the same time-distance as the outer suburban rail terminals in the much bigger area of London. Copenhagen could have dealt with the problem of future growth by using the London solution of green belt and new towns; instead its planners decided to increase accessibility to the central city, by new forms of higher-speed transport (suburban railways) along certain preferred axes or fingers, thus extending the 45-minute zone much farther from the city centre. Between these axes, wedges of open space would naturally be preserved in the lower-accessibility areas.

The plan was implemented, but Copenhagen – like many other European city regions – grew faster than had been expected; by 1960 the population had already reached 1.5 million, the long-term figure in the 1948 Finger Plan. The revised estimates showed that in the absence of comprehensive controls on industrial location, such as those in Britain, the total could swell further to 2.5 million by the end of the century; and rising space standards would create additional demand for land. With a city growing at such a rate, it was no longer possible to think merely of increasing accessibility to the centre; as in the Abercrombie London plan, jobs, too, must now decentralize. But the Copenhagen planners continued to reject the principle of the green belt and self-contained new town. Instead, they proposed new 'city sections', or major centres, developed on further extensions of the fingers; these would contain both manufacturing and service jobs, and the level of urban services would be appropriate to the average size of each major centre: approximately 250,000, the size of the largest provincial cities of Denmark. Thus jobs for many of the new residents would be provided near home; but for those who must still commute to the centre, very high-speed transport links along the fingers would be available. Overall, it was calculated by the Copenhagen Regional Planning Office that savings in travel costs for such a decentralized structure could be of the order of £50 million per annum.

A split developed over how the principle should be implemented. The four necessary new city sections could be grouped in one sector, with a concentration of the transport investments in that sector; in that case, the logical sector to choose would be that running westwards towards the town of Roskilde and south-westwards towards the town of Køge, both medium-sized country towns about 20 miles from the centre of Copenhagen. Alternatively, they could be developed in a number of different sectors, in order to relieve overloading in any one of them; thus, while the first development would take place towards the west and south-west, later emphasis would shift to the north-west. But the latter development would invade high-quality landscapes, important for recreation, which many planners thought

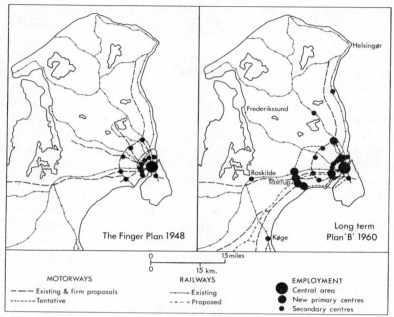

64. *Plans for Copenhagen: The 1948 Finger Plan, and the 1960 Plan 'B'.*
Copenhagen early reacted against the green belt ideas of the 1944 London plan,
substituting a design based on fingers of urban development with intervening green
fingers. The later plan extends the fingers with major new employment centres along
them, relieving pressure on the city.

should be conserved. Even deeper down, there was a division between those who wanted to encourage rapid decentralization of
people and jobs from the city of Copenhagen, and those who wanted
to encourage replanning and redevelopment within the city; this, of
course, was as much a political as a professional controversy. As a
provisional step, development during the 1960s was concentrated in
the south-west area, with the development of a new centre next to the
suburban railway station at Tåstrup, about 12 miles from the centre
of the city. By 1971, with a population of 1.8 million expected to
increase to 2.1 million by 1985, the regional planning council was
providing alternative sketches based on concentration along main

transportation corridors − not merely the radial lines, but also a north–south line bypassing the main urban agglomeration on the west side.

In Stockholm the story has been a simpler one − partly, perhaps, because until recently most of the new development took place within the city limits and on land actually owned by the city. An important fact is that the Stockholm agglomeration is smaller than the corresponding Copenhagen one: while Copenhagen reached 1.1 million people by 1945 and 1.5 million by 1960, expecting to reach 2.5 million by the year 2000, the corresponding figures for Stockholm are 850,000 in 1945, 1.2 million by 1960 and an expected 2.2 million by the end of the century. In fact, by the mid-1940s − when plans for comprehensive future development were under discussion − Stockholm had already spread to an average distance of about 8 miles from the centre, mainly on the basis of tramways; in certain directions, where suburban railway service was available, it extended farther. But in general, the city could not extend much farther on the basis of existing transport systems.

This was one critical fact in the plans produced in the late 1940s, which were embodied in a general plan for the city in 1952. While still a relatively small city by European standards, Stockholm determined that its future growth should be based on an underground railway system consisting of lines radiating from a central interchange station in the city centre, with stations at approximately half-mile intervals. Then, to ensure that the improved accessibility would not be followed by low-density suburban spread, as in London during the 1920s and 1930s, new suburbs would be deliberately planned around the new railway stations on the principle of local pyramids of density: higher densities around the stations, lower farther away. The railway station areas were also logically to become centres for shopping and other services, ordered according to a hierarchical principle; thus, the new shops would have the maximum number of customers easily placed within walking distance, in the surrounding high-density flats. Lastly, the system of suburban areas thus created would be physically defined by local green belts, which would wrap around and interpenetrate them.

These principles were faithfully followed in the rapid urban development of the 1950s and 1960s. By the mid-1960s the underground system extended over a 40-mile network, serving the new suburban areas, and bringing them all within a 40 minute ride of the city centre. At the railway stations, shopping centres were built at one of two levels in the hierarchy: local 'C' centres serving 10,000–15,000 people, mainly within walking distance of a station, and sub-regional 'B' centres serving several suburban areas, with 15,000–30,000 people within walking distance and another 50,000–100,000 served by underground, feeder bus or private car. To meet the rising demand for shopping by car, parking provision at the 'B' centres has

65. Plans for Stockholm: 1952 and 1966. The 1952 plan established the idea of planned suburban satellites, with a hierarchy of shopping centres, linked by the new underground railway system. This plan was largely implemented by the late 1960s, when a wider-ranging regional plan extended the principle through new developments along main-line railways and motorways radiating from the city.

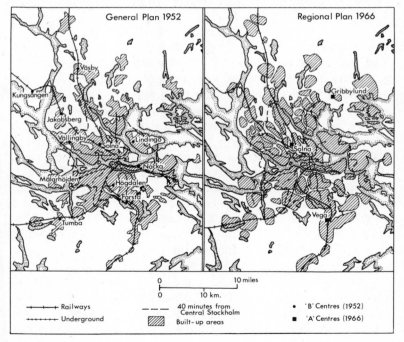

231

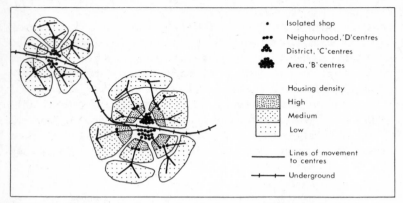

66. Stockholm: schematic diagram of a suburban group. The principle of the
hierarchy of suburban shopping centres in the 1952 plan. The bigger 'B' centres are
surrounded by high-density residential areas from which the inhabitants can walk to
the shops or to the underground station. Densities fall away from the centre toward
the edge.

sharply increased since the original design of the mid-1950s; and
these centres are served by high-capacity arterial highways, which
were being upgraded to motorway standard in the late 1960s and
early 1970s. Thus, in a typical suburban group, four local 'C' centres
will be grouped around their 'B' centre, the whole being tied together
both by the underground line (running usually above ground in the
suburbs) and by the highway system.

Together with the British new towns, the Stockholm suburbs
represent one of the most admired planning achievements of the mid-
twentieth century. But by the late 1960s, limitations were apparent.
One was that unlike the British new towns policy, the 1952 plan did
not ensure large-scale decentralization of jobs; indeed, in the early
1960s the central area (Hötorget), over and around the central
underground station, was reconstructed to provide for a big increase
in office jobs and shopping, while the new suburban areas failed to
become self-contained towns for working and living on the British
model. In a relatively small city with exceptionally good public
transport, this ideal was probably unattainable and undesirable. But
as the size of the developed area grew, a new scale of thinking was

necessary. This is the basis of the Greater Stockholm regional plan of 1966 – a plan which takes in not merely the city, but also adjacent suburban and rural areas up to 20 miles in all directions.

The 1966 plan starts from certain principles, which emerge from research studies and forecasts. One is that though space-using types of industry will seek peripheral locations, an increasing number of decision-making service industry jobs will still seek locations at or near the centre. Another is that people will seek more space in and around their homes, leading to a big extension of the total developed area. Taken together, these suggest an increasing demand for long-distance commuter journeys to the centre; and since the structure of central Stockholm will not allow for more than a small proportion of these to be made by private car, major investment in rail

67. Aerial view of Farsta, Sweden. The centre of one of the planned Stockholm suburbs, designed in the early 1960s. The underground station is seen in the right centre of the picture, surrounded by higher-density residential developments. The shopping centre is easily accessible by car, underground train or on foot from the apartment blocks.

transport is a priority. Because, however, the underground system is too slow to serve effectively those areas more than about 12 miles from the centre (the effective radius of the London system), future growth outside these limits must depend on faster long-distance commuter services on the main-line Swedish railways system. The new suburbs themselves will not concentrate so closely around the stations, but will take a more dispersed form, following feeder bus routes. Thus the future city region will tend to take a star-shaped form, with long fingers of development following the main-line railways and parallel national motorways, westwards to Södertäjle, northwards to Arlanda airport, south-westwards to Kungsängen. Along these axial extensions, most development will still take the form of small neighbourhoods built at pedestrian scale; groups of these neighbourhoods will constitute physical units, separated from each other by belts of open land that contain the major highways for longer-distance movement. Overall the urban structure will be rather discontinuous, with large areas of open land – which will be heavily used for summer homes and recreation – in contrast to the compact nineteenth-century town.

The Netherlands: Randstad and Regional Development

For the last case-study in this chapter, we return southwards to the heart of the Common Market. The western Netherlands sit in the centre of that smaller Golden Triangle, located near the north-western end of the EEC area, where such a high proportion of the economic life and urban population are concentrated. In the great port and industrial complex at the Rhine mouth (Rijnmond), the Dutch may fairly claim to have the principal point of exchange between the EEC and the rest of the world. By any reasonable standards of international comparison, here is one of the most important city regions of the European continent, with a population of close to $4\frac{1}{2}$ million.

It is, however, a city region of an unusual kind. 36 per cent of the population of the Netherlands is concentrated here, on 5 per cent of the land area – a degree of metropolitan concentration greater even

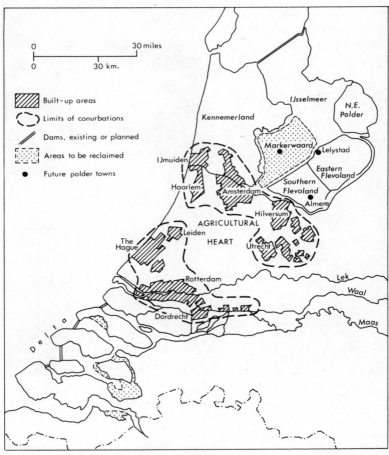

0   30 miles

0   30 km.

Built-up areas

Limits of conurbations

Dams, existing or planned

Areas to be reclaimed

Future polder towns

IJsselmeer

N.E. Polder

Kennemerland

Markerwaard

Lelystad

IJmuiden

Eastern Flevoland

Haarlem

Southern Flevoland

Amsterdam

Almere

Hilversum

AGRICULTURAL

The Hague

Leiden

HEART

Utrecht

Lek

Waal

Rotterdam

Delta

Maas

Dordrecht

68. Map of Randstad Holland. Urban development in the western Netherlands has taken the form of a horseshoe-shaped ring of cities, each performing specialized functions (government in the Hague, commerce in Rotterdam, shopping and culture in Amsterdam) with a central 'green heart' which it is planning policy to preserve.

69. View of Randstad Holland near Rotterdam. The mixture of new housing and intensive agriculture is typical of the Randstad – a polynuclear urban region in which town and countryside rapidly alternate.

than in Britain or in France. Yet the impression on the observer is certainly not one of metropolitan over-growth. This is because the Dutch metropolis, which the Dutch themselves call *Randstad* (or Ring City) *Holland*, takes the form of a ring of physically separate cities, running in an approximately horse-shoe-shaped line approximately 110 miles in length. In the 1960s it incorporated three cities – Amsterdam, Rotterdam and the Hague – with between $\frac{1}{2}$ million and 1 million people within their corporate limits; one – Utrecht – of 250,000; one – Haarlem – of 170,000; and one – Leiden – of nearly

100,000. Each is separated from its neighbours by a green zone, even though this is sometimes wafer-thin in the extreme western part of the horseshoe. All the cities look inwards into a central area of open space, carefully preserved by regional planning, which has earned the whole complex the nickname (in the words of the British planner Gerald Burke) of Greenheart Metropolis.

Unlike London or Paris or Stockholm, but like the Ruhr area of Federal Germany, the Randstad is therefore an example of a poly-centric metropolis. This quality is not merely physical; it is also functional, in that different cities within the complex perform broadly different functions. Thus government is concentrated in the Hague; the port, wholesale business and heavy industry in Rotterdam; finance, retailing, tourism and culture in Amsterdam; lighter manufacturing and more local service-provision in a number of smaller centres. By splitting functions into separate cities in this way, the Randstad avoids several of the more grievous problems of larger single-centred metropolitan cities: journeys to work tend to be shorter, traffic congestion less widespread. But there is one problem that the Netherlands share with their EEC neighbours: it is the problem of regional imbalance between the booming growth of the Randstad and the more laggardly development (or stagnation) of peripheral areas such as Limburg (in the southern part of the country) or Groningen (in the north-east, on the far side of the former Zuiderzee). Thus there have developed ambitious pro-grammes of regional development, in the form of incentives to locate in these regions, coupled with the provision of infrastructure; but as is usual throughout the Common Market, in contrast to Britain, this has not extended to an attempt to limit economic growth in the western Netherlands by actual restraints on new factories or other industry.

By the 1960s it appeared that the policy of encouraging the peripheral regions was having an effect; the proportion of national population growth in the western provinces was falling, though much of the increase was passing to immediately adjacent regions. But because of the very rapid natural growth of the whole population, this still meant a very rapid increase in the Randstad itself. Therefore, in order to encourage further decentralization, the government physical planning service proposed that the Randstad should grow outwards along lines of good accessibility, especially into areas where land reclamation or new lines of communication, or both, create new opportunities: outstanding among these are the reclaimed polders of the former Zuiderzee, where Lelystad, the central city, will have a population of some 100,000 by the end of the century, and the delta region south of Rotterdam. Other opportunities for growth will occur on older reclaimed land, in the northern tip of the province of North Holland adjacent to the west end of the Enclosing Dyke across the former Zuiderzee. The Randstad, thus extended, is expected to contain no less than ten concentrations of 250,000 and more people by the year 2000. The critical factor, therefore, is the way population and employment are distributed within these major concentrations, or city regions; and this is a main theme of the *Second Report on Physical Planning in the Netherlands*, published in 1966.

This report starts from several theses about present trends and future projections. Jobs are expected to decentralize somewhat from city centres, and even out of the Randstad altogether. Residential areas will spread out even more, because a majority of the population – 50–70 per cent – will wish to live in single-family homes. Densities can be lower in smaller urban units, but these will offer less variety of urban services. Whereas the smallest towns can accommodate fairly widespread car usage, this becomes progressively more difficult as the urban size increases; and above about $\frac{1}{2}$ million in size, the problems will increasingly demand rail-based systems for their solution. The urban structure which emerges from this analysis is based on a hierarchy of differently sized units, which could theoretically be combined in different ways: these range from a local unit for about 5,000 people, through a unit of about 15,000 and another of 60,000 to one of 250,000 which can offer a very complete range of urban services. (The two middle levels of this hierarchy seem similar in many respects to the 'C' and 'B' levels of the Stockholm planners' hierarchy.) The problem is how these units are to be combined on the ground.

The preferred solution, in the *Second Report*, is termed 'concentrated deconcentration'. Essentially, this is a compromise between the two extremes of concentration – which would give high accessibility to jobs and services, but poor environment for living – and deconcentration, which would use too much space. The preferred solution would offer a good choice in terms of job opportunities, housing patterns, modes of transport and types of recreation; and it is flexible, since it does not put a rigid shape on the future development of the city region. Units at each level of the hierarchy are separated, but are grouped closely together. In the biggest clusters (such as Amsterdam) all four levels are represented; in smaller ones

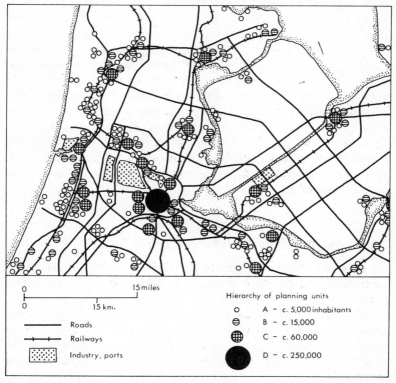

0   15 miles

0   15 km.

―――――― Roads

―+―+―+― Railways

[::::] Industry, ports

Hierarchy of planning units

O   A – c. 5,000 inhabitants

⊖   B – c. 15,000

⊕   C – c. 60,000

●   D – c. 250,000

70. *The principle of 'concentrated deconcentration', from the* Second Report on Physical Planning in the Netherlands. *For the future development of the Dutch Randstad, government planners suggest grouping the population into urban agglomerations which could then be allowed to decentralize to give a variety of living conditions – urban, suburban and semi-rural.*

(such as Haarlem) the top-most regional level is missing, but is available not far away. About one quarter of the population would live in the smallest units and about one quarter in the largest; the average housing density would be four times as great in the latter as in the former (about 24 dwellings per acre against 6). Applied to the Randstad, the scheme gives six top-level units (based on Dordrecht, Rotterdam, the Hague, Amsterdam, Utrecht and Arnhem), and some 40 centres at the next level, some of them independent, some in the form of suburbs attached to the bigger centres. The two lower levels of the hierarchy form either outer suburban centres for the biggest city regions, or independent villages and small town centres, or systems linking these regions along major routeways. The central green heart of the Randstad would be preserved to a remarkable degree, with only a few urban centres of the lowest status; all the emphasis is on outward development northwards, north-eastwards, eastwards and southwards. But it would be a mistake to treat this as another version of the axial plans of Stockholm or Copenhagen (or, for that matter, Paris); the future urban structure of the extended Randstad, based on the careful articulation of a number of differently sized building blocks, is a very complex one which has no real parallel elsewhere.

The European Experience: Some Conclusions

To generalize from such diverse cases may seem impossible. But in their different ways, the countries of the West European mainland do illustrate some common points.

The first concerns national/regional planning and the centre–periphery contrast which, in one form or another, recurs in all these countries. (Though it was not treated for lack of space, it can be found too in Scandinavia, in the problems of development of such areas as northern Jutland and the whole north of Sweden.) A real danger, which concerns many European planners, is that the European Economic Community may actually reinforce, rather than diminish, this imbalance. The original six signatories of the Treaty of Rome, and the three additional nations which joined in 1973, are clearly tied together by strong trade lines which connect up their major urban areas – lines like the Rhine and the more important Alpine passes, or the Rhone–Saône corridor plus the Mediterranean coast of France and northern Italy. The increased economic links between these urban areas, along the above lines, may have the effect of making the peripheral areas seem even more remote. Moreover, by increasing economic opportunity in the urban areas, they may accelerate the process of rural depopulation. This at any rate seems to have been the experience of the 1960s.

Against this, the peripheral areas may be able to offer low labour costs – an advantage that may become more telling, since with inflation labour costs tend to become a steadily larger proportion of total costs. British development areas in particular have some of the lowest money wages in Europe outside the Italian south, and firms from the European mainland may find this a considerable magnet if they can invest in efficient new plant – as American electronics firms, for instance, found in Scotland during the 1950s.

A second point about the national/regional scale concerns the measures which the European countries have taken to deal with the problem. Overall, with the exception of the French controls on new establishments in the Paris region, these countries have conspicuously avoided the sort of negative controls which the British have operated for industrial development since 1945 and for office development since 1964–5. They have relied heavily on inducements, generally in the form of grants and loans for building or equipment of new industry in the development areas, coupled with provision of State infrastructure, especially in the form of improved communications with the outside world. To varying extents they have also operated a policy of trying to channel aid into cities or towns which seemed to be favourably located within the development areas – though the expression of this policy varied very greatly, from the giant *métropoles d'équilibre* of France to the much more modest *Bundesbauorte* of Germany's remoter rural areas. The policies have met with mixed success, but in general it cannot be said that the results have been spectacular.

Here, however, a word of reservation is necessary: both the problems at the regional/local scale, and the solutions, are necessarily rather different from those in postwar Britain. The problem is one of agricultural depopulation rather than decline of industrial staples; the solution has been to encourage industry to move into the country-side, rather than to build up new industry to replace the old. Only in a few places, such as Germany's Ruhr area, have the problems of industrial adaptation arisen on the mainland of western Europe. Where they have arisen, an international agency – the European Coal and Steel Community, a precursor of the Common Market itself – has been closely concerned, as in future years it will in Britain.

A significant point about the European Communities, however, is how slow they have been to develop a common regional policy. The Treaty of Rome allows the EEC Commission to challenge policies which distort competition. But this cannot affect a national policy which is non-discriminatory with regard to the national origin of the product and which does not distort national competition. Because of this, as we have seen, different EEC countries have vigorously pursued various forms of aid to industry without interference. There are now firm Commission recommendations as to the extent of aid to industries in needy regions outside a central zone; ironically the limits of these regions have not yet been closely defined, though by 1973 there was agreement that the critical criteria should be unemployment, income per head, migration and over-dependence on agriculture. And though the EEC Social Fund provides help for retraining and resettling workers, and the Agricultural Fund can now be diverted to provide for regional development, these supplement national policies rather than by-passing them.

During the 1970s, as the EEC moves towards complete fiscal and economic union, it is certain that regional policies will become a bone of contention – if only because, at that stage, the community itself must take from member countries their cherished power to control their own economies. The 1972 proposals of the Commission – a Guarantee Fund for regional development and a Society for Regional Development with direct investment powers – represent a first, tentative attempt to grapple with these emerging problems.

On the regional/local scale, all these countries have faced the problem of the continued growth of large metropolitan areas. Though there are no parallels elsewhere in Europe to the scale of problem represented by London or Paris, the solutions adopted for smaller-scale metropolitan cities – such as Copenhagen or Stockholm – may prove apposite for many other cities of similar size in other countries. Most significantly, perhaps, the experience of multi-centred metropolitan areas, such as the Dutch Randstad or the Rhine–Ruhr region, provides some possible object-lessons for the future internal organization of very large city regions. Certainly, in so far as comparisons can ever be meaningful between such individual and varied urban areas, these polycentric urban regions do seem to avoid some of the acuter problems that afflict their monocentric equivalents, such as London, Paris or New York.

Further Reading

Useful general sources are: Peter Hall, *The World Cities* (World University Press, 1966), Chapters 3–5, on Paris, Randstad Holland, and Rhine–Ruhr; and on Amsterdam, Copenhagen, Paris, Rome and Stockholm: William A. Robson and D. E. Regan, *Great Cities of the World* (Allen & Unwin, second edition, 1972). *The Mastery of Urban Growth: Report of the International Colloquium, Brussels, 2–4 December 1969* (Brussels: Mens en Ruimte, 1971) contains useful reports on planning in several European countries. *Economic Planning and Policies in Britain, France and Germany* (PEP, 1968) is a useful source on national/regional planning.

On particular countries or cities, there are a number of important sources. For French regional planning: Lloyd Rodwin, *Nations and Cities* (Boston: Houghton Mifflin, 1970), Chapter 6, and Niles M. Hansen, *French Regional Planning* (Edinburgh University Press, 1968). For Swedish urban planning and urban studies: Ella Ödmann and Gun-Britt Dahlberg, *Urbanization in Sweden: Means and Methods for the Planning* (Stockholm: Allmänna Förlaget, 1970). For the Netherlands: Gerald Burke, *Greenheart Metropolis* (Macmillan, 1966) is useful.

Additionally, important material is found in articles in the journal *Regional Studies*, including: Peter Hall, 'Planning for Urban Growth: Metropolitan Area Plans and their Implications for South-East England', *Regional Studies*, 1 (1967), pp. 101–34; A. Mayhew, 'Regional Planning and the Development Areas in West Germany', *Regional Studies*, 3 (1969), pp. 73–9; and S. K. Holland, 'Regional Under-development in a Developed Economy: the Italian Case', *Regional Studies*, 5 (1971), pp. 71–90.

9. Planning in the United States since 1945

To many Europeans, even well-informed ones, planning in the United States is a contradiction in terms. The country is seen as a land where rampant individualism provides the only guide to economic development or physical use of the land. Planning, either in the sense of positive programmes for the regeneration of depressed regions, or in the sense of control over land use in the interest of the community, is thought to be virtually non-existent. Thus the United States is seen as a land where the phenomenally rapid settlement process has been accompanied by unprecedented destruction of irreplaceable natural resources; where extreme affluence marches hand in hand with large-scale pockets of poverty, often close by; where urban areas sprawl unregulated into fine open country, leaving a trail of ugliness and economic inefficiency. Fiercely critical as it may be, this is the stereotype which many European professional planners, and many intelligent European citizens, hold.

It contains both elements of truth and elements of complete distortion. Of course, pollution and destruction of resources and depressed regions and urban sprawl do exist – on a much larger absolute scale than in western Europe. But at the same time the United States in the postwar era possesses a vast and complex system of planning agencies and of planning measures – both of a positive and a negative kind. Furthermore, just as in Europe, these operate at two distinct levels: first, the level of national/regional economic development planning; and secondly, the level of regional/local physical development planning. Both systems have had profound effects on the pattern of postwar economic and physical change in the United States; though, it can be said at the outset, some of them do not seem to have been very effective in relation to their scale and cost.

More perhaps than in any European country, because of the vast scale of the continental United States, these two levels of planning can be regarded as distinct. Indeed, one major recurring criticism of United States planning is that while economic planning tends to deal with very large regions, physical planning is excessively local and small-scale; the intermediate level of planning for the city region, though much written about and reported upon, is not very effective in practice. So the two scales of planning can usefully be treated at distinct levels.

Economic Development Problems

Though international comparisons are notoriously difficult and possibly misleading, it appears clear that regional disparities in economic development are greater in the United States than in western Europe. In Britain, for instance, official statistics show that if the median national personal income is set at 100, regional variations (in 1969–70) range from over 118 (in Hertfordshire) to 80 (in County Tyrone, Northern Ireland). In the United States, the range of average family income in the early 1960s is from 122 (in Connecticut) to 51 (in the Deep South State of Mississippi). Of course, the size and geographical grain of the two analyses is very different; if the whole of western Europe were taken as an apter comparison with the United States, the discrepancies (as between Sweden at one extreme and the Italian south on the other) would appear much more extreme. But in addition it must be remembered that the American analysis is in terms of States, which are often large and very varied areas; there are great differences in economic development between the New York City area and up-state New York, between the Detroit–Flint axis and northern Michigan, or between the Dallas–Houston zone of Texas and the north-western part of that State. Whatever the scale and the grain, levels of economic development and of personal income remain stubbornly large in the United States.

By and large, these variations can be related to the character of the economy. The high-income areas of the United States tend to be urban regions specializing in the newer, more technically sophisticated manufacturing or service industries; they include the major urban areas of the western States with their dependence on the aerospace industrial complex (Seattle, Los Angeles, Phoenix), the Texan cities of Houston, Dallas and Fort Worth with their combination of petro-chemicals and newer engineering industries, and the Great Lakes industrial area. Conversely, and more relevantly here, the low-income areas tend to be zones where the employment base is declining, either under the influence of falling demand or of increasing efficiency of production; in some cases, too, the basic industry makes extensive use of rather low-skilled, poorly paid labour. One extensive group of such areas includes the agricultural regions of the south-east (the Old South) and south central parts of the country; these include both the former slave plantation areas which were converted to sharecropping of cotton (or to a lesser extent tobacco) after the Civil War, and the mountain areas of the Appalachians and Ozarks which have traditionally been inhabited by poor subsistence farmers. In many parts of this vast zone, which sweeps in a great crescent from the Carolinas through the Deep South States of Georgia, Alabama, Louisiana, Mississippi, Kentucky and Tennessee to Arkansas and eastern Oklahoma, average personal incomes are one quarter or less of the American national average; indeed, parts of these areas exist largely outside the mainstream of American life, resembling quite closely the traditional peasant economies of Europe. Overlapping geographically with this zone is another type of depressed area: the declining mining communities of the central Appalachians, extending from Pennsylvania and West Virginia down into eastern Kentucky. Within this zone, too, are many cities and towns dependent on iron, steel and heavy engineering, whose income is considerably lower than the national average. Other industrial areas, where demand has fallen or competition from other regions has been severe, may also exhibit the symptoms of decline; among them, the textile towns of New England are the most notable.

This regional analysis, however, omits the important fact that income levels may vary locally. Characteristically, and increasingly, many American urban areas display the pattern of a low-income inner core – often extending over a fairly wide area, to embrace most, if not all, of the incorporated city, and consisting largely of those residential areas developed before the Second World War – surrounded by higher-income suburbs. The explanation of this pattern lies both in economic and in social causes. Though in most American cities there is still a considerable concentration of highly paid managerial and professional jobs in the central business districts of the cities, increasingly these jobs are migrating to suburban business or research centres; the better-paid, more highly skilled factory jobs have already decentralized in large part. In any case, even if the jobs remain in the cities, the people who work in them live in far-flung suburbs, commuting over increasingly long distances each day. This is not a new phenomenon; it goes back almost to the beginnings of rapid urban growth in the United States, around the mid-nineteenth century. But since the Second World War it has accelerated under two influences: the suburban building boom, which will be described later in this chapter, and the mass migration of low-income, low-skill workers from the declining agricultural areas of the South (and, in the case of New York City, the island of Puerto Rico in the Caribbean) into the inner areas of the great northern cities. Again, the latter phenomenon is not new; traditionally, poor immigrants to America first established themselves in the inner city, moving out as they acquired income and knowledge. But because the vast majority of the new immigrants are black, they suffer from race prejudice in their attempts to follow this traditional route outwards; and since the higher-paid jobs move out while the lower-paid, less skilled jobs tend to remain, they tend increasingly to be trapped in a vicious circle of inner urban poverty and lack of opportunity.

In summary, therefore, the contemporary United States presents a picture of islands of relative poverty amidst general affluence. Though it needs to be stressed that this is relative poverty – by world standards, the poor in America are certainly quite well off – nevertheless, for people actually experiencing it, this poverty will be intensely felt simply because people will judge themselves by the standards they see in their own society generally. These islands of poverty occur within two scales: first, on the broad regional level, in wide tracts of the southern and Appalachian States; and secondly, on the local level, within the inner cores of many metropolitan areas. These are the problem areas with which any development programme will need to deal.

Machinery for Economic Development

Until the 1960s, the machinery for regional economic development in the United States tended to be quite local and *ad hoc* in character, even if it resulted from initiatives from the Federal government. Thus the great scheme for regenerating the Tennessee Valley, which runs through seven States in the heart of the South, was a highly successful piece of integrated development planning, which combined power, water supply, flood and erosion regulation, recreational planning, new industry, and agricultural development; but, though a centre-piece of the Roosevelt administration's New Deal policy of the mid-1930s, it was not emulated on any similar scale elsewhere. After the Second World War, as in Britain, the impetus for regional development tended to fade under the influence of general full employment and widespread affluence. But, again as in Britain, there was a general realization that – at any rate in times of economic recession – many areas were not sharing in the general prosperity. Thus, by the early 1960s, two thirds of the labour-market areas of the United States had unemployment rates of 6 per cent or more.

The early attempts to deal with these disparities took a familiar form. The Area Redevelopment Administration (ARA), set up in 1961 within the Department of Commerce to help areas with high unemployment or low local incomes, was empowered to grant loans to small businesses and to make loans or grants (up to 100 per cent of cost) in respect of public infrastructure; as a condition of help, a local region must prepare an overall economic development programme (OEDP). The Public Works Acceleration Act, in 1962, gave the ARA still further funds for grants to provide infrastructure. But there was no overall strategy for distributing help from the centre, partly because there was too little research into needs and, because of constant political pressure, the constant tendency was for help to be spread too widely to achieve the necessary impact. There was an over-emphasis on expensive construction projects and not enough attack on the problem of aiding individuals to readapt themselves to economic change through retraining programmes.

By 1965 this criticism was being faced; the Public Works and

Economic Development Act, in that year, converted the Area Development Administration into an Economic Development Administration, with bigger funds which were to be concentrated in a restricted number of major regions whose character was defined in the Act. First there were redevelopment areas with serious economic problems and with median family income 40 per cent or more below the national average; secondly there were economic development areas, combining at least two redevelopment areas, and a substantial city capable of acting as a growth centre for them; and thirdly, regional planning commissions could be set up for areas which overran State lines, such as the Ozarks, the Upper Great Lakes and the Four Corners (Arizona–New Mexico–Colorado–Utah) in the western mountains and deserts (Illustration 71). Even then, though, the experience was still that help was scattered among too many small areas and small cities; while most of the actual help was too concentrated on loan capital subsidies to businesses rather than direct help to the disadvantaged; that, where such help was available, it was geared too much towards training for the sorts of low-skill, low-pay jobs that were traditional in those depressed regions; that programmes often did not help the most disadvantaged groups; and that the machinery for implementation, which required widespread local agreement, was weak.

The Appalachian Regional Development Act of 1965, which established the Appalachian Regional Commission, in many ways represented a more hopeful experiment. Here, in this great upland mass which stretches from New England to the Deep South and which separates the huge concentration of population on North America's East Coast from the almost equally dense grouping in the mid-western States, the problems were both physical and human. The natural resources of the region, once extremely rich – resources of timber, soil, coal and other minerals – had been removed by ruthless exploitation. The people were depressed and impoverished by centuries of isolation; their incomes were among the lowest in the United States and their standards of education, health and housing were often abysmally low. To grapple with these problems the Commission supervised the injection into the region of no less than $679 million in the years 1965–9 (inclusive) alone. But it is significant

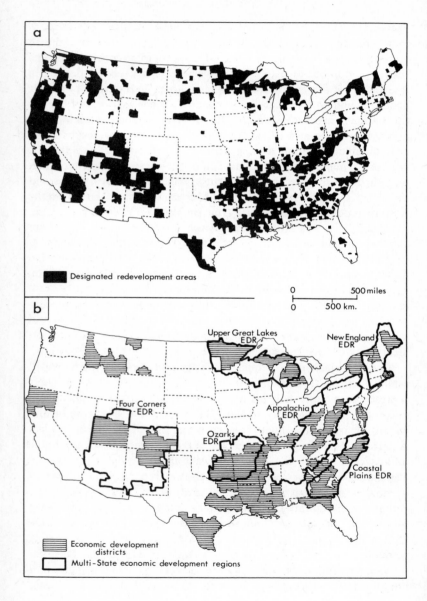

a

Designated redevelopment areas

0   500 miles
0   500 km.

b

Upper Great Lakes EDR

New England EDR

Four Corners EDR

Appalachia EDR

Ozarks EDR

Coastal Plains EDR

Economic development districts

Multi-State economic development regions

250

that no less than $470 million went on an ambitious programme of super-highway construction, the avowed objective of which was to increase both the accessibility of the region to the outside world and the contacts within the different parts of the region itself. Doubtless this was a useful objective, but the concentration on expensive construction contracts seems to represent a real distortion of investment; once again, as so often in the history of American regional programmes, the benefit passed mainly to outside business interests rather than to the hard-pressed people of the region. It is only fair to say, though, that educational programmes (especially vocational training), health and housing improvements were also part of the total package; and that welfare of the population was a more prominent objective than in the ARA or EDA programmes earlier discussed. Administratively, too, the Appalachian programme broke new ground in developing joint Federal–State developments; and it provided a model for other regional exercises in other depressed areas, such as the Ozarks, the Four Corners region in the mountainous area of the west (where poverty was a problem among the many Indians on the reservations) and the coastal plains of the South where poor black sharecroppers had similar problems.

One important point about all these regional programmes – threatened with virtual closure by the Nixon administration in 1973 – is that by ear-marking aid for particular areas, they represented a conscious attempt to break away from the bad American tradition of spreading help thinly among all States and all areas, however different their problems. But all of them, like the ARA/EDA programmes, seem to have been conceived very largely in terms of the broader regional problem. By definition, in the United States this was difficult to solve because of the great size of such regions and their isolation from the areas of real economic dynamism; thus, though the Appalachian Commission made a conscious attempt to develop a policy of growth centres within its region, these were still many hundreds of miles distant from the main industrial areas of the

---

71. Area development programmes in the United States. During the 1960s the Federal government developed a wide variety of assistance and development programmes, concentrated especially on the more remote rural areas where regional incomes were below the national average.

country to which migrants were still moving. Almost ignored, on the other hand, was the growing and perhaps more readily soluble problem of localized poverty within the major urban areas. The great non-white migration from the rural South to the Northern cities, which doubled the black population in the Northern States between 1940 and 1966, ironically provided a potential solution to the biggest of the major regional problems by transferring poor agriculturalists *en masse* to areas of greater economic opportunity; but only at the expense of distributing it in smaller pockets within the cities. Yet, perhaps because of lack of recognition and perhaps because of political apathy, the problem does not seem to have been grasped clearly by the Federal government.

Metropolitan Growth and Change

The postwar United States, in fact, has witnessed two great human migrations: one, of black workers and their families from the mainly rural areas of the South to the Northern cities; a second, of white families from the central cities of metropolitan areas to their suburban rings. In quantitative terms, the second was the more important. Whereas 1,457,000 blacks migrated from the South between 1950 and 1960, and another 1,216,000 between 1960 and 1970, the corresponding estimates for white migration to the suburbs were 5.8 and 4.9 million. Together, the two migrations resulted in a progressive occupation of Northern cities by non-white populations. In the central cities of metropolitan areas of 1 million and more people, the proportion of non-whites doubled between 1950 and 1970, reaching 25 per cent; the twelve largest central cities by then contained two thirds of the black population outside the South. Chicago had 14 per cent non-white population in 1950, 23 per cent in 1960 and 33 per cent in 1970; Washington, with the highest non-white proportion of any major city, had 35 per cent in 1950, 54 per cent in 1960 and no less than 71 per cent in 1970.

The motive for both migrations was the same: improved economic and social status. But it operated in very different ways in each case. Whereas many of the blacks who migrated north did so out of necessity — their traditional economic base, sharecropping, had been suddenly removed by the development of cotton-picking machinery in the early 1950s — the new white suburbanites were voluntary movers in search of better housing and general environment. Furthermore, though the blacks moved unaided, the suburban white migration was powerfully assisted by Federal policies. The Federal Housing Administration (FHA) had been created in 1934, a product of the Roosevelt New Deal; in 1949 the Housing Act established a Housing and Home Finance Agency (HHFA) to coordinate the activities of FHA and other official agencies. From the start, the emphasis of HHFA was on purchase of new homes; loans were easily available, on a 10 per cent down payment basis from FHA, and interest rates were low at first. Further, FHA established standards of construction and of appraisal, which became current throughout the building industry and which improved the quality and reliability of new home construction.

Logically, the new housing was built on land that was previously undeveloped. The widespread use of the septic tank — a device which is normally restricted to rural areas in Britain — together with almost universal car ownership, allowed a great deal of freedom in location; in particular, it meant that housing areas did not need to be as compact as in the interwar years. Thus sprawl developed in two ways: first, the house itself, and even more so its garden space (in American English, 'yard space') tended progressively to occupy more land, so that typical net residential densities dropped from ten to six and finally to between one and four houses to the acre; and secondly, the individual housing subdivisions tended to leap-frog, leaving areas of undeveloped land between them. Such far-flung development would have been inconceivable without mass dependence on the private car; but in turn the pattern encouraged further scatter, since the new suburban areas were typically too far from the city to make use of its shops or services. Thus big new shopping centres developed in, or between, the new suburbs, rivalling the older urban centres in scale and generally excelling them in design. Jobs tended to decentralize too; in particular, blue collar manufacturing jobs and those service jobs that were tied to the needs of the suburban population. After the mid-1950s an ambitious programme of inter-

72. Levittown-Fairless Hills, New Jersey, USA. Postwar suburban development in the Atlantic urban region. Low-density single-family homes occupy subdivisions, with much leap-frogging of urban development over patches of vacant land. Commuting and movement generally in such areas depend almost exclusively on the private car.

State highway (motorway) construction greatly improved the case of making long suburb-to-suburb work journeys, thus further aiding the trend.

The suburban housing boom certainly performed a valuable service for many millions of Americans – in particular, those marrying and founding families, who made up record totals in the 1950s. Such people – ranging from highly paid managerial and professional groups, through the range of white collar clerical workers, to the more skilled factory workers – enjoyed solid benefits from life in

73. Milford Center, Milford, Connecticut. Located in the fast-growing suburban zone outside New York City, this is a good example of the suburban, edge-of-town, new shopping centres that have developed on a large scale for car-based shoppers in the United States since the Second World War.

suburbia, whatever popular sociology might say by way of criticism. They moved straight into new, well-equipped housing in generally pleasant neighbourhoods (though in many cases, because of insensitive bulldozing of natural vegetation, less pleasant than they might have been); with neighbours they felt they could relate to; and, with constantly rising prices, they found hire purchase a useful hedge against inflation. In fact, the main criticism of the new suburbia was not that it was inadequate, ugly, or particularly inefficient – for it was not, given the preferences and the life styles of these who lived in it;

rather, it is that the benefits were restricted to too narrow a spectrum of the American population. Comparing average mortgage payments with figures of annual earnings, it is not difficult to calculate that the possibility of buying a new house has been beyond the capacity of at least the whole lower half of the income scale. True, many of these could still hope to buy second-hand houses in the older residential neighbourhoods of the central city or the inner suburbs. But a substantial proportion were condemned to live in rented housing which, because of failings in the tax laws, tended to be left by its owners to decay. In contradistinction to Britain and many other European countries, the United States does not cushion this group to any extent by providing new public housing; over the period 1945–70, less than 3 per cent of all non-farm housing starts were in the public sector, as against about 57 per cent in Britain. Nor, until the Housing and Urban Development Act of 1970, was there any Federal funding to develop new towns on the British model.

In fact, many Federal programmes actually rebounded against the disadvantaged low-income inner city resident; urban renewal programmes, carried through under the 1949 Housing Act, became synonymous in many cases with bulldozing the homes of low-income residents, and there was all too little provision of alternative housing for those displaced. The proposals for rehabilitation of existing housing under the 1954 Act – designed to meet criticisms of the earlier urban renewal programmes – failed to have the expected impact on the condition of inner-city housing. In the 1960s, it is true, policies were redesigned to focus help on central city residents; more Federal mortgage aid was concentrated on cheaper central city housing, and the Federal government took the lead in trying to coordinate welfare and social service programmes for low-income families there.

This trend towards social planning, which is well marked in the later 1960s, really indicates recognition that the problems of American low-income city residents – above all the non-white ones – have to be viewed as a whole; housing and physical planning form only a small part of the bundle of policies needed to deal with a complex problem. The report of the Kerner Commission on Civil Disorders, in 1968, summarized a good deal of useful evidence on this point. Black median incomes, they pointed out, were only 58 per

74. A ghetto area. This is fairly typical of the racial ghettos that exist on a large scale in the inner areas of many American cities. Black people – many of whom have moved from the rural South since 1945 – find it difficult to escape into the suburbs where the better housing and job opportunities are found.

cent of white median incomes; and the gap was increasing. Very-low-income families, counted as below the official poverty line, constituted 32 per cent of all non-white families in 1966, and about two thirds of this group appeared to be making no gains in income at all. Unemployment, which is higher among non-whites, contributes to this; but the main cause is simply the fact that many more non-whites are in unskilled manufacturing or service jobs. In addition, nearly one quarter of non-white families were fatherless in 1966; and it must be remembered that non-white families are, on average, larger than white ones. Many black families are thus caught in a vicious circle of poor job opportunities, poor education, and family breakdown. It is small wonder that indices of social malaise – such as crime (especially violent crime), illegitimate births, drug abuse and poor health – are much higher in those areas where non-whites are concentrated. Within large urban areas, over 60 per cent of non-whites (as of 1967) lived in 'poverty areas' defined on an index of deprivation that included low family income, children in broken homes, persons with poor educational achievement, males in unskilled jobs, and sub-standard housing. To try to cope with these problems, the welfare budgets of the cities rose to levels that could only be described as staggering. In particular, police and fire services, aid to dependent children and educational expenditures were disproportionately high in cities like New York, Chicago, Boston and Detroit.

Many non-whites, therefore, found themselves trapped in a vicious circle of social problems and rising expenditures from which they could not escape. Racial disturbances in the cities during 1967–8 intensified the desire of many blacks to leave, but hardened the barriers against them in the white suburbs. Continued migration from the South, coupled with a high rate of natural increase, was expected to make many major cities more than half black by 1980. To make matters even more problematic, by the 1960s employment as well as white population was leaving the cities for the suburbs; not only did this intensify the cities' financial crisis, but it reduced the pool of well-paying jobs available to the black city populations within easy travelling distance. As the proportion of black population in the cities rose and as frustration increased, militant blacks urged their own version of apartheid as a solution – particularly since by the late 1960s black control in the central cities at last seemed a feasible political proposition.

In this impasse, the only feasible liberal solution was somehow to bring the black cities and the white suburbs into some sort of closer relationship. As in most other countries, the political geography of the twentieth-century United States has long ceased to represent social or economic reality. City boundaries have been hardly extended for half a century, during which time suburban expansion has extended the effective urban area many times. From the start, it suited many suburban communities to go their own way and make their own rules; in the 1950s and 1960s, as the cities plunged into their vicious circle of poverty and civic bankruptcy, to maintain independence became for the suburbs a matter of survival. Consequently, though intellectual voices were raised in favour of metropolitan governments which would plan city and suburbs as a single unit for the common good of both, real-life experiments in this direction were few. Only Greater Miami went for full-scale metropolitan government, while Minneapolis and its suburbs adopted a looser form of federation.

Planning Powers and Planning Policies

This raises the critical question of the machinery of planning, its geographical basis, and its effectiveness. To discuss this for a European readership is difficult, because in many ways the American system of government is unlike that in other countries. In the first place, it is Federal; and traditionally matters of domestic importance, which would certainly include planning and local government, have been matters left to the States to determine. (The township system of government in the New England States, for instance, is quite different from the county system used elsewhere.) The power and influence of the Federal government in domestic affairs, especially through the use of Federal funds, has admittedly increased very strikingly since the Second World War – in this particular area of interest, above all in the 1960s. But State differences must constantly be borne in mind. Secondly, American local government is typically less tidy and more complex than European; services are supplied by a multiplicity of *ad hoc*, single-purpose agencies, such as planning commissions, boards of education or sewer commissions, so that a citizen may live within the area of a score of different local government units, some of them with different boundaries. Since these agencies are separately controlled (and separately elected) there is no logical reason for them to cooperate; very often they are at loggerheads. Coupled with the very strong role of private agencies in the urban development process, this means that there are very many more different agents or actors associated with urban growth and change than in the typical European situation; a fact that makes the whole process both more difficult to describe, and more difficult in practice to control.

At the top level there is the Federal government agency for housing and planning: the Department of Housing and Urban Development (HUD). This is the nearest equivalent to a European

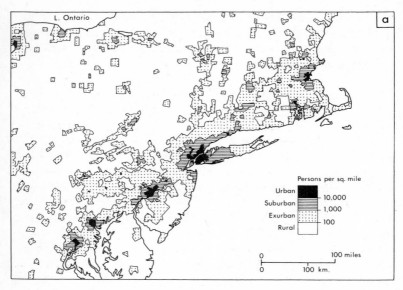

L. Ontario

Persons per sq. mile

Urban
Suburban
Exurban
Rural

10,000
1,000
100

0   100 miles
0   100 km.

a

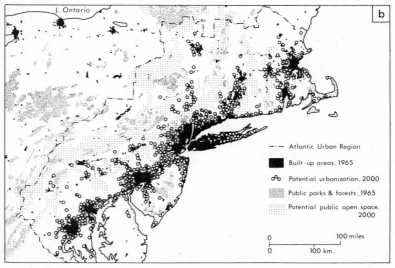

L. Ontario

—·— Atlantic Urban Region

■   Built-up areas, 1965

⍺   Potential urbanization, 2000

   Public parks & forests, 1965

   Potential public open space, 2000

0   100 miles
0   100 km.

b

department such as Britain's old Ministry of Housing and Local Government before its incorporation in the Department of the Environment; it deals neither with transportation, which is handled by a separate Department of Transportation (DOT), nor with national parks, which since their inception have been traditionally a responsibility of the Department of the Interior. But perhaps the most significant point about HUD is that it was set up only in 1965, after fairly bitter political opposition; up to that time, there was actually no central agency at Federal level handling the complex of problems presented by urban growth. HUD inherited the responsibility for a variety of agencies concerned with housing, themselves brought under the umbrella of the Housing and Home Finance Organization in 1949; but perhaps more importantly, it was given extensive new responsibilities in the field of metropolitan area planning, which it has pursued with energy. In the years since 1965, HUD first became responsible for the Model Cities programme authorized by Congress in 1966, under which cities were aided by Washington to adopt a comprehensive, across-the-board, integrated approach to problems of housing, renewal, job training, education, health and welfare in poor city neighbourhoods. Then in 1968 HUD turned to the creation of new communities with Federal aid. The Housing and Urban Development Act of that year made funds available to cover the difficult transitional period when heavy investments were needed but when returns were low. A further Housing and Urban Development Act, in 1970, gave modest extra funds for new community creation. The specific aims were to channel a significant part of future metropolitan population growth – estimated in 1968 as 75 million by the year 2000 – away from contiguous suburbs and towards reasonably self-contained communities; and to work towards a social balance by ensuring reasonable proportions of low-income and non-white residents.

---

75. The Atlantic Urban Region: (a) Population densities c. 1960; (b) Potential development by the year 2000. The Atlantic seaboard from Boston to Washington – 'Megalopolis', in the term of the geographer Jean Gottmann – is one of the greatest massings of humanity in the world, with over 30 million people. It is an example of a highly complex multinuclear urban structure, where the growth of one city impinges on that of another.

HUD can exert considerable leverage on local governments across the United States by its control over Federal funds. Even before it came into existence in 1962, it had been laid down that to obtain Federal highway moneys, local areas would have to engage in a comprehensive planning exercise. Similar Federal funds were available for wider metropolitan planning under Section VII of the 1954 Housing Act; later, progressively during the early 1960s, comprehensive metropolitan plans were made mandatory for any authority that required Federal funds for a wide variety of purposes – whether for sewers, open space, education, or urban renewal. But HUD does not have the same power as its British counterpart: the power to require local authorities to submit plans (and regular revisions of those plans) to it for approval. Nor may it designate land for a new community, with consequent restrictions on the amount of public liability for compensation, as happens in Britain. As so often in American government, the powers are permissive rather than regulatory.

Indeed, it would be difficult to see how this could be otherwise. Even national programmes funded largely by Federal funds, such as the 41,000-mile, $41,000 million Interstate Highways Program, must be executed by the individual State governments. Powers of compulsory purchase for the creation of new communities would have to be exercised with the States' approval, through their courts. Local government structure itself, as previously indicated, varies from State to State. Any Federal department is, therefore, necessarily more circumscribed than its British equivalent.

At local government level, two complications obtrude. The first is the multiplicity of agencies; this means that even where a number of separate boards or commissions operate over the same geographical area (usually a county) their operations are not likely to be coordinated in any way by a central managing unit, as would occur in the average British or European local government unit. Thus the sewer commission may have as big a potential influence on urban development as the so-called planning commission; so may the commissioner for highways; but all these are separate agencies, each going its own way independent of (and sometimes in spite of) the others. The other complication, exceedingly difficult to grasp for the average European, is that the use of land may be affected by two different operations, planning and zoning; but that these two are in principle (and not seldom also in practice) separate. In 1968 there were over 10,000 local government units in the United States with a planning board or similar organization; but the great majority of these had either no staff, or a completely inadequate one, and the plans they prepare generally lack legal status or binding power. If there is a central governing board for the country, that board will not be governed by the decisions of the planning board; nor, of course, will any specialized agency. In this situation the sewer agency may be in effect the real planning authority rather than the nominal planning board.

In fact the real core of the American system of land-use control is not planning, but zoning. But it is formally separated from the planning system; it is administered by a separate zoning commission for each local authority area, it need take no account of the plan (if any), and it is essentially a limited and negative system of control over changes in land use. By definition, zoning is a device for segregating different types of land use, usually on a rather coarse-grained basis. What zoning cannot do in practice is to stop a potential developer from developing altogether; he must be left with some profitable development of the land. This, essentially, is because the American system – in contradistinction to the British one – does not involve any method of compensation for lost development rights, such as was embodied in Britain's historic 1947 Town and Country Planning Act. Rather, the American zoning system rests on the concept of *police power* – a term hardly known in Britain – which is a general residual power of government to pass laws in the interests of general public health, safety and welfare. Zoning, in a fairly rough and ready way, has achieved some of the same objectives in practice as land-use planning in Britain; it has segregated land uses thought to be incompatible, such as factory industry and homes. But by definition, it cannot protect open countryside against development; that could usually be assured only by public purchase as a national or State park or similar facility. In practice, zoning is more subject to abuse than land-use control in Britain; notoriously, if the landowner or prospective developer is persistent enough, he can usually get the change he wants. So, with ineffective planning and only semi-effective zoning, controls over the physical growth and change within urban areas are much weaker in the United States than in Britain – or many other parts of Europe. The developer and, behind him, the consumer of his product, is still sovereign in a way that in Britain he is not.

Some Conclusions

The results, in the eyes of many European and not a few American observers, are deplorable. These critics quote the waste of land and the inefficiency represented by continuing low-density, leap-frogging urban sprawl, the profligate use of natural resources, and the pollution and cost in lives, resulting from the widespread dependence on the private car; the lack of choice, and the homogeneity of standards, brought about by suburbanization; and the ugliness which may result from failure to control the more bizarre manifestations of commercialism. But, while conceding the force of all these arguments, it is worth while to put some points in defence of the process of mass suburbanization – points which are fairly obvious, but which are perhaps too seldom stressed.

First, the process has been remarkably effective, in that within a relatively short period of a quarter-century it has produced millions of new homes and hundreds of new shopping centres, together with schools, community facilities, and other services. Secondly, in terms of sheer quality, the process has actually produced a great deal of rather good housing and pleasant neighbourhoods. Though the style of life in these areas may not appeal to the cosmopolitan intellectual critic, it does seem to have met effectively the needs of millions of young families who wanted a suitable environment in which to rear children. There is absolutely no evidence that for these people the suburbs were a failure. And thirdly, the dispersed decision-making structure that guided the whole process did avoid massive social errors; like democracy in politics, it may have avoided the spectacular success, but it equally avoided spectacular failure.

The criticisms in fact are rather different. They are that the whole process could have been carried through so as to have given an

76. *Freeway interchange in Los Angeles. The southern Californian metropolis, with a population of over 10 million in the early 1970s, has developed almost entirely in the era of mass car ownership since 1920. Thus it has grown quite differently from older cities, with wide dispersion of jobs and homes and a generally low density of development. Long-distance commuting is made possible by hundreds of miles of freeways which criss-cross the vast urban area – now nearly one hundred miles across.*

equally good environment (or perhaps a better one) with less use of land and with lower resulting costs for public services, if the intervening undeveloped areas of land had been developed first; that sometimes the new suburbia was not as attractive visually as it might have been; and that, most seriously, the benefits have been denied to a substantial proportion – at least half – of the total population. By concentrating so heavily on house construction for sale in an inflating market, and by failing to provide a stock of new well-designed housing for lower-income groups, American postwar housing policies have in effect condemned a large part of the people to live in poor, run-down, overcrowded neighbourhoods. As a result, American society is becoming increasingly stratified by income, occupation and race. Even if the suburban development process cannot bear the whole blame for this, it must bear a part. Moreover, and associated with this last criticism, the United States has had as little success as most other countries in remodelling its local government structures to grapple with the metropolitan problems which face it. The local pressures against change have been too strong; and, in the nature of the American system, the leverage exerted at the centre has been too weak.

Finally, there is no doubt that at the wider regional level, the vast cost of the various development programmes has not yielded anything like a satisfactory return. Far too much funding has been spread indiscriminately across the country, both among areas in great need and areas in less need. This is because a philosophy of economic development, based on careful analysis of goals and objectives, has not been clearly worked out at the centre. Such a presentation of objectives would need to take into account the often conflicting considerations of geographical relationships, management of natural resources, and the conservation of the environment. From it would emerge – hopefully – a set of guidelines as to the regions and areas where growth should be positively encouraged, those where no particular aid was needed, and even those where growth should be positively discouraged for various reasons – whether of conservation, congestion, or simply lack of economic prospects. Only against this background could the Federal government begin to pursue a policy of selective aid through support of educational, health and job training programmes. Up to now, this has not been done in a clear or conscious way.

As a result of these failures, there is no doubt that the contemporary United States – perhaps to a greater extent than any Western European country – presents strange anomalies which must be regarded as failures of urban policy. On the one hand, widespread diffusion of a remarkably high level of material wealth; on the other, minorities living in poverty which is striking just because it is so far below the general level. On the one hand, massive construction achievements in areas such as suburban housing and new highways; on the other, paralysis and decay in the inner cities. On the one hand, general private affluence at a level not witnessed elsewhere in the world; on the other, in places, real public squalor in the form of blighted landscapes and obvious failures to get to grips with the problems of pollution. These are contrasts of which increasing numbers of Americans are aware; and hopefully the time will not be far off when the resources are marshalled to grapple with them.

Further Reading

For regional economic planning, the standard source is Lloyd Rodwin (see reading list, Chapter 8), Chapter 7; this also deals in passing with the urban problem. More detail on economic planning is provided by John H. Cumberland, *Regional Development Experiences and Prospects in the United States of America* (Paris and The Hague: Mouton, 1971). A wealth of material on the background to American regional development is found in Harvey S. Perloff, Edgar S. Dunn, Eric E. Lampard and Richard F. Muth, *Regions, Resources and Economic Growth* (Baltimore: Johns Hopkins University Press, 1960; paperback edition available).

Marion Clawson, *Suburban Land Conversion in the United States: An Economic and Governmental Process* (Baltimore: Johns Hopkins University Press, 1971), is the standard source on postwar American urban growth; Marion Clawson and Peter Hall, *Planning and Urban Growth: An Anglo-American Comparison* (Baltimore: Johns Hopkins University Press, 1973) draws on this source to provide an account for the general reader of contrasts between the British and American patterns of postwar urbanization. For the character of postwar changes in American metropolitan areas, see the *Report of the National Advisory Commission on Civil Disorders* (in paperback edition, New York: Bantam Books, 1968); and Advisory Commission on Inter-Governmental Relations, *Urban and Rural America: Policies for Future Growth* (Washington DC: Government Printing Office, 1968).

On the legislative and administrative basis of planning and zoning in the United States, see John Delafons, *Land Use Controls in the United States* (Cambridge, Mass.: MIT Press, second edition, 1969).

10. The Planning Process

Up to now this book has been an introduction to the problems and the content of spatial planning, treated historically. That has been its aim, as the preface indicated. But now, this last chapter tries to make a bridge to the actual process of planning, as it is carried out by progressive planning authorities at the present time. This process is based strongly on theoretical concepts, which are well set out in modern textbooks of planning. Therefore, this chapter, which tries to distil the central content of these more advanced texts, will perhaps serve as an introduction to them for the student of planning.

Planning as a Continuous Process

Modern planning theory, as it has evolved since about 1960, is based on the notion that all sorts of planning constitute a distinct type of human activity, concerned with controlling particular systems. Thus spatial planning (or, as it is called here, urban and regional planning) is just a sub-class of a general activity called planning; it is concerned with managing and controlling a particular system, the urban and regional system. It follows from this that all planning is a continuous process, which works by seeking to devise appropriate ways of controlling the system concerned, and then by monitoring the effects to see how far the controls have been effective or how far they need subsequent modification. This view of planning is quite different from the one held by an older generation of planners, such as Geddes or Abercrombie, or even the generation which set up the planning system in Britain after the Second World War. These older planners saw planning as concerned with the production of plans, which gave a detailed picture of some desired future end state to be achieved in a certain number of years. It is true that under the 1947 Planning Act in Britain, deliberate provision was made for review of the plans every five years. But the philosophy behind the process was heavily oriented towards the concept of the fixed master plan.

Arising from this basic difference of approach, there are also detailed differences between the old planning and the new. The old planning was concerned to set out the desired future end state in detail, in terms of land-use patterns on the ground; the new approach, embodied in Britain in the new structure plans prepared under the 1968 Planning Act, concentrates instead on the objectives of the plan and on alternative ways of reaching them, all set out in writing rather than in detailed maps. Again, the old planning tended to proceed through a simple sequence, best set out in the terse instructions of Patrick Geddes: Survey–Analysis–Plan. The existing situation would be surveyed; analysis of the survey would show the remedial actions that needed to be taken; the fixed plan would embody these actions. But in the new planning, the emphasis is on tracing the possible consequences of alternative policies, only then evaluating them against the objectives in order to choose a preferred course of action; and, it should be emphasized, this process will continually be repeated as the monitoring process throws up divergences between the planner's intentions and the actual state of the system.

The new concept of planning derives from one of the newest sciences: cybernetics, which was first identified and named in 1948 by the great American mathematician and thinker, Norbert Wiener. Rather than dealing with a completely new subject matter, cybernetics is essentially a new way of organizing existing knowledge about a very wide range of phenomena. Its central notion is that many such phenomena – whether they are social, economic, biological or physical in character – can usefully be viewed as complex interacting systems. The behaviour of atomic particles, a jet aeroplane, a nation's economy – all can be viewed, and described, in terms of systems; their different parts can be separated, and the interactions between them can be analysed. Then, by introducing appropriate control mechanisms, the behaviour of the system can be altered in specific ways, to achieve certain objectives on the part of the controller. The point here is that it is necessary to understand the operation of the system as a whole (though not necessarily in complete detail throughout) in order to control it effectively; unless this is done, actions taken to control one part of the system may have completely unexpected effects elsewhere. A good example is the design of a motorcar: if the designer produces extra power without considering the total impact on the rest of the complex system that makes up the car, the result could be instability or rapid wear of other parts, with disastrous results.

Cybernetics has already had considerable practical applications in modern technology, especially in the complex control systems which monitor spacecraft or automatic power stations. Its applications to the world of social and economic life are still tentative. Some observers think that human mass behaviour is too complex and too unpredictable to be reduced to cybernetic laws. Others find ethically repellent the idea that planners should seek to control mass human behaviour in the same ways that they seek to control the operation of machines. All that can be said with certainty is that in some areas where men and machines interact – as for instance in urban traffic control systems – cybernetics is already proving its effectiveness. It still remains to be proved definitively whether the application can be extended equally well to all areas of human behaviour.

Fundamental to the concept of systems planning – as the cybernetics-based planning has come to be called – is the idea of interaction between two parallel systems: the planning or controlling system itself, and the system (or systems) which it seeks to control. This notion of constant interaction should be kept in mind throughout the following account of the systematic planning process. More particularly, we are concerned with this process as it applies to spatial planning, using the word 'spatial' in its widest sense: it need not be limited to the three-dimensional space of Euclidean geometry, but may extend for instance to include notions of economic space (the costs involved in traversing distance), and psychological or perception space. Nevertheless, there can be little doubt that in some sense, however distorted by psychological or economic factors, the relationship of parts of the urban and regional system in geographical space must be the central concern of the urban and regional planner.

To control these relationships, in a mixed economy such as the United States or the countries of western Europe, the planner has two main levers: one is the power to control public investment, especially in elements of infrastructure such as roads, railways, airports, schools, hospitals and public housing schemes; the other is the power to encourage or discourage initiatives from the private sector for physical development. Both these forms of power, of course, vary in their scope and effectiveness from one nation or society to another. Different countries invest different proportions of their gross national product in public infrastructure (though in advanced industrial countries there are limits to this variation); different nations have very widely differing controls over physical development (though in none, apparently, is there either a complete lack of such controls, or a completely effective central control). Therefore, almost by definition, the urban or regional planner will never be completely ineffective, or completely omnipotent. He will exist in a state of continuous interaction with the system he is planning: a system which changes partly, but not entirely, due to processes beyond his mechanisms of control.

Against this background, it is now possible to appreciate the schematic summaries of the planning process set out by three leading British exponents of the systematic planning approach: Brian McLoughlin, George Chadwick and Alan Wilson. McLoughlin's account (Illustration 77a) is the simplest: it proceeds in a straight line through a sequence of processes, which are then constantly reiterated through a return loop. Having taken a basic decision to adopt planning and to set up a particular system, the planner then formulates broad goals and identifies more detailed objectives which logically follow from these goals. He then tries to follow the consequences of possible courses of action which he might take, with the aid of models which simplify the operation of the system. Then he evaluates the alternatives in relation to his objectives and the resources available. Finally he takes action (through public investment or controls on private investment, as already described) to implement the preferred alternative. After an interval he reviews the state of the system to see how far it is departing from the assumed course, and on the basis of this he begins to go through the process again.

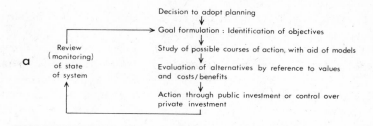

Decision to adopt planning
↓
Goal formulation : Identification of objectives
↓
Study of possible courses of action, with aid of models
↓
Evaluation of alternatives by reference to values and costs/benefits
↓
Action through public investment or control over private investment

Review (monitoring) of state of system

a

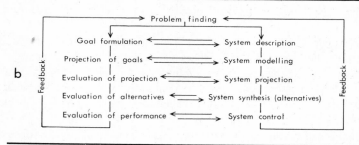

b

Problem finding

Goal formulation ⟷ System description

Projection of goals ⟷ System modelling

Evaluation of projection ⟷ System projection

Evaluation of alternatives ⟷ System synthesis (alternatives)

Evaluation of performance ⟷ System control

Feedback   Feedback

c

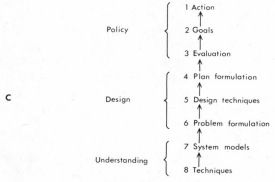

Policy
  1 Action
  2 Goals
  3 Evaluation

Design
  4 Plan formulation
  5 Design techniques
  6 Problem formulation

Understanding
  7 System models
  8 Techniques

N.B. The diagram is to be read *upwards*; but constant interaction takes place between all eight levels

77. Three concepts of the planning process: (a) Brian McLoughlin; (b) George Chadwick; (c) Alan Wilson. During the 1960s interest developed in systematizing the process of planning, with a new stress on modelling and evaluating alternative designs or courses of actions. These formulations drew heavily from the new sciences of cybernetics and systems analysis.

273

Chadwick's account of the process is essentially a more complex account of the same sequence (Illustration 77b). Here, a clear distinction is made between the observation of the system under control (the right-hand side of the diagram) and the planner's actions in devising and testing his control measures (the left-hand side). Appropriately, there are return loops on both sides of the diagram, indicating again that the whole process is cyclical. But at each stage of the process, in addition, the planner has to interrelate his observations of the system with the development of the control measures he intends to apply to it.

Wilson's account (Illustration 77c) is even more theoretically complex, but again it can be related to Chadwick's. In it, there are not two sides of the process which interact, but three levels presented vertically. The most basic level, corresponding to part of Chadwick's right-hand sequence, is simply called 'understanding' (or, in the terminology of the American planner Britton Harris, 'prediction'). It is concerned wholly with devising the working tools, in the form of techniques and models, which are needed for the analysis of the system under control. The intermediate level, corresponding to another part of Chadwick's right-hand side, is concerned with the further use of these techniques in analysing problems and synthesizing alternatives which will be internally consistent. The upper level, corresponding roughly to the left-hand side of the Chadwick diagram, is essentially concerned with the positive actions which the planner takes to regulate or control the system: goal formulation, evaluation of alternatives, and actual implementation of the preferred alternative.

All three accounts are helpful ways of looking at the planning process. But since simplicity must be the essence of this summary chapter, the following accounts of the separate stages of the process are based principally on the classification of Brian McLoughlin.

Goals, Objectives and Targets

Planning, as a general activity, may have one objective or many. There is no necessary relationship between the scale and expense of a planning programme, and the complexity of the objectives behind it; thus the American moon-shot programme, one of the costliest pieces of investment in the history of mankind, had a fairly obvious single main objective. Most urban and regional planning activities, however, have multiple objectives. The first step in the planning process, then, is to identify these purposes which the planner seeks to achieve, to order them in terms of their importance, and to consider how far they are reconcilable each with the other. This might seem obvious, yet surprisingly most plans of the past prove to be very perfunctory in their treatment of objectives; it seems almost as if the aims of the plan were so well understood that no one needed to set them down. But unless objectives are made explicit, no one can be sure that they are shared by the people they are being planned for; nor is it possible rationally to prefer one plan to another.

Modern plan methodology, therefore, lays great stress on this first step in the process. In particular, it distinguishes rather carefully between three stages in the development of aims: *goal* formulation, identification of *objectives*, and *target* setting. *Goals* are essentially general and highly abstract; they tend to fall into broad categories such as social, economic and aesthetic (some of which categories may overlap), and they may include qualities of the planning process itself, such as flexibility. Some authors, notably Wilson, define goals in a rather different way, as areas of concern: in this view, the planner starts by identifying broad functional sub-systems which are of interest to him, because they appear to present problems which may be amenable to the controls he proposes to manage. Examples of areas of concern would include public health, education, income and its distribution, mobility (both physical and social), and environmental quality. *Objectives* in contrast are rather more specific; they are defined in terms of actual programmes capable of being carried into action, though they fall short of detailed quantification. They also require the expenditure of resources (using that word in its widest sense, to include not merely conventional economic resources but also elements like information) so that they imply an element of competition for scarce resources. Thus if 'mobility' is a general goal, the resulting objectives might include: a reduction of travel time in the journey to work, an improvement in the quality of public transport (or of a part of it), or a programme of motorway construction to keep pace with rising car ownership. Notably, as in the cases just quoted, objectives can only be devised as the result of a more detailed scanning of the system being planned, in order to identify specific malfunctioning or deficiencies. Finally, as a further stage of refinement, objectives are turned into *targets* representing specific programmes in which criteria of performance are set against target dates. Thus the detailed targets developed from the above objectives might include: construction of a new underground railway line within ten years to reduce journey times in the north-western sector of the city by an average of 20 per cent; or construction of a new motorway link within five years in order to cut traffic delays by some specific amount. Targets, by their nature, tend to be very specific and particular; one problem that emerges from the whole goals–objectives–targets process, therefore, is that of integrating rather disparate individual programmes into a coherent plan.

Already, this first stage in the planning process involves great difficulties of a conceptual and technical nature. In the first place, it is not entirely clear who should take the lead in the process. Broad goals for society, it might be argued, are a matter for the politicians, though the professional planner can play a valuable role by trying to order the choices. But politicians are largely involved with acute short-term issues; their time scale is very different from that of the planner, whose decisions may have an impact for generations. The public themselves form a very heterogeneous mass of different groups, whose value systems are almost certainly very different if they are not in open contradiction. Even the identification of these groups poses difficulties, because most people will belong to more than one group for different purposes; they will have interests and values as members of families living at home, as workers in a factory or office, as consumers, and perhaps as members of voluntary organizations, and the values of these groups may actually come into conflict with each other. Public opinion polls and other surveys may throw limited and distorted light on preferences, because most people find difficulty in thinking about highly abstract goals that do not concern them immediately, and because they will not easily imagine long-term possibilities outside their immediate range of experience.

Because of differences and even conflicts of view, it is almost certainly impossible even to devise a satisfactory general welfare function, which would somehow combine all the individual preferences and weightings of different individuals or groups.

It is no wonder, then, that in his comments on goal formulation Chadwick points out that 'the gap between theory and possible practice is pretty wide'. Planners do the best they can by trying to amass as much information as possible about their clients and their values; by trying to identify acknowledged problem areas, where by fairly common agreement something needs to be done; and by using logical argument to proceed from general goals to more specific objectives. Evolving research tools, such as simulation and gaming – whereby members of the public are faced with imaginary choice situations which test their preferences – will also help to throw light on one particular dark area: the weighting of different objectives and the trade-off between them. But it should not be expected that there will be a dramatic breakthrough in this intellectually very difficult area.

Forecasting, Modelling and Plan Design

Having defined objectives and given them some precise form in the shape of targets based on performance criteria, the planner will turn to description and analysis of the urban or regional system he wishes to control. His aim here is to find ways of representing the behaviour of the system over time – both in the recent past, and in the future – in such a way that he can understand the impact of alternative courses of action that are open to him. To do this, he will produce a model of the system (or, more likely, a number of interconnected models which seek to describe the behaviour of its sub-systems). A model is simply a schematic but precise description of the system, which appears to fit its past behaviour and which can, therefore, be used, hopefully, to predict the future. It may be very simple: a statement that population is growing by 2 per cent a year is in effect a model of population growth. But it may be, and often is, computationally quite complex.

There are two important questions that the planner needs to resolve about the modelling process: first, what aspects of the urban system he wishes to model; second, what sorts of model are available. The answer to the first question will, of course, depend on the planner's precise interests; the planner must first say what questions the model is required to answer. But usually, the urban and regional planner is concerned with the spatial behaviour of the economy or of society. In particular, he is interested in the relationships between social and economic *activities* – such as working, living, shopping, and enjoying recreation – and the *spaces* (or structures) available to house them. He will need to know the size and location of both, as well as the *interrelationships* between activities (transportation and communication) which use special spaces called *channel spaces* (roads or railways, telephone wires). Together, these aspects of the urban system can be said to constitute activity systems. Particularly important among them, for the urban planner, is the relationship between work-places, homes, shops and other services, and the transportation system that links these three.

The answer to the second question – the choice of type of model – will again depend on the object of the planning exercise. Models, whether simple or complex, are capable of being classified in a number of different ways. They may be *deterministic* in character, or *probabilistic* (i.e. incorporating an element of chance). They may be *static* in character, or *dynamic*. Many of the best-known urban development models are static; that is, they project the system only for one future point in time, at which point the system is regarded as somehow reaching equilibrium. This, of course, is a totally unrealistic assumption which is not supported by knowledge of how the system actually behaves, and one of the main challenges is to produce better dynamic models which are useable. Another separate but related question is whether the model chosen is to be simply *descriptive* of the present (or recent past) situation, or *predictive* of the future, or even *prescriptive* in the sense that it contains some element of built-in evaluation. Self-evaluating models are not very common in urban and regional planning, though they do exist: the linear programming model, which automatically maximizes the achievement of some variable subject to certain constraints, is the most notable example and has been used in planning contexts both in the United States and in Israel. But more commonly the model merely predicts the future; it can be run a number of times with different policy assumptions underlying it, but finally the choice will be made through a quite separate evaluative process.

Yet another question is the choice between *spatially aggregated* models and *spatially disaggregated* models. A model which projects some sub-system for the town or region as a whole is termed spatially aggregated; a model which examines the internal zone-by-zone allocation of that system is spatially disaggregated. Urban and regional planners, of course, require both sorts of model, but the results of their spatially disaggregated models must accord with the control totals given by the spatially aggregated ones. Well-known population projection models, such as the cohort survival model (which operates through the survivorship rates of successive five-year age cohorts of the population), are spatially aggregated; so are the common economic models, such as input-output models. Models which predict future distributions of people and service industries within urban areas, such as the well-known Garin—Lowry model used in a number of planning studies, are, of course, spatially dis-aggregated.

Some models also combine an aggregated with a disaggregated element; this is true of Garin—Lowry. This model (Illustration 78) starts with an assumed amount, and an assumed distribution, of basic industry — that is, industry the produce of which is exported from the city or the region, and which thereby provides an economic base or support for the people of that region. The model then calculates simultaneously both the aggregate amount, and the spatial distribution, of residential population and of the local service industry employment which is dependent upon that population. The aggregate totals are obtained by using two simple ratios, a basic employment—population ratio and a population—service industry employment ratio. The distributions are obtained by using a so-called spatial interaction model which, like most of this type, is derived from the well-known gravity theory. This states that the interaction between any two areas which form part of a wider set of areas is directly proportional to their sizes (as defined, for instance, in terms of

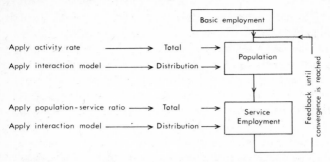

78. The Garin–Lowry model structure. First developed in the United States but employed extensively in Britain, Garin–Lowry is the best-known of the mathematical models used to project the amount and distribution of residential population and local services. It depends on prior knowledge or assumptions about the amount of basic employment.

employment or population concentrations) and inversely proportional to the distance between them. Such a model contains a number of parameters and constants, which are values capable of being altered so that the model provides the best possible fit to the observed past or present facts; this process of fitting is called calibration of the model.

The Garin–Lowry model, then, starts with a simple distribution of basic industry – however this is defined for the purpose of the exercise. It ends with a picture of the urban area at some future point in time, showing the patterns of residential population, of service provision, and of the work journeys and service journeys which link up these varied activities. It is capable of being run with different planning policy assumptions in it: different assumptions, for instance, about the distribution of basic industry, or of the pattern of transportation facilities which will affect the accessibility of the systems to each other. This, plus its relative simplicity and economy, have made it one of the most commonly used models in British and North American urban planning practice. Its chief disadvantage – that it is a simple, one-shot model requiring constant repetition to make it fit a dynamic planning framework – may be overcome within the next few years, by the development of an operational dynamic version.

Model design is one of the most complex and intriguing stages of the modern planning process. Designing a model, or models, to suit the precise problem involves logical analysis of a set of interrelated questions. Once it is determined precisely which questions the model is supposed to answer, the next problem is to list the concepts to be represented, which must be measurable. It is also necessary to investigate which variables can be controlled by the planner, at least in part; if the assumption is that no parts are controllable, then the model is a pure forecasting model, but if at least some of the factors are under the planner's control then this is a planning model. The planner must also consider what behavioural theories about systems are to be embodied in his model. He must consider technical questions, such as how the variables shall be categorized or subdivided (as, for instance, population can be categorized by age, sex, occupation, or industry group); how explicitly time will be treated; and how the model is to be calibrated and tested. The answers to these questions will depend in part on the techniques that are available, and on the relevant data that can be used to illustrate them, as well as on the computational capacity of the computer which will be used to run the models.

Plan Design and Plan Evaluation

Many standard accounts of the modern planning process refer to a stage which is called plan design, or plan formulation. To the layman, this would appear to be the critical point where, when all technical aids have been used to the utmost, the planner takes command and exercises his creative abilities, just as he did in a simpler age before computer modelling had become an integral part of the planning process. In an important way, this is true: there must be at least one point in the whole process, and in all probability more than one point, where the planner exercises a power to synthesize disparate elements into a coherent plan. But in fact, this power has to be manipulated in close relationship to the machine. What the computer has done is to speed up, many times, the power to generate and to evaluate alternative formulations of the plan. The capacity to design is essentially the capacity to use this power critically and creatively.

The design process, therefore, really starts as soon as the planner begins to design his models. At that point, the critical questions – what elements of the urban system should the models represent, and in how much detail – will finally determine the content of the plan design. To all intents and purposes, the model is the design, and alternative assumptions built into the model generate alternative design possibilities. Of course, the word 'design' here is not being used in a conventional sense. In most cases, the urban and regional planner does not end by producing a blueprint for actual physical structures on the ground. What he tries to do is to specify a future state or states of the urban and regional system which appear, from the operational model, to be internally coherent and consistent, and to be workable and feasible; and which also best satisfy the objectives which have been set. The content of the design, and of the model which embodies it, will depend on the focus and the objectives of the planner. Thus, if his plan stresses transportation, it will chiefly consist of a design for channel spaces to accommodate projected traffic flows. If his plan stresses social provision, it will embody locations for social service facilities in relation to the distribution of projected demands from different sections of the population. Invariably, following the modern stress on planning as process, the design will not be a one-shot plan for some target date in the future; rather, the model or models which incorporate the design will represent a continuous trajectory from the present into the predictable future.

Design, therefore, essentially consists of two elements. The first is the *choice of system models* to represent the main elements which the design should incorporate, and the running of these models to give a number of coherent and realistic pictures of the future state of the system through time. The second is the process of *evaluation* of the alternatives to give a preferred or optimum solution. At the stage of evaluation, the goals and objectives which the planner has generated are applied directly to the alternative simulations of the future system.

Like most other terms in the planning process, the word 'evaluation' needs careful definition. To most lay observers, it conveys a connotation of economic criteria: evaluation, crudely, represents the best plan for money. Many notable modern planning exercises have in fact made extensive use of economic evaluation procedures; some of these will be described in summary a little later. But essentially, evaluation consists of any process which seeks to order preferences. Strictly speaking, it need not refer to money values, or to use of economic resources, at all.

What is essential is that evaluation derives clearly from the goals and objectives set early on in the planning process. The first question must be how well each design alternative meets these objectives, either in a general sense, or (preferably) in terms of satisfying quantified performance criteria. Very commonly it is found that many objectives contain an element of contradiction in practice. It is difficult for instance to reconcile the objective: 'preserve open countryside' with the objective: 'give people the maximum freedom to enjoy the private environment they want', or alternatively to reconcile: 'provide for free movement for the car-owning public' with: 'preserve the urban fabric'. Somewhere along the line, either in the original formulation of objectives or in the evaluation process, it is necessary for the planning team to devise weights which rank some objectives above others, and indicate how much different objectives are worth in relation to each other. This may involve a conscious decision to favour one group of the client population more than another, because quite often the interests of these groups are in conflict: car-owners versus non-car-owners, for instance, or old-established rural residents versus new interests. Such value judgements are hard to make, and the political process must inevitably have a large hand in them.

To try to make plan evaluation more rigorous, since about 1955 at least three techniques have gained widespread currency in the planning world. The best known of these among the general public, *cost-benefit analysis*, is explicitly economic in its approach. It assumes that the best plan will be the one which delivers the greatest quantity of economic benefits in relation to economic costs; these latter being defined, as is usual in economic analysis, as alternative opportunities foregone. (A simpler form of economic analysis, cost-effectiveness analysis, assumes that benefits from alternatives are equal, and analyses merely the variable cost; it is of limited use in urban and regional planning.) Essentially, cost-benefit analysis is useful in situations where decision-makers want to know which of several alternatives represents the best economic value, but where normal market measures are not available. The businessman in private industry has no such problem: he can predict the demand for his product or service in the market, and so calculate expected return on capital invested. But public decision-makers have no market as a guide: they are producing services which are not sold at a price. Cost-benefit analysis, therefore, works by trying to create 'shadow prices' for items outside the market. The value of a road investment is defined in terms of savings in petrol, tyres, drivers' and passengers' time, and reductions in accidents; these last are valued in terms of lost capacity for earning wages, and on this basis even the value of a death in a road accident can be calculated in money terms.

This approach, however, throws up many problems – some so intractable that critics claim cost-benefit analysis to be of very limited use, and even positively harmful, in planning decisions. Valuing people's time, or the risk of accidents, in terms of wage rates may mean that poor people (and housewives, and children) are valued less than rich people, especially businessmen. Many important elements in planning, such as the value of a fine landscape or of an old building, are almost literally imponderables: there is no easy way that a value can be put on them. If an attempt is made to do so – landscapes can be valued in terms of the lengths of journey that people make in order to look at them, and old buildings can be valued in terms of the insurance value put upon their possible destruction – many people will argue that it is ethically wrong to use such commercial judgements in such situations; the result of following the approach consistently, they say, would be that no building or landscape could ever be preserved if there were a good economic case for removing it, so that a motorway could be driven with impunity through Westminster Abbey, or London's new airport be located in Hyde Park. These very fundamental objections are closely related to another: cost-benefit calculations have to be applied to the planner's models of the future state of the system, and if these models prove to be wrong in even small particulars, this may seriously affect the outcome of the analysis. In the celebrated controversy surrounding the Roskill Commission inquiry into the siting of London's third airport during 1968–70, for instance, the cost-benefit analysis developed for the Commission contained a very large element for the value of air travellers' time, and this in turn was highly sensitive to assumptions made about the future pattern of travel by air in Britain. Critics argued that it would be unwise to reach firm conclusions on such speculative, and easily upset, projections.

Fundamentally, the objection to cost-benefit analysis is that it is too arbitrary in character. By trying to represent all types of costs and benefits, to all groups in the population, in terms of a single aggregate metric, it conceals the very considerable value judgements that underpin it behind an appearance of value-free objectivity. To some extent cost-benefit analysis can meet this criticism by producing sensitivity analyses; these show the impact of altering some of the basic assumptions in the analysis, and allow the decision-maker to consider just how much he would be willing to sacrifice of one element in order to achieve another. Cost-benefit analysis, in this argument, is not a magic touchstone but an educative device, which makes the decision-making process more rigorous by stressing the economic argument about the costs of alternative choices. But this still does not meet completely the counter-argument about imponderables.

The second best-known evaluative device in planning, Professor Nathaniel Lichfield's *Planning Balance Sheet*, specifically tries to deal with this criticism. It is essentially a modified cost-benefit analysis, which tries to render in economic terms those items which are capable of being treated in this way, but which resorts to simpler devices for the imponderables. Unlike cost-benefit analysis in the strict sense, it makes no attempt to render all values in a common metric; it does not produce a 'rate of economic return', as cost-benefit analysis does, and it is not, therefore, very suitable for comparing a range of different investments. It is, however, specifically devised for the consideration of alternative plans for the same urban or regional system, and has been successfully applied to problems of urban renewal and of new town construction. Its merits are that it is highly disaggregative, stressing advantages and disadvantages of alternative plans for different groups in the population; and that it

285

spells out its value-assumptions very carefully, so that the decision-maker is aided without having the decision taken out of his hands. Its disadvantage lies in its inevitable complexity, which means that the decision-maker needs a strong effort of will to question each successive weighting that is made in the course of the exercise; if he fails to do this, he will tend to accept the weightings or trade-offs made by the professional evaluator, which he (or his electorate) may not necessarily share.

The *Goals Achievement Matrix* of Professor Morris Hill, third of the evaluation devices which have gained currency in urban and regional planning, tries to deal with this problem by starting from the agreed objectives which the plan-making machine sets up. It compels decision-makers to make specific judgements about the weights they attach to the various objectives; these judgements are then applied to further judgements as to the degree to which alternative plans meet these objectives, expressed on a numerical scale. Like Lichfield's method, Hill's matrix recognizes that different groups of the public may have different value-systems, so that they may place quite different weights on different objectives; it allows for this by disaggregating its analysis. As with the Lichfield method, which it so closely resembles, the chief defect of the Goals Achievement Matrix is its complexity. But it has to be recognized that plan evaluation is bound to be a complex and often a controversial process, in any event.

Most serious planning exercises now use some form of systematic plan evaluation technique, though they may not go as far as employing one of the three methods just described in its full rigour. Many are content with a considerably simplified version of the Goals Achievement Matrix technique, in which alternatives are judged against a check list of objectives, with some simple attempt at weighting. Many in addition try to involve the public in the process of evaluation, by trying to obtain the views of a sample of the public on the question of the weights to be applied to different objectives, as well as on their preferences among the plan alternatives which have been generated. These pioneer attempts at public participation are open to the objection that many ordinary people cannot easily appreciate abstract qualities, such as flexibility or environmental quality, especially when they are applied to rather large-scale, diagrammatic plans which do not make specific reference to the local areas that people really know and understand. But they represent a beginning.

One important question about the whole plan–design process is whether it should be linear or cyclical. The version so far outlined in this chapter is linear: that is, the alternative plans are developed and modelled, all in equal detail, up to the point where they are all evaluated side by side with a common set of evaluation procedures. In fact several recent major British planning exercises – such as the sub-regional studies for Nottinghamshire and Derbyshire and for Coventry, Solihull and Warwickshire – have instead used a cyclical approach. A number of very crude alternatives are developed, modelled and evaluated. Certain among them are eliminated, one or more are retained, and these (or combinations and permutations of them) are developed and modelled in greater detail. This process may be repeated three or four times, with the modelling–evaluation process progressively testing finer and more subtle variations of detail. The cyclical or recursive approach appears more complex, particularly when it is described in the plan report. But it can be argued that it is more economical of the planning team's skills and of computer time, and by logically eliminating alternatives and concentrating on detailed variations it acts as a systematic educative process for the team. It seems likely in future to become the standard method.

Implementing the Plan

By systematic evaluation of alternatives, the planner can select a preferred course of action for implementation. But it needs to be stressed again that this is no once-for-all decision. In the planning process outlined here, the whole exercise of modelling, evaluation and selection is continuously repeated. The objective is to have on the one hand a monitoring system, which checks the response of the urban or regional system to the various planning measures which are taken to control its progress; and on the other hand the control system itself, which responds flexibly and sensitively to the information conveyed by the monitoring system. The analogy, of course,

Urban and Regional Planning

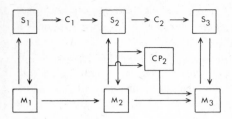

S – Surveys of the real world
C – Control mechanisms
M – Models, forecasts and plans
CP – Comparative analyses of models versus the real world

79. The plan implementation process, according to Brian McLoughlin. This formulation, in which models interact with surveys of the real world through comparative analyses, and in which control processes are then applied to the real-world situation, draws heavily on analogies and insights from the science of cybernetics.

is with piloting a ship or an aeroplane. A course is set; a battery of instruments confirm that the craft is on course, or that it is deviating from course; appropriate control devices, either automatic or man-minded, take appropriate corrective action. The monitoring system thus tests the correspondence (or lack of correspondence) between the real-world situation and the model (or 'navigation chart') that has been set up to describe it. If there is a divergence, then either controls must be operated to bring the real world situation again in confor-mity with the model design, or the model must be altered to make it a more realistic description of the way the world works, or both.

This is, frankly, a description of a planning ideal rather than of present planning reality. The world that urban and regional planning seeks to control is much bigger and richer in content than the rather limited piece of reality represented by the course of a ship or an aeroplane. To reduce it to schematic terms by means of a model is correspondingly more difficult, and the likelihood of error much greater. Because of the complexity of the human responses involved, the control systems open to the planner are much cruder and less effective than those available to the ship's master or airline pilot. The history recounted earlier in this book proves definitely that even in strong and effective planning systems, the world changes in all sorts of ways that planners fail to predict, so that plans may fail grievously to correspond to reality, even after a very few years. In any event, even if we did know how to control the responses in the urban and regional system, to exert pressure effectively might well prove politically unfeasible.

In practice, as revealed in some notable planning controversies of recent years, a tidy systems view of planning may go wrong in a variety of ways. In the first place, knowledge about the external environment of the planning decision may increase rapidly, with unpredictable results. The changing economics of nuclear and conventional power production may invalidate a programme of power-station location; variations in the noise-emission levels from jet aeroplanes, and improvements in ground level city-to-airport transportation, may completely change the framework of a decision about airport location (while increases in the size of planes may make a new airport unnecessary); the development of quieter, or completely silent, motorcars might render much of the current controversy about urban motorways irrelevant. In practice it ought to be possible to predict technical changes and their impact rather better than is now generally done. (It seems extraordinary, for instance, that just after the Second World War, at a time when jet aircraft were already flying, their noise impact seems to have been ignored in planning the major civil airports of the world.) But even so, it must be recognized that there will be a considerable element of unpredictability and chance.

Secondly plans can go wrong because of the complex interrelationships between different levels of the planning system, and between different actors in the planning situation. Thus a general, high-level strategic policy may be laid down by a national or regional planning authority, for apparently good cause, but with unexpected results at the more local planning level. In Britain, office development control is a good example; it was introduced in 1964–5 with the aim of restricting office growth in London and other major cities, and of promoting decentralization to new towns and development areas. But the restrictions had the result of holding up for many years some important pieces of redevelopment in central London, such as

Piccadilly Circus, which depended for their commercial viability on office development. The process can, however, work in reverse. Thus, though almost everyone was agreed on the need for a national motorway from London to South Wales to relieve traffic congestion and reduce the accident toll on the old road, work on the new highway was held up for over ten years as one local amenity society after another successfully diverted the line of the road from its own area. The fact that, as finally built, the motorway probably follows the least environmentally damaging line is perhaps some consolation.

Thirdly there is the fact that over time human values – or at least the values of those actively concerned – tend to change. In recent years there is some evidence that the pace of such changes is actually increasing: fashions in planning tend to change almost as fast as fashions in clothing. Since complex plans inevitably take time to prepare and then to execute, the result may be controversy. Urban redevelopment provides a good example. In the late 1950s and early 1960s, the key word was 'comprehensive redevelopment': to provide a better environment and separate people's activities from the danger and pollution of traffic, it was necessary to make a clean sweep of many old urban areas. But by the late 1960s and early 1970s, there had been virtually a reversal: the key words now were 'conservation' and 'urban spontaneity', and younger planners in particular wanted to keep the chaos and disorder of the older city. Plans which represented the older scheme of values, such as the Greater London Council redevelopment of Covent Garden or the reconstruction of the La Défense area of Paris, were bitterly attacked for just those qualities which would have made them admired a few years before. Similarly, the late 1960s saw a revulsion against motorway-building in cities, with protest movements as far apart as San Francisco and London, New Orleans and Paris. Earlier, it had been almost axiomatic that urban traffic should be channelled on to special segregated routes designed for the purpose. But now, opponents began to stress the disadvantages of the motorways: noise, visual intrusion, and severance of traditional neighbourhoods. Since it was impossible for the city ever to cater adequately for the rising tide of car traffic, objectors argued, the right policy was to restrict the use of the car in cities and to build up good public transportation instead.

Finally, however, the problem is that it is very difficult to reconcile different sets of values. Most planning controversies, even though the bitterness of the debate may obscure the fact, involve a conflict of right against right. Other things being equal, it is right to build urban motorways to cater for traffic; if it can be assumed that there is no way of stopping people buying and using cars, and that in fact these cars do provide desirable personal mobility, then urban motorways are the best way of handling the resulting problem. The trouble is that this is not the only consideration. As opponents are not slow to point out, motorways are intrusive and disruptive, even if better designed than they are now (which it is certainly possible to achieve); funds spent on them may well be diverted away from public transport investment; even when the great majority of families own cars, as has been the case since the mid-1950s in the United States and should be true by the early 1980s in Britain, the great majority of individuals at most times will still be without free access to one. The controversy, then, is essentially about priorities. In a perfect world without an economic problem, there would be unlimited resources for very well-designed motorways, integrated into the urban fabric, and for a superb public transport system available to all — not to mention all the other competing investments such as the replacement of old schools and mental hospitals and prisons, and the construction of new homes for those who are still wretchedly housed. But, of course, the resources are far from unlimited; and the community as a whole has to decide which of many good things it wants the most.

In the final analysis, therefore, most major planning decisions are political in character. Unfortunately, as is well-known, political decision-making is a highly imperfect art. Ordinary people are given the choice of voting every four or five years for a national government, and perhaps every three years for a local government; in either case, they must vote on a confusing bundle of different policies, in which planning issues may be well down the list. Many of these issues, as stressed more than once in this chapter, may be so general and abstract in character that it is difficult for the ordinary citizen to appreciate their impact until critical — and perhaps irrevocable — decisions have been taken. Pressure groups may achieve effective action on particular issues, but they tend to be formed and manned disproportionately by those groups in society which are better educated, better informed, and better organized – which, in most cases, also means richer. The recommendations of the Roskill Commission on London's third airport were finally overruled by the Minister after a great public outcry; and many planners thought that the Minister was right to do so. But many also took little comfort in the fact that whereas the Commission's work had cost just over one million pounds, the pressure group against it had spent three quarters of a million in getting the recommendation overturned. The danger here is that the greater the call for public participation in planning decisions, the greater the likelihood that decisions will go in favour of the richer and better organized – and against those who can least look after their own interests.

A particularly acute problem of divergent values, which is evident in many planning situations, concerns the trade-off between the interests of different generations. In such situations, the best is truly the enemy of the good. Should public housing, for instance, be built to reflect the standards and aspirations of the first generation of occupiers, or the second or third? If it is built merely to minimal contemporary standards, the risk is that it will be regarded as sub-standard within a generation or two; and it may not be possible then to redesign it except at unacceptable cost. But if it is built in advance to satisfy the standards of tomorrow, then less resources will be available to satisfy the pressing housing needs of today. Similarly, many decisions about preservation and conservation involve questions of the interests of different generations. It may be cheaper to pull down a Georgian housing area in a city, and replace it by new flats than to rehabilitate it; the community is then faced with a choice between the needs of those who are ill-housed, and the value of the area for generations of future citizens. Similarly, the establishment of green belts round many British cities after the Second World War involved certain sacrifices on the part of those who were housed farther away from their jobs in the cities, while the majority of the urban populations of the time were unable to enjoy any benefits because they lacked cars to make excursions into the protected countryside; the true benefits will probably be experienced by the next generation, who will use cars to travel out to the new country parks established in the green belts long after they were designated. Here, the planner may with justification claim that by his intervention he is guarding the interests of posterity, including generations now unborn.

Planning in practice, however well managed, is therefore a long way from the tidy sequence of the theorists. It involves conflicts of values which cannot be fully resolved by rational discussion or by calculation; the clash of organized pressure groups and the defence of vested interests; and the inevitable confusions that arise from the complex interrelationships between decisions at different levels and at different scales, at different points in time. The cybernetic or systems view of planning is a condition towards which planners aim; it will never become complete reality. But it does represent a systematic attempt to use reason and logic to reduce confusion and increase man's control over his social, economic and physical environment; and for that, it should be welcomed.

Further Reading

The best introductory textbook on the systems view of planning is J. B. McLoughlin, *Urban and Regional Planning: A Systems Approach* (Faber, 1969; paperback version, 1970). It should be supplemented by George Chadwick's *A Systems View of Planning* (Pergamon, 1971), which is more complex and theoretical in character. F. Stuart Chapin's *Urban Land Use Planning* (Urbana: University of Illinois Press, second edition, 1965) is the best general textbook on planning from the modern viewpoint.

Much of the theory behind projections, forecasts and models for planning is set out in Walter Isard's monumental *Methods of Regional Analysis: An Introduction to Regional Science* (Cambridge, Mass.: MIT Press, 1960). Alan Wilson's *Papers in Urban and Regional Analysis* (London: Pion, 1972) is a collection of his most important papers on the subject of spatial interaction models and their use in a systematic planning framework; written between 1968 and 1971, they form the best available source on the use of models in planning.

A more elementary introductory treatment of the techniques used in modern urban and regional planning is found in Peter Hall, *The Theory and Practice of Regional Planning* (Pemberton, 1970), Chapters 3 and 4.

Index

Page numbers printed in heavy type indicate illustrations

Abercrombie, Patrick, and C P R E, 40; County of London Plan (1943), 61, 64, 103, 123; Bloomsbury Precinct, **63**; contribution to planning, 64, 81, 93, 269

Greater London Plan (1944), 66–7, 103, **105**, 112, 162, 229; and decentralization, 103; accommodation of overspill, 103–4, 114; proposed green belt, 104, **120**; expansion of country towns, 112

Acts of Parliament: Clean Air, 1956, 193

Commonwealth Immigration, 1962, 169

Control of Office Development, 1965, and an O D P, 145

Countryside, 1968, 193; Trent Park, **164**; country parks, **192**, 193, **194**

Cross Acts, 1875, 28

Distribution of Industries, 1945, 99; development areas, 108–9, 125; omissions, 109, 125; limitations of incentives, 109; loopholes, 109–10

Housing, 1918, 36

Industrial Development, 1966, 147, 149

Industry, 1972, 150–51

Land Commission, 1967 (repealed post 1970); compensation and betterment provisions, 118; inflationary results, 118–19

Local Employment, 1960; concept of development districts, 141; reversal of its policy, 142–4

Local Government, 1888, 1894, new structures, 29

Local Government, 1972, 29; suggested two-tier system, 181, **183**; and planning, 181; and national parks, 193

Local Government Reform, 1963, 178, 181

Municipal Corporations, 1835, 28; 1882, 29

National Parks and Access to the Countryside, 1949, 99, 119; and local government powers and responsibilities, 121

New Towns, 1946, 99, 110, 114, 170 and Commissions for the New Towns, 110, 112

Nuisance Removal, 1868, 28

Planning, 1968, 178

Public Health, 1848, 28; 1875, local government reform, 28–9

Sanitary, 1866, 28

Special Roads, 1949, 40

Torrens Acts, 1868, 28

Town and Country Planning, 1947, 8, 99; five-year development plan, 12, 270; I D C certificate, 108; importance, 114–15; nationalization of right to develop land, 115, 116; new local planning authorities, 115–16, 119; and compensation, 116–18, 263; payment of 'development charge', 116–17; changed financial provisions, 117–19; and national parks, 119, 121;

Index

Acts of Parliament – *contd.*
assessment, 112–14, 178; and urban regions, 160, 162

Town and Country Planning, 1968, 8, 119; new structure, 270

Town Development, 1952, 99, 112–14; and new towns, 162

Town Planning, 1909, 1925, 1932; and private developer, 39; control of ribbon development (1935), 40

Transport, 1968, 178

Acts of United States Congress:

Appalachian Regional Development, 1965, 249

Housing, 1949, 253, 256; 1954, 262

Housing and Urban Development, 1968, 1970, 256, 261

Public Works Acceleration, 1962, 248

Public Works and Economic Development, 1965, and ARA, 249

Agriculture, consumption of its land, 39, 100, 167; 19th c. depression, 51, 83; British and W. European labour force, 200; depopulation, 242; US depressed areas, 246; out-migration from the South, 247–52; German, 218, 219; Italian, 222, 225; Scandinavian, 226

Alexander, Christopher, condemns neighbourhood units, 59; *A City Is Not a Tree*, 59

Amsterdam, **235**, 236, 240; socio/economic, 237; 'concentrated deconcentration', 239

Ancient Rome, population, 19; urban noise, 20

Appalachian Region, socio/economic conditions, 249; development programme, 249–52; super-highway, 251

Architecture, Baroque, 20–21

Area Redevelopment Administration (ARA) (US), and unemployment or low income, 248, 251

Atlantic Urban Region (US), **260**, 261

Baldock, creation of Knights Templar, 20

Barlow Commission, provoked by Great Depression, 87; importance to postwar planning, 90, 93; terms of reference, 93; omission of service industries, 109; meaning of word 'industry', 109; control of inter-regional migration, 158–9

Report (1940), 17, 85, 93 ff., 153, 155; location of industry and population, 94, 108; 'structural effect' and industrial growth, 95, 131; analysis of disadvantages of conurbations, 95–7; suggested remedies, 97; major and minority reports, 97, 125; resulting studies and legislation, 98, 99, 108

Barnard, Chester, 10

Bath, residential development, 21

Belgium, 214; coalfields, 200

Birmingham, 201; factory estates, 39; Bournville, 45, **47**; 'new' industries, 85; control of office building (ODP), 145; population growth, 159; proposed new town, 164; under Redcliffe Maud reform, 181

Blache, Vidal de la, 64

Black country, industrial landscape, 22

Board of Trade, IDC certificate, 108, 109, 125; operation from 1956–60, 1966–70, 126–7; proportion of new floor space in relation to employment, 128–9; growth in industries outside control, 138–9; improvement in development areas, 152–3

Booth, Charles, social investigator, 50–51

Boston, ethnic ghettoes, 43, 258

British Isles *see* Great Britain

Buchanan, Sir Colin, and environmental factors, 189, 191; London's West End, **190**, 191; *Traffic in Towns*, 189

Buckingham, James S., idea of a model city, 45

Building materials, brick and stone, 30; interwar cheapness, 34, 37

Building standards, increased control, 28

Burke, Gerald, 237

Cadbury, George, Bourneville estate, 45

Canals, 65

Centre for Environmental Studies, use of transportation models, 188

Chadwick, George, systematic planning approach, 272, **273b**, 274; and goal formation, 277

Coal-mining, and industrial location, 22, **24**, **25**, 65, 84, 85–7; associated economic problems, 81–2; in decline, 82, 131; numbers employed, 83; replaced by oil, 84; nationalization, 116; designated special areas, 141, 147

Committee of Inquiry on the Intermediate Areas, designation, 149; report (1969), 150, 151; regional variation in employment and incomes, 151; unemployment areas, 151–2; inter-area migration, 152; overall conclusions, 152–3

Chapin, Stuart, 188

Chicago, ethnic ghettoes, 43, 258; non-white population, 252

Community, eventual victim of poor social provisions, 48; neighbourhood units, 56, **58**; and betterment, 101–2; new-towns ownership, 110; in local government reform, 180; choosing priorities, 291

Commuter, the, demand for long distance journeys, 233; US, 247

Compulsory purchase, and compensation, 101; by public authorities, 115, 117; payment of existing use value, 117; return to full market value, 117; US States' approval, 262

Computerization, in management and planning, 10–13; new problems and dangers, 13–14; potentialities, 186; and transportation, 186–7

Copenhagen, 243; Finger (linear) Plan, 1948, 72, 227, **229**; population, 226, 227, 228; new higher-speed transport, 227–8; rejects green belt and new town solution, 227, 228, 229; 'City sections' decentralization, 228; Plan 'B', 1960, **229**, 229–30

Copenhagen Regional Planning Office, 228

Cost-benefit analysis, and urban planning, 101, 283–4; evaluation of alternatives, 189, 283–5; and London's third airport, 191, 285; Lichfield's modification, 285–6

Council for the Protection of Rural England (CPRE), 40

Country parks, 193; Elvaston Castle, **194**; Wirral Way, **192**

Countryside, *vis-à-vis* the city, 48, **49**, 51; inclusion in planning, 100, 119, 121–3; long distance footpaths, 121; and AONB, 121, **163**; and value judgements, 284

Coventry, postwar reconstruction, 64, 287; and 'new' industries, 85

Crime, index of social malaise, 257; US concentration in non-white areas, 257–8

Cullingworth, Barry, *Housing Needs and Planning Policy*, 167

Cumberland, West, area of economic problems, 81–2

Cybernetics, definition, 11 and n., 270; source of new concept of planning, 270; technological application, 271;

Index

Cybernetics – *contd.*
and control of mass human behaviour, 271; evaluation, 293
Czechoslovakia, 215

Decision-making, 233, 264; as a science, 10; in cybernation, 14; European quarternary industry, 201, 203; and cost-benefit analysis, 284, 286
Demangeon, Albert, 64
Denmark, 214, 227; Greater Copenhagen region, 226; population, 228
Dennison, Stanley, and Scott report, 101
Department of Economic Affairs, National Plan on French system, 145, 146; abolition, 146
Department of Housing and Urban Development (HUD) (US), Federal area of control, 259–60, 261; Model Cities programme, 261
Department of the Interior (US), 261
Department of Trade and Industry, 108
Department of Transportation (DOT) (US), 261
Derbyshire, 85; cotton-making areas, 22; industrial concentration, 94; sub-regional studies, 287
Developer, the, lack of control, 39; suggested 'onus of proof', 100–101
Development, final form of urban planning, 7; influence of cybernetics, 11–12; suggested embargoes, 100; and higher urban density, 101; in special areas, 108
Development Areas (Districts), wait for analysis of economic problems, 82, **148**; 1945 nomination, 108, 140–41; and unemployment, 126, **134**, 141, 152, 153; operation of IDC machinery, 126–7, **128**, **129**; actual creation of employment, 127, **128**, **129**, **130**,

131; effect of bad industrial structure, 131–2, **132**; additional labour waste, 133; lower activity or participation rates, 133; regions of lower-than-average income, 135, **136**; outward migration, 135, 152, 189; implantation of growth industries, 138–9; replaced by districts, 141, **148**; disparity with London and SE, 144; change in Government incentives, 147; criticisms of anomalies, 147, 149; SET-REP inducements, 149–50, 154; investment grants, 150, 153; evidence of improvement, 152–3; financial and infrastructure inducements, 153; population increases, 159; need for overspill policy, 172; low labour costs, 241; Central Scotland, 108, 112, 140–42, 168, 170; Merseyside, 108, 140, 168, 170; North-East England, 108, 112, 140, 142, 168, 170; South Wales, 108, 112, 141; West Cumberland, 108, 140; Halewood, **140**; Port Talbot, **139**
Disease, cholera, 26, **27**; identification, 28
Dougill, Wesley, LCC architect, 61
Dower, John, Report on National Parks, 99, 107, 119
Drucker, Peter, 10
Durham, Co., 82; coal mining, 22; population, 23

Economic Development Administration (EDA) (US), 249, 251
Education, planning for, 4, 5–6; neighbourhood schools, 59; growth of higher sector in SE, 145; US non-white, 257
Edinburgh, New Town, 21
Edward I, fortified towns, 20
Employment, 'density gradient' in residential areas, 73, 75; postwar

stagnation in manufacturing, 109; a political obsession, 126; index of regional performance, 126–7, **128**, **129**, **230**; changes by Industrial Orders, 1953–65, **130**; effect of bad industrial structure, 131–2, **132**; in development areas (1960s), 151, 159; decentralization, 177; (US) movement to the suburbs, 258; use of Garin–Lowry model, 279–80

Engineering industry, 15; in decline, 82; numbers employed, 83; coalfield location, 84

England and Wales, enclosure movement, 23; expectation of life at birth, 1841, 26; 'Megalopolis', 135, **137**; inter-regional migration, **138**; SE growth and prosperity, 144; birth rates, 1871–2004, 156, **157**; size of average household, 158 *see also* Great Britain

Environment, a factor in planning costs, 185, 189, **190**, **191**, **192**, 193; world-wide issue, 193; use of public pressure, 195

Europe, continental, Baroque town planning, 20; rural landscapes, 21; academic planners, 42, 70–78; urban spread, 43; villa life in new suburbs, 43; high-density housing, 43, 44; 'density gradient', 73; inner-city apartments, 78; industrial location, 87 *see also* Western Europe

European Coal and Steel Community (ECSC), and the Ruhr, 219, 242

European Economic Community (EEC), population distribution, 200, **202**, 203; agglomerations, 201; 'Golden Triangle', 201, 223, 234; Gross Regional Product per capita, **202**, 203; development programmes and problem areas, **202**, 203; regional development, 203, 219, 242;

Common Market agreement, 219; and periphery/centre imbalance, 240; and rural depopulation, 241; Social and Agricultural Funds, 242; criteria of aid, 242; and fiscal/economic union, 242

Farr, William, rural/urban expectation of life, 1841, 26

Fawcett, C. B., *Provinces of England*, 175

Federal Housing Administration (FHS) (US), 253

Forest parks, **163**

Forshaw, J. H., postwar London reconstruction plan, 61, **63**

France, 20, 218; and human geography, 64–5, 205; economic planning system, 145, 205; planning regions, 145, 207, **209**, 210; urban agglomerations, 201, 204; out-migration of young, 203; centralist political tradition, 204, 205, 214, 216; national/regional and regional/local organizations, 204, **206**, 206–8, 210; operation of mixed economy, 205–6; Commissariat général au plan (CGP), 206, 207; regional coordination (DATAR), 207; city-level planning (OREAM), 207; *métropoles d'équilibre*, 208, **209**, 210, 214, 219, 225

Gardens, absence in urban spread, 31; later provision, 35, 36–7, 43; increase size (US), 253

Geddes, Patrick, classic planning sequence (survey–analysis–plan), 12, 65, 66, 115, 189, 270; influence, 58, 65–6, 79, 81, 104, 123, 269; and human ecology, 64–5; concept of conurbations, 65, 83; decentralization, 66, 104; 'neotechnic' industries, 85

Index

Geography, economic, concept of 'growth pole', 141; definition of 'spheres of influence', 170; 'have' and 'have not' regions, 201, 208

Germany, 6, 83; Baroque town planning, 20; Krupp housing settlement, 45; Ruhr coal-fields, 65, 200, 215, 219, **220**, 221, 237; Rhine pollution, 215

Democratic Republic, border areas, 201, 214, 215, 218

Federal Republic (West Germany), urban *Ballungsräume*, 201, 214–15; service industries, 203; administrative tradition, 204, 215 (by *Länder*), 216, 219; market economy system, 204; urban/rural contrasts, 215; air and water pollution, 215; national/regional planning, 216–19, 221; Development areas, **217**, 218–19; Frontier Zone, **217**, 218–19; special areas, **217**, 218, 219; regional/local planning, 219–21; *Landschaftverbände*, **220**

Glasgow, 23; new towns, 104, 112, 170; urban motorway programme, 142; reconstruction plan, **142**; slum clearance, 143

Gottmann, Jean, 'Megalopolis', 261

Gravier, Jean-François, *Paris et le désert français*, 205, 214

Great Britain, early urban development, 17, 20–21, 85; rural exodus, 23; population distribution, 1801, 1805, **24**, **25**; changed landscape, 76, 78; areas with economic problems, 81–2; era of industrial greatness, 82–4; specialization, 83, 84; effect of world economic changes, 84–5, 87; numbers of insured workers, 1923–37, **94**; postwar need for change, 155; existence of 'two Nations', 135; pattern of regional development, 1945–

72, **148**, 149, 155; financial crises, 150, 168; birth-rate fluctuations, 156, **157**, 158; fall in average size of households, 158; mixed economy, 160; restraints on land development, 162, **163**, **164**; new towns, **171**; population growth, 1961–71, 175, **176**, 177; control of office development, 289

Great Depression, 1929–32, 87; regional imbalance, 17, 87; and suburban growth, 34; and national/regional planning, 81, 82; unemployment, 132

Greater London Council (GLC), creation, 178

Greater London Development Plan, 196; Covent Garden, 290

Green belts, round garden cities, 51, 52, 55; Abercrombie and, 104, 114, 120; Government circular (1955), 162, 164; function, 162, 164; attempts to infringe, 164, 166; leap-frogged by developers, **167**, 168, 175; under county control, 181; divergent interests, 292–3; GB, **163**; London, 33, **120**, **164**; Stockholm, 230

Gropius, Walter, and modern architecture, 72

Hague, the, **235**, 236, 237, 240

Hampstead Garden Suburb, 53, 55

Harris, Britton, use of term 'prediction', 274

Heathrow Airport, 39, 194

Hill, Prof. Morris, *Goals Achievement Matrix*, 286

Hobhouse Committee, Report on National Parks Administration, 99, 107, 119

Holmans, A. E., limited application of IDCs, 138–9

Homelessness, in conurbations, 96

Housing, use of planning, 4; 19th c. overcrowding, 26; by-laws for construction, 29, 48; 'net density' to the acre in urban areas, 30, 37, 43, 55, 73; interwar ownership, 34; prices, 37; garden-city, 44 ff., 55; neighbourhood units, 56, **58**; 'density gradient', 73, 75; part played by new towns, 113, 114; and birth-rate fluctuations, 158; total postwar needs, 158; demands of mass car-ownership, 159–60; entry of private sector, 160, 167–8; character of Federal aid (US), 256; 'industrial dwellings', **29**; by-law, 29–30; semi-detached with gardens, **35**; single-family council, 36–7, 43, 78; ribbon development, **38**, 40; factory estates, 39, 44–5

Housing and Home Finance Agency (HHFA), 253; Housing and Home Finance Organization, 261

Howard, Ebenezer, Garden City concept, 44, 45, 48, 51, 71–2, 110; career, 44; Three Magnets, 48, **49**; Social City, **50**, 52, 65, 106; residential density, 51–2; followers, 52–6, 64; inter-urban railways, 56; neighbourhood units, 56; and decentralization, 66, 177; practical concerns, 79; and regional planning, 81, 83, 93, 104; *Garden Cities of Tomorrow*, 44, 48, **49**

Human beings, complex inter-relating systems, 11, 288; and computerization, 14; and their environment, 64; in cost-benefit analysis, 284; variation in value judgements, 286; changing values, 290

Hunt, Sir Joseph, Report on intermediate areas, 150

Immigrants, Commonwealth, and London and SE, 135, 138, 144, 169; restrictions on, 158

US, ethnic ghettoes, 43, 247, 252; housing patterns, 247, 252; inter-State movements, 251–2; South to North non-white, 252–3

Income, low rate in 1930s, 82; and retention of unproductive industries, 126; as index of economic health, **133**; relationship to unemployment and activity rates, 135; regional disparities, 135, **136**, **137**, 151, 244; US, 244, 245–6, 249; black/white comparison, 256–7

Income tax, source of income rates, 135, **136**, **137**

Indian subcontinent, industrial growth, 84–5

Industrial Revolution, 10, 17, 21–2; socio/economic results, 19; housing settlements, 45; staple industries, 83; UK/W. Europe comparison, 200–201

Industry, early dispersal, 21–2; impact of coal, 22; creation of new towns, 22–3, 45; port towns, 22–3; rural exodus, 23; northern depressed areas, 37, 40, 81–2, 87; factory movement into suburbs, 39, 45, 65; importance of home market over export, 85; efforts to reinflate, 90; 'trading estates', 90; disadvantages of conurbations, 96; peripheral and central seeking locations, 233; (US) low income rates, 246

Infant mortality, industrial city rates, 26; reductions in regional variations, 96

Intermediate areas, 150–52

Ireland, exodus after potato famine, 23; population distribution, 1821, 1841, **24**, **25**; problem area, 201; Northern new towns, 170, **171**

Israel, linear programming models, 279

Italy, southern problem area, 201, 221, **222**, 225; 'Mezzogiorno', 202, 222–3, **223**, 224; out-migration of young,

Index

Italy – *contd.*
203, 222, 223; regional development, 221–6; centre/periphery socio/economic contrasts, 222–3, 225; industrialized Lombardy Plain, 222; ineffective land reform movement, 222–3, 224, 225; 'Golden Triangle', 223; geographical limitations, 224, 226; state public utility corporations, 225

Japan, 6, 84–5
Jarrow, closure of Tyne shipyard, **91**
Job opportunities, imbalance in location, 87; in development areas and elsewhere, 138; for US non-whites, 257, 258

Kerner Commission on Civil Disorders, 1968, and black/white median incomes, 256–7

Labour, effect of Great Depression, 34, 37; inter-regional migration, 135, 137, **138**, 158–9; low costs in peripheral areas, 241
Laissez-faire, impediment to social reform, 28
Lancashire, cotton-industry, 22, 31–2, 84, 147–8; coal-mining, 22; industrial growth, 23, 65, 94; slower-than-average employment growth, 151; economic problems, 152; new towns, 168, 170
Land, prices, 36, 96, 100, 117, 118; suggested nationalization, 102–3, 115, 117; proposed Commission, 118; designated protected areas, 162, **163**
Le Corbusier, 67; and mass car-ownership, 59; contribution to urban planning, 72–8; notions concerning densities, 78; Alton West Estate, 75–6, **77**; Chandigarh capital city, 72; Notre Dame en Haut, 72; Paris plan (1922), 73, 75; Unité de Habitation,

Marseilles, 72; Villa Savoye, 72; *The City of Tomorrow*, 72–3; *The Radiant City*, 72–3, **74, 76**
Leicestershire, 22, 85, 94
Le Play, P.G.F., human geography, 64–5; triad Place-Work-Folk, 65
Letchworth Garden City, 52, **53, 54**, 55, 104
Lever, Wm Hesketh (later Lord Leverhulme), Port Sunlight, 45, **47**
Lichfield, Nathaniel, *Planning Balance Sheet*, 285–6
Liverpool, 23, 140, 181; Irish immigrants, 23; cellar dwellings, 26; expectation of life at birth, 1841, 26; infant mortality, 1841, 1970, 26; public transport, 36; Halewood factory, **140**
Local authorities, and social reform, 27–8; slum improvement, 28, 30, 36; net density in housing, 55; and land purchase, 102; new towns, 106, 113; new planning authorities, 115–16, 119, 121, 122; payment of compensation, 117–18; and use of the countryside, 119, 121; experimental structure plans, 178; and management techniques, 186, 196
Local government reforms, 1875–94, 28–9; 1965–72, 173, 175–85; 1967, 196; Redcliffe Maud report, 180–85; new social services departments, 196–7
Local government (US), 259, 262–3
Local Planning authorities, creation and powers, 115–16, 119, 121, 155; negative powers of control, 122–4, 155; need for overall coordination, 123–4, 162, 172, 173; and inter-regional migration, 158–9; and private enterprise, 160, 162; major inquiries, 164; new area of control, 178
Location of Offices Bureau (LOB), 144

London, 19–21; industrial and population growth, 23, 26, 30, **33**, 34, **35**, 36, 94, 96, 97, 144, 159, **166**, 167; 'net density' to the acre, 30, 32; decentralization, 34, 39, 66; County of London Plan (1943), 61, 64, 103; postwar reconstruction plans, 61, **63**, 64; Tripp's precinct plan, 61, **62**; Greater London Plan, 66–7; MARS plan, 72; location of marketing industries, 85, 109; new towns, 112; control of office development, 144–5, 289–90; reconstruction of East End, **165**; migration outwards, **166**, 167, 177; third airport controversy, 285

London County Council, 61; influence of Le Corbusier, 75–6, **77**

Los Angeles, Freeway interchange, **265**

Lowry, Ira, 188

Mackinder, H. J., and human geography, 64

McLoughlin, Brian, systematic planning approach, 272, **273a**, 274 ff.; implementation process, **288**

McNamara, Robert, Department of Defence, 197

Madrid, remnants of El Ciudad, 70, **71**

Management, education in, 10; development of cybernetics, 11; and local government, 186, 196

Manchester, 19th c. overcrowding, 26; expectation of life at birth, 1841, 26; 1880s, 50; public transport and housing, 36; factory estates, 39; Wythenshawe satellite town, 55, **57**, 104; proposed new town (Lymm), 164, 167, 170; population decrease, 177

Marketing services, 95, 117; economic demands, 201, 203; location, 203

Marshall, Alfred, idea of new towns, 45, 48

Maud Committee on management, 196–7

Middle classes, commuter population, 32; assimilation of working classes, 34; house-ownership, 37; movement outwards, 43; continental European housing, 43

Middlesex, suburban development, 34, **35**; consumption of market garden land, 39, 100

Milan, 201, 223; underground railways, 221

Milton Keynes, 52, 59, 169

Mining (US), depressed areas, 246

Ministry of Housing and Local Government, 146, 147

Ministry of Town and Country Planning, 110; right of appeal to the Minister, 116; closure of regional offices, 123–4, 126

Models, deterministic or probabilistic, static or dynamic, descriptive or predictive, 278; linear programming, 278–9; spatially aggregated or disaggregated, 279, 285; Garin–Lowry, 279–80, **280**; spatial interaction, 279–80; calibration, 280; complexity, 281, 286; design process, 282; subject of cost-benefit calculations, 284–5; monitoring system, 287–8

Monnet, Jean, economic planner, 205

Motor car, mass ownership, 291; 1939, 36; 1900–2010, **186**; US, 43, 253, 264, 291; 1900–2010, **186**; and urban workers, 51; implications, 59, 67, 70, 159, 177; manufacturing location, 85; use of computerization, 186, **187**; use in Italy, 221

Motorways, delayed provision, 40; computerized forecasting, 187; and the environment, 195; reaction against, 290–91; M56 N. Cheshire, 56; London orbital, 178; M1 studies, 189; Stockholm, 232, 234; US inter-

Index

Motorways – *contd.*
    state, 253–4; London–S. Wales, 290
Mumford, Lewis, *The Culture of Cities*, 66

National Parks, Reports on, 107, 119
National Parks Commission, creation, 121, **163**; powers, 121, 122, 193; long-distance footpaths, 121
Natural Environment Research Council, 122
Nature Conservancy, 122
Nature Reserves, **163**
New Jersey (US), Radburn new town, 59, **60**, 61; Levittown Fairless Hills, **254**
Netherlands, Randstad and Regional Development, 201, 204, 234–40, **235**, **236**, 237; tertiary industries, 203; water supply, 215; importance in EEC, 234; metropolitan concentration, 234, 236, 237; agricultural heart, **235**, 236, 237, 240; population, 236–7; decentralization, 237–8; land reclamation, 238; Second Report on Physical Planning, 238, **239**; 'concentrated deconcentration', 238–9, **239**, 240
New Towns, 147; community ownership, 110; in development areas, 112, 143, 169–70; post 1961, 112, 143, 169–70; reception of overspill, 114, 143, 169–70, 172; and birth-rate predictions, 158; and population growth, **161**; Conservative policy, 162, 168; Cumbernauld, Scotland, **143**; Dawley, 170; Irvine, 170; Livingston, 170; Lymm, 164, 167, 170; Runcorn, 170; Skelmersdale, 168, 170; Slough, **86**; South-East, **174**; Stevenage, 110, **111**; Warrington, 170; Washington, 170; Wythenshawe, 55, **57**, 104

New York, 243; ethnic ghettoes, 43; Regional Plan (1920s), **58**; Manhattan Island, 73; 'density gradient', 73; income variations, 245; Puertoricans, 247; welfare budgets, 258; Milford Center, **255**
Northamptonshire, 94, 169
Northern Economic Planning Council, new factory jobs, 153
Northern Region Planning Council and Board, 82
Northumberland, 81–2, 94
Nottinghamshire, 85; coal-mining, 22; industrial concentration, 94; sub-regional studies, 287

Osborn, Sir Frederick, and new towns, 53
Overall Economic Development Programme (OEDP) (US), 248
Owen, Robert, New Lanark settlement, 45, **46**

Paris, 20, 201, 243; linear plan (1965), 72; agglomerations, 204, **211**; socio/economic dominance, 205, 210; PADOG plan, 206; restrictions on future growth, 206, 208; central planning group (GCPU), 207; research association (IAURP), 207; increase in *départements*, 208; Schema directeur (1965), 208, 210–11, **211**; under-investment in infrastructure, 210; new towns, 210, 214; Metro system, 210; attempted decentralization, 211, 214; Reconstruction of *La Défense*, 210, 212, 213, 290
Parker, Barry, garden city architect, 53, 55–7, **57**; and parkways, 55–6, 57; and mass car-ownership, 59
Perroux, François, 'growth pole' concept, 141

Perry, Clarence, neighbourhood units, **58**, 59, 61

Philanthropists, housing ventures, 44–5, **46, 47**

Planners, and computer-controlled development, 11–12; use of continuous information, 13; multi-purpose and dimensional objectives, 14–17; reaction against urban spread, 37, 39–40; professional status, 39; Anglo-American and Continental groups, 42–4, 44–70, 70–78; assessment, 78; idea of a linear city, 71; concern with end-state product, 78; failure to produce alternatives, 79; belief in physical solutions to problems, 79–80; and birthrate predictions and realities, 156, 158–9; and mass car-ownership, 159; interaction between ineffectiveness and omnipotence, 272; relations with the public, 277, 286; and modelling process, 278–81; content of design and his objectives, 282; and value judgements, 283, 284, 286

Planning, definition, 3–4, 5; detailed *v.* general controversy, 7; pre-Industrial Revolution, 19–20; complexity in mixed economy, 79, 145; socio/economic framework, 185–6, 195–6; winners and losers from decisions, 195; who benefits and who suffers, 196; key questions needing research, 198; US/European differences, 259; recent controversies, 289, 291; imponderables and changing economies, 289; changing fashions, 290; conflict of right against right, 291, 293; political motivation, 291; interests of different generations, 292

Planning, economic, 4; factors involved, 8; concept of 'growth pole', 141; attraction of French system, 145; boards and councils, 145–7; demar-cation dispute, 147; concern with spatial expansion, 173; new emphasis, 185

Planning Advisory Group (P A G), two-tier system of plan-making, 178, **179**

Planning process, post-1960 concept, 269; a continuous operation, 269, 282, 287; older view, 270; evaluation of alternative policies, 270, 273, 277, 282, 285–6; notion of constant interaction, 271, 272; systems concept, 271–2, 282; main control levers, 272; three exponents, 272–4; goals, objectives, targets, **273**, 274–7, 282, 283; conceptual and technical difficulties, 276; forecasting, modelling and plan design, 277–81; and plan evaluation, 281–7; definition of evaluation, 282–3; economic evaluation procedures, 283–6; implementing the plan, 287–8; real life situations, 288–9

Planning-Programming-Budgeting System (P P B S), 197

Plans, variation in meaning, 3; spatial, 7; structural and local, 178; changes in content, 185; modern methodology, 275; design process, 278–87; linear or cyclical?, 287; S. Hampshire, 1972, **179**

Pollution, pre-Industrial Revolution, 20; government powers, 193–4; industrial, 194–5; Germany, 215; US failure to deal with, 267

Population, 23; distribution in G B, 1801, **24**; 1851, **25**; 20th c., 87; interwars, 87; expectation of life at birth (rural/urban), 1841, 26; growth in net density, 31–2, 34; relative growth in G B, 1861–91, 1921–39, 87, **88, 89**; birth-rate predictions and fluctuations, 156, **157**, 158; decentralization and car ownership, 160; in- and outwards migrations, 160;

Index

Population – *contd.*
    urban decentralization, 167; rural increase (1950s–60s), 175, **176,** 177; W. European, 203; urban/rural (French) comparison, 205; projected growth, 211; Garin–Lowry projection models, 279–80, **280**

Port towns, 22–3

Poverty, US, 247; Indian, 251; in major urban areas, 252, 257–8; definition of 'areas', 258

Poverty line, numbers living below, E. London, 1880s–90s, 50–51; US non-white numbers, 257

Powell, Geoffrey, population growth in Home Counties, 167

Preston, high density housing, **31**

Private enterprise, speculative building, 34, 37, 114; garden cities, 52, 53; initiation of physical development, 79, 122–3, 156, 160, **161**; in Italy, 225, 226; and US urban development, 259

Public health services, early scarcity, 23, 25–6; cholera epidemics, 26; impediments to reform, 27–8; improvement by 1890s, 48, 96

Public transport, lack of and industrial location, 26; and urban spread, 31, 32, **33,** 34; influence of electric trains and motor buses, 34, 36, 37; Corbusier's mass-system, 73, 75, 78

Pullman, George M., model town, 45

Radburn layout, 60, 61

Railways, transport of coal, 22; and urban development, 22, **33,** 34, 65; commuter trains, 32; electrification, 32, 33, 34; underground, 53; (Italian), 221; Stockholm, 230–31, 233–4; nationalization, 116; Stockton and Darlington, 22

Redcliffe Maud, Sir John (later Lord), and local government reform, 180; unitary and two-tier solutions, 180–81, **182**; position of planning, 180, 181, 185; Metropolitan Counties, 181, **183**

Regional economic boards, civil service membership, 146; activities, 146–7; and spatial planning, 172–3

Regional economic councils, membership, 145–6; activities, 146–7; demarcation dispute, 147; and spatial planning, 172–3

Regional planning (regional/local), 83; modern usage, 81; distinguished from 'regional economic', 81, 82; pattern of development, **148,** 149

Regional economic planning (national/regional), 83; birth due to Great Depression, 81, 82; distinguished from 'regional', 81–2; appropriate units, 82; nature of problem, 82–9; efforts to reinvigorate the economy, 90; 'structural effect' of industrial growth, 95; record of controls, 125; overall concern with employment, 126; continuance of bad industrial structure, 131; movement of labour, 135, 138, 158–9; small impact on total problem, 138; post-1960 policy changes, 140–72; concept of development districts, 141; of 'growth pole' (zone), 141, 142–3; new organization, 145; verdict on its policies, 151 ff.; major studies, 168–70, 172; efforts at central and local government cooperation, 173; multi-centre growth zones, 173–5, **174**

Regional Employment Premium (REP), 149–50

Reith, Lord, Committee on New Towns, 99, 106, 110; and BBC, 106; decentralization, 177

Roadways, arterial developments, 40; multi-level free-flow highways, 75;

and mass car-ownership, 159–60; Great West, **38**

Rochdale, spectacular growth, 23

Rome, 16th to 17th c. reconstruction, 20; 'Mezzogiorno', 201; underground railways, 221

Roosevelt, F. D., New Deal, 248, 253

Roskill Commission, on London's third airport, 191, 285, 292

Rotterdam, **235**, 236, 240; port-industrial, 237

Royal Commissions: Distribution of the Industrial Population, 90 and n., 93, 99

Constitutional arrangements, 175, 185

Local Government, England, 180, **182**; Scotland, 180, 181, **184**; Wales, 180

Local Government in England, 1967, 58–9, 180

State of Large Towns, 28

Royal Town Planning Institute, 197–8

Ruhr Coalfield Association, **220**

Salt, Titus, Saltaire settlement, 45, **46**

Scandinavia, social-democratic tradition, 204; population distribution, 226; later industrial revolution, 226–7; regional/local planning, 227; periphery/centre contrasts, 240

Schuster Committee, training planners, 198

Scotland, 84, 131; depressed areas, 40; European type slums, 44; urban concentration areas, 65; Clydeside shipping, 84; Commission for 'special areas', 90; industrial areas, 94; new towns, 112 (Cumbernauld), **143**; need for new jobs, 140; injection of growth industries, 140; less-than-average rise in incomes, 151; drift southwards, 158; local government reform, 180, 181, **184**; problem areas in EEC, 201; US electronic firms, 241

Scott, Sir Leslie, Report on Land Utilization in Rural Areas, 99, 100; suggested 'onus of proof', 100–101

Select Committee on the Health of Towns (1840), 28

Selective Employment Tax (SET), 149–50

Shipbuilding, declining industry, 82, 131

Shropshire, Coalbrookdale ironworks, 22

Sicily, oil, 222; regional development, 224

Simon, Herbert, 10

Skyscrapers (high-rise flats), Le Corbusier's concept, 73, 75, **76**, 77; replace slums, 76, **165**; inhumanity, 76, 165; cost compared with agricultural land, 167; Stockholm, 230

Slough, 'new' industries, 85, **86**; 'trading estate', 90, 91

Slums, European/English comparison, 43–4; effect of clearance on landscape, 76; E. London reconstruction, **165**; lack of land, 167; Merseyside, 168

Smailes, A. E. and Green, F. H. W., 123

Smith, Adam, division of labour, 83

Snow, Dr John, and cholera, **27**, 28

Social sciences, and academic geography, 9; and control of human processes, 14; and training of planners, 198

Social services, planning, 4; factors involved, 8; eventual community provision, 48; (US) development areas, 251; lack of public housing, 256; and non-white areas, 258

Soria y Mata, Arturo, Linear City (El Ciudad lineal), 70, **71**

South East Planning Council, 173, **174**

Index

South East Study (1964), ban on office building, 168–9; major conclusions and recommendations, 168–9, **174**

Southampton–Portsmouth, new town, 169

Soviet Russia, State ownership, 205

Special development areas, **148**, 149, 150

Stamp, Sir Laurence Dudley, and agricultural land, 100

Standard Industrial Classification, % increases in employment, 1961–71, **130**, 131

Standing Conference on London and South-East Regional Planning, 172, 173

Stein, Clarence, and neighbourhood units concept, 59; segregation of pedestrian roads, 59, 61; and Radburn, 59, **60**

Stevenage, 110, **111**, 112; pedestrian precinct, **113**

Stewart, Sir Malcolm, and Special areas, 90, 93

Stilwell, Frank, 'shift and share' analysis, 131–2, **132**

Stockholm, linear plan (1966), 72; suburban developments, 78, 227, 230–32, **232**, 233–4; transport services, 230–31, 233–4; General Plan, 230, **231**, 232; Regional Plan, **231**, 233; highways, 232; hierarchical shopping centres, 231–2, **233**, 238; Farsta planned suburb, **233**; axial extensions, 234

Stone, Peter, costs of high-density redevelopment, 167

Strategic Plan for the South East (1970), **174**, 185

Strategy for the South East (1967), 173, **174**

Streets, minimum width, 30; precincts, 61

Suburban growth, effect of electric trains and motor buses, 32, **33**, 34; underground railways, 34, **35**; and decentralization, 39, 45, 65, 176–7; private developments, **161**, 167–8; Heswall, Cheshire, **161**

Suburban growth (US), 246–7, **254**, **255**, 258; in search of a better environment, 252, 253; shopping centres, 253, **255**; dependence on private car, 253; social status, 254–5; limited benefits, 255–6, 264, 266; unavailable to black people, 256, 258; achievements, 264

Sweden, urban population, 226; planning achievement, 232

Systems control and analysis, 10–11; use of cybernetics, 270; production of models, 277–80

Technology, and urban spread, 34, 35, 36; and demand for export staples, 84; and planning forecasts, 289

Tennessee Valley redevelopment scheme, 248

Tertiary industries, city-centre location, 39, 177, 203; lack of government control, 109, 125, 145; fastest employment growth, 1961–71, 131, ·138–9; aims of SET, 149; in W. Europe, 201, 203; high income areas (US), 245

Textile industry, numbers employed, 83; coalfield location, 84; in decline, 131, (US), 246

Town and country planning, 1947 Act, 8; Association, 52

Town Planning Institute, 39

Traffic congestion, due to decentralization, 39–40, 177; in conurbations, 96; environmental considerations, 189, **190**; Italian cities, 221; use of cybernetics, 271

Transportation planning, 196; *ad hoc* studies, 177, 178, 186–7; computerization of analysis and prediction, 185, 186–7; new structure pattern, 187–8, **187**; integrated public and private programmes, 188; and high density concentrations, 188; inadequate training programmes, 189; interrelationship with channel spaces, 278

Treasury, the, economic planning function, 146

Treaty of Rome, 204, 219; links between signatories, 240–41; and competition, 242

Tripp, Sir Alker, idea of precincts, 61, **62**, 63; high-capacity free-flow highways, 61, **62**; *Town Planning and Traffic*, 61

Tudor Walters report, housing recommendations, 36–7, 55

TV closed circuit, educational use, 6

Tyne and Tees estuaries, 81–2; Team Valley Estate, 90, **92**

Unemployment, 82, 125; uneven distribution, 87, 132; planning for reductions, 126; higher rates in less prosperous areas, 132–3, 151–2, 153; regional differentials, 1961–8, **134**; a criteria for aid, 141, **148**, 149, 242; (US), rates in early '60s, 248; among non-whites, 257

United Nations: Conference on Human Environment, 193

United States (US), 6, 17, 279; management education, 10; urban outward migration, 43; ethnic ghettoes, 43, **257**; idea of parkways, 55–6; neighbourhood units, **58**, 59; industrial power, 83; Wall St crash, 87; National Parks Service, 107, 261; pioneer transportation studies, 177, 186–7; social aspects of planning, 195, 256–7; Interstate Highway Program, 195, 262; metropolitan

development, 195–6, 252–9; stereotype opinion of its planning, 244; national/regional economic development, 244–5, 248–52; regional/local physical development, 244–5; regional variation in family incomes, 245–6, 249; character of its economy, 245–6; depressed areas, 246, 247, 249; industrial communities, 246; islands of poverty amidst affluence, 247, 267; area development programmes, 249, **250**, 251; distortion of investment, 251; nonwhite S. to N. migration, 252, 258; low-income city residents, 256–8; racial disturbances, 258; urban poverty and civic bankruptcy, 258; planning powers and policies, 259–64; Federal control, 259–62; land use control ('planning' and 'zoning'), 262–4; concept of *police power*, 263; increasing social stratification, 266

Urban and regional planning, precise meaning, 6–7; spatial character, 7, 8, 14–17, 278; and other social sciences, 8–9, 14, 16; multi-dimensional and multi-objective, 14–16, 274–5; academic thinkers, 42 ff., 168–70, 172; reports leading to postwar system, 99–107; resulting legislation, 107–21; lack of effective organization, 162; omission of social policy, 172; new regional structure (1968), 173; sub-class of general planning, 269; production of models, 278–81; evaluation devices, 283–7

Urban Renewal Programmes, 122

Urban spread, urbanization, 19; lack of socio/economic provision, 23, 25–6; post-1870 development, 30 ff.; effect of public transport, 32, **33**, 34, **35**; tentacular growth, 34, 70; changed pattern of accessibility, 36; reaction against, 37–9; separates homes from

Index

Urban spread – *contd.*
  workplaces, 39; development of conurbations, 65; linear development, 71–2; extent in Britain (1901), 83; (US), 246–7, 253–5
Unwin, Raymond, 55, 56; and Letchworth, 53; *Nothing Gained by Overcrowding*, 55
Uthwatt, Sir Augustus (Lord Justice), Expert Committee on Compensation and Betterment, 99, 101, 102, 117; recommendations, 102–3, 115, 118

Van der Rohe, Mies, and modern architecture, 72

Wakefield, Edward G., 45
Wales, 20; depressed areas, 40, 201; industrial location (South), 84, 94; unemployment, 87; Commission for 'special areas', 90; Treforest trading estate, 90, 92; low income rates in Mid-, 135; Port Talbot, **139**
Warrington, new town, 170
Washington, linear plan (1961), 72; non-white population, 252
Water transport, and location of industry, 84, 139
Webb, Beatrice (later Lady Passfield), 51
Welwyn Garden City, 52, 55, 104
Western Europe, 17, 200 ff.; Great Depression, 81; form of industrialization, 200–201; exodus of farm workers, 200–201, 242; long distance migrations, 201; rural/urban comparison, 201, 203, 205; manufacturing and tertiary industries, 201–3; socio/economic problems, 203–4; differentiated political traditions, 204; variation in land control, 204; national/regional planning, 240, 241;

centre/periphery contrast, 240; policy in development areas, 241; regional/local problems, 241–2; metropolitan growth, 242–3; regional variations in income, 235 *see also* Europe, continental
West Hartlepool, growth, 23
West Midlands, 65, 85; new towns, 104, 170; industrial structure, 131; growth control, 168; strategic regional study, 169–70, 174
Wheatley, Mr Justice, local government reform (Scotland), 180, 181
White Papers: Investment Incentives, 1966, 147
Wibberley, Gerald, cost of high-density development, 166
Wiener, Norbert, and cybernetics, 270; *Human Use of Human Beings*, 10–11
Wilson, Alan, 188; systematic planning approach, 272, **273c**, 274; definition of goals, 275
Women, regional variations in employment customs, 133; areas of small job opportunities, 135
Working classes, 19th c. distance from work, 31–2; social mobility, 34, 37, 43; house ownership, 37; increased income by 1890s, 48; continuing high-density living, 48, 50; decentralization, 51
Wright, Frank Lloyd, 72; variance with Continental school, 67, 69; influence on US planning, 67; concept of a dispersed, low-density urban spread (Broadacre City), 67, **68–9**

Yorkshire, West Riding industries, 22, 84; industrial concentration, 94; slower-than-average employment and income growth, 151; economic problems, 152

More about Penguins and Pelicans

Penguinews, which appears every month, contains details of all the new books issued by Penguins as they are published. From time to time it is supplemented by *Penguins in Print*, which is a complete list of all titles available. (There are some five thousand of these.)

A specimen copy of *Penguinews* will be sent to you free on request. For a year's issues (including the complete lists) please send 50p if you live in the British Isles, or 75p if you live elsewhere. Just write to Dept EP, Penguin Books Ltd, Harmondsworth, Middlesex, enclosing a cheque or postal order, and your name will be added to the mailing list.

In the U.S.A.: For a complete list of books available from Penguin in the United States write to Dept CS, Penguin Books Inc., 7110 Ambassador Road, Baltimore, Maryland 21207.

In Canada: For a complete list of books available from Penguin in Canada write to Penguin Books Canada Ltd, 41 Steelcase Road West, Markham, Ontario.

Human Identity in the Urban Environment

Edited by Gwen Bell and Jaqueline Tyrwhitt

By the year 2000 there may be over 1,000 cities in the world with a million or more inhabitants. Already thirteen areas deserve the title of 'megalopolis', including the eastern seaboard and the Great Lakes complex in the United States, the smaller denser area of England and the huge population surrounding the Rhine.

How is man to remain human in the coming wilderness of steel, concrete and tarmac?

It is to this problem that this collection of more than forty essays is addressed. The governing factors of nature, the needs of man, society, buildings and construction, and the networks of transport and communications provide headings for articles by W. H. Auden, C. A. Doxiadis, Bertrand de Jouvenel, Margaret Mead, Buckminster Fuller, Arnold Toynbee, C. H. Waddington and a number of architects, planners and sociologists.

Finally the editors have assembled a group of articles which provide a case study of the greatest complex of all, the Tokaido megalopolis in Japan, where nearly 70 million people live.

Man and Environment

Crisis and the Strategy of Choice

Robert Arvill

What will the world look and be like tomorrow? Must the landscape be an extension of today's spreading deterioration? More air fouled by noise and poisoned fumes; more water polluted by chemicals and oil slicks; more land crushed under the sprawl of towns, super-highways, airports, factories, pylons and strip-mines? Is man bound to build a stifling steel-and-concrete hell for himself? Or can effective steps be taken now to preserve our open-spaces, seashores and life-sustaining elements from the assaults of technology?

This is a book about man – about the devastating impact of his numbers on the environment and the decisions and actions he can take to attack the problem. The author is an expert on conservation and planning. Land, air, water and wildlife are treated by him as both valuable resources in very short supply and as precious living entities. He contrasts present management of these resources with man's future needs. British experience and examples from all over the world illustrate the critical and practical aspects of the problem. Past conservation programmes are reviewed and evaluated, and the book offers a complete set of proposals for regional, national and international action on environmental protection. The approach is farsighted, informed, urgent.

Shape of Community

Realization of Human Potential

Serge Chermayeff and Alexander Tzonis

Technology is creating an ever-expanding environment which is becoming increasingly hostile to the natural one. The conflict between the natural and the man-made has reached a point of unprecedented crisis: life's total habitat is endangered. One of the most devastating threats is created by transport and communications which destroy meeting places and the sense of community.

Affluent societies in their narrow-minded preoccupation with quite material gains are losing sight of long-term consequences which, however, are tragic to man's survival. The simple remedial steps that are being taken now have become ineffective and obsolete.

Shape of Community is a manifesto urging the re-thinking of technology as a catalyst of human evolution, rather than simply as a blind destructive force. It proposes a design methodology and an urban model that may lead to a peaceful coexistence of man and nature, and man with man within the community.

Mental Maps

Peter Gould and Rodney White

Mental Maps is a study of the 'geography of perception': of the mental images we form of places, which are inevitably shaped by a selective channelling of information. A New Yorker's 'mental map' of the United States is significantly different from a Californian's; and it is well known that most southerners think Carlisle is inside the Arctic Circle.

The mental images we construct are crucial in deciding where to live, in the siting of factories and new towns, in our choice of holidays and in our attitude to other people. Geographers are now trying to measure 'mental maps', to discover how they are formed and how they differ. Peter Goulding and Rodney White have written an exciting and sometimes surprising survey of this new area of inquiry; they include accounts of mental maps at work in America, Sweden, Southeast Asia, parts of Africa and Britain, and an analysis of the implications of their findings.

The opening up of this new field of study will be of vital importance for future planning and for widening our perception of the environment.

The Pebble First Guide to

Horses

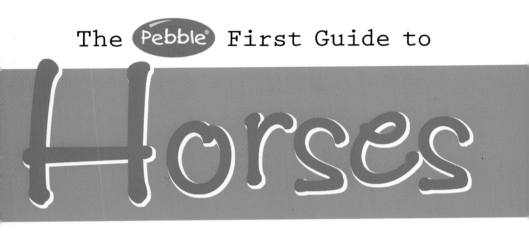

by Zachary Pitts

Consulting Editor: Gail Saunders-Smith, PhD

Capstone
press®
Mankato, Minnesota

Pebble Books are published by Capstone Press,
151 Good Counsel Drive, P.O. Box 669, Mankato, Minnesota 56002.
www.capstonepress.com

Copyright © 2009 by Capstone Press, a Capstone Publishers company.
All rights reserved. No part of this publication may be reproduced in whole
or in part, or stored in a retrieval system, or transmitted in any form or by any
means, electronic, mechanical, photocopying, recording, or otherwise,
without written permission of the publisher.
For information regarding permission, write to Capstone Press,
151 Good Counsel Drive, P.O. Box 669, Dept. R, Mankato, Minnesota 56002.
Printed in the United States of America

1 2 3 4 5 6 13 12 11 10 09 08

Library of Congress Cataloging-in-Publication Data
Pitts, Zachary.
    The Pebble first guide to horses / by Zachary Pitts.
    p. cm. — (Pebble books. Pebble first guides)
    Includes bibliographical references and index.
    ISBN-13: 978-1-4296-1708-6 (hardcover)
    ISBN-10: 1-4296-1708-X (hardcover)
    ISBN-13: 978-1-4296-2802-0 (softcover pbk.)
    ISBN-10: 1-4296-2802-2 (softcover pbk.)
    1. Horses — Juvenile literature. I. Title. II. Series.
SF302.P58 2009
636.1 — dc22   2008001396

Summary: A basic field guide format introduces 13 horse breeds.

About Horse Sizes

The height of a horse is measured in hands. One hand equals 4 inches (10 centimeters). Shetland ponies are measured in inches. A horse is measured from the ground to the highest point on its shoulders.

Note to Parents and Teachers

The Pebble First Guides set supports science standards related to life science. In a reference format, this book describes and illustrates 13 horse breeds. This book introduces early readers to subject-specific vocabulary words, which are defined in the Glossary section. Early readers may need assistance to read some words and to use the Table of Contents, Glossary, Read More, Internet Sites, and Index sections of the book.

Table of Contents

American Paint Horse 4

American Quarter Horse 6

American Saddlebred Horse 8

Appaloosa Horse 10

Arabian Horse 12

Belgian Horse 14

Clydesdale Horse 16

Friesian Horse 18

Lipizzan Horse 20

Percheron Horse 22

Shetland Pony 24

Tennessee Walking Horse 26

Thoroughbred Horse 28

Glossary 30

Read More 31

Internet Sites 31

Index 32

foal

4

Height: 14 to 16 hands

Weight: 1,000 to 1,200 pounds
          (450 to 540 kilograms)

Colors: bay, brown, chestnut, black;
          has white spots

Home country: United States

Uses: rodeos, western riding

Facts: • smart and calm
          • good with children

foals

Height: 15 to 16 hands

Weight: 1,200 to 1,500 pounds
(540 to 680 kilograms)

Colors: bay, brown, sorrel, roan

Home country: United States

Uses: rodeos, western riding, racing

Facts:
- most popular horse
- strong and quick

foal

Height:	15 to 17 hands
Weight:	1,000 to 1,200 pounds (450 to 540 kilograms)
Colors:	bay, brown, chestnut
Home country:	United States
Uses:	riding, driving
Facts:	• has large eyes • smart and friendly

foal

Height:	14 to 16 hands
Weight:	1,000 to 1,200 pounds (450 to 540 kilograms)
Colors:	bay, chestnut, black; has spots
Home country:	United States
Uses:	riding
Facts:	• first used by Native Americans • named for Palouse River in northwestern United States

11

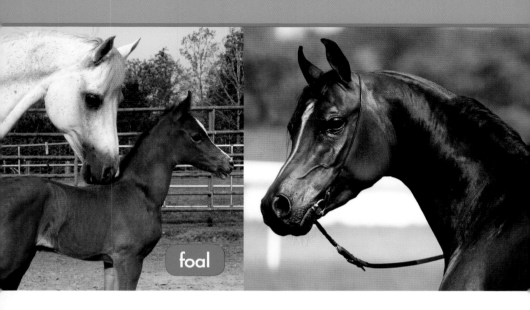

foal

Height:	14 to 15 hands
Weight:	800 to 1,100 pounds (360 to 500 kilograms)
Colors:	chestnut, bay, gray, black
Home country:	Saudi Arabia
Uses:	riding
Facts:	• very old breed • gentle and graceful

13

Belgian Horse

14

foal

Height: 16 to 18 hands

Weight: 1,800 to 2,000 pounds
           (815 to 900 kilograms)

Colors: chestnut, sorrel, roan

Home country: Belgium

Uses: driving, farm work

Facts: • able to pull heavy loads
           • nicknamed "gentle giant"

15

Clydesdale Horse

16

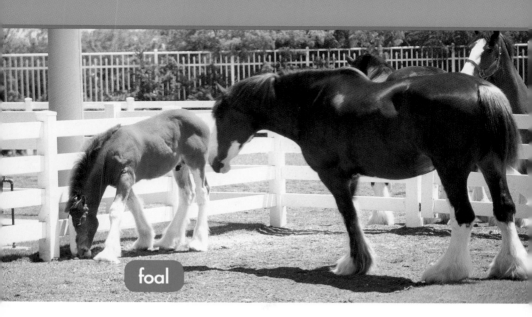
foal

Height:	16 to 18 hands
Weight:	1,600 to 1,800 pounds (725 to 815 kilograms)
Colors:	bay, brown, black
Home country:	Scotland
Uses:	driving, farm work
Facts:	• foot is size of dinner plate • hardworking and easy to train

17

foal

Height:	15 to 17 hands
Weight:	1,300 to 1,400 pounds (590 to 635 kilograms)
Colors:	black
Home country:	Netherlands
Uses:	driving, English riding
Facts:	• has a thick mane and tail • calm and willing to learn

19

foal

Height: 14 to 16 hands

Weight: 1,000 to 1,300 pounds
            (450 to 590 kilograms)

Colors: gray, but darker when young

Home country: Slovenia

Uses: riding, driving

Facts: • strong and graceful
            • lives up to 35 years

21

foal

Height:	15 to 17 hands
Weight:	1,600 to 2,400 pounds (730 to 1,100 kilograms)
Colors:	gray, black
Home country:	France
Uses:	driving, farm work
Facts:	• proud and smart • often used in parades

23

foal

Height: 40 to 42 inches
(102 to 107 centimeters)

Weight: 300 to 450 pounds
(140 to 200 kilograms)

Colors: bay, brown, chestnut, black

Home country: Scotland

Uses: children's ponies, driving

Facts:
- smart and independent
- small but very strong

25

foal

Height:	15 to 16 hands
Weight:	900 to 1,200 pounds (410 to 540 kilograms)
Colors:	black, bay, chestnut
Home country:	United States
Uses:	trail riding
Facts:	• comfortable to ride • calm and friendly

foal

Height:	15 to 17 hands
Weight:	1,000 to 1,200 pounds (450 to 540 kilograms)
Colors:	brown, chestnut, gray
Home country:	England
Uses:	racing, riding
Facts:	• smart and brave • famous for its speed

Glossary

bay — brown with a black mane and tail

chestnut — a reddish-brown color

driving — using a harness on a horse so it can pull a cart, wagon, sleigh, plow, or carriage

English riding — a style of horseback riding based on European traditions and equipment

hand — a measurement of horse height that is equal to 4 inches (10 centimeters)

roan — sorrel, chestnut, or bay body color, sprinkled with gray or white

rodeo — a contest in which people ride horses and bulls and rope cattle

sorrel — light red body color with a lighter mane and tail color

trail riding — a type of horseback riding where riders follow marked trails

western riding — a style of horseback riding first created by Spanish and American cowboys in the western United States

Read More

Criscione, Rachel Damon. *The Quarter Horse*. The Library of Horses. New York: PowerKids Press, 2007.

Dell, Pamela. *Arabians*. Majestic Horses. Chanhassen, Minn.: A Child's World, 2007.

Internet Sites

FactHound offers a safe, fun way to find Internet sites related to this book. All of the sites on FactHound have been researched by our staff.

Here's how:

1. Visit *www.facthound.com*
2. Choose your grade level.
3. Type in this book ID **142961708X** for age-appropriate sites. You may also browse subjects by clicking on letters, or by clicking on pictures and words.
4. Click on the **Fetch It** button.

FactHound will fetch the best sites for you!

Index

children, 5, 25
driving, 9, 15, 17, 19, 21, 23, 25
farm work, 15, 17, 23
Native Americans, 11
parades, 23

racing, 7, 29
riding, 5, 7, 9, 11, 13, 19, 21, 27, 29
rodeos, 5, 7
speed, 7, 29

Grade: 1
Early-Intervention Level: 25

Editorial Credits
Erika L. Shores, editor; Alison Thiele, designer; Jo Miller, photo researcher

Photo Credits
©2004 Mark J. Barrett, cover (Friesian), 19
Alamy/blickwinkel, 21; Mark J. Barrett, 18
Deer Creek Walkers/Mary Bittner, 27
Far Field Farm/Barbara Molland, 9
Getty Images Inc./Robert Harding World Imagery/David Tipling, 24
iStockphoto/iofoto, 15 (right); Karen Givens, cover (Arabian); Nancy Kennedy, cover (Belgian)
©Lynn Cassels-Caldwell, 23 (right)
Peter Arnold/Biosphoto/Grenet M. & Soumillard A., 23 (left); S. Stuewer, 26
Shutterstock/C. L. Triplett, 5; Condor 36, 28; Elena Elisseeva, 25 (right); Eline Spek, 10, 25 (left); Greg Randles, 4; Jeff Banke, 8; Karen Givens, 12; Laila Kazakevica, 13 (right); Lorraine Kourafas, 14; Maryellen Zwingle, 16; Sharon Morris, 13 (left); Stephanie Coffman, 6, 7 (right); Tan Kian Khoon, 29; Thomas Barrat, 22; Tyler Olson, 7 (left); Yan Simkin, 20; Zuzule, cover (American Paint)
UNICORN Stock Photos/Deneve Feigh Bunde, 15 (left); Dick Young, 17; Joel Dexter, 11

Capstone Press thanks Robert Coleman, PhD, associate professor, Equine Extension, Department of Animal Sciences at the University of Kentucky in Lexington for reviewing this book.